THE ROMANCE OF RACE

The Romance of Race

Incest, Miscegenation, and Multiculturalism
in the United States, 1880–1930

JOLIE A. SHEFFER

Rutgers University Press
NEW BRUNSWICK, NEW JERSEY, AND LONDON

LIBRARY OF CONGRESS CATALOGING-IN-PUBLICATION DATA

Sheffer, Jolie A.

The romance of race : incest, miscegenation, and multiculturalism in the United States, 1880–1930 / Jolie A. Sheffer.

   p.   cm. — (American literatures initiative)

Includes bibliographical references and index.

ISBN 978-0-8135-5463-1 (hardcover : alk. paper)

ISBN 978-0-8135-5462-4 (pbk. : alk. paper)

ISBN 978-0-8135-5464-8 (e-book)

   1. American literature—Minority authors—History and criticism.   2. American literature—Women authors—History and criticism.   3. Ethnic groups in literature. 4. Multiculturalism in literature.   5. Identity (Psychology) in literature.   6. Minorities—United States—Intellectual life.   I. Title.

PS153.M56S54   2013

810.9'920693—dc23

2012012094

A British Cataloging-in-Publication record for this book is available from the British Library.

Copyright © 2013 by Jolie A. Sheffer

Visit our website: http://rutgerspress.rutgers.edu

Manufactured in the United States of America

THE
AMERICAN
LITERATURES
INITIATIVE

A book in the American Literatures Initiative (ALI), a collaborative publishing project of NYU Press, Fordham University Press, Rutgers University Press, Temple University Press, and the University of Virginia Press. The Initiative is supported by The Andrew W. Mellon Foundation. For more information, please visit www.americanliteratures.org.

For Daniel

Contents

Preface   ix

Acknowledgments   xi

Introduction   1

1   Mulattos, Mysticism, and Marriage: African American
Identity and Psychic Integration   27

2   Half-Caste Family Romances: Divergent Paths
of Asian American Identity   55

3   The Mexican Mestizo/a in the Mexican American
Imaginary   91

4   Half-Breeds and Homesteaders: Native/American Alliances
in the West   119

5   Blood and Blankets: Americanizing European Immigrants
through Cultural Miscegenation and Textile Reproduction   149

Conclusion   171

Notes   179

Bibliography   209

Index   225

Preface

The seeds of this project were planted many years ago, when I took an undergraduate course on nineteenth-century women writers with Julia Stern at Northwestern University. One of our texts was Louisa May Alcott's *Little Women* (1869), which had been one of my childhood favorites. What struck me upon reencountering the novel was its deep anxiety about immigrants, particularly German and Irish immigrants, who appeared as pathetic wretches and invading hordes. I wanted to know the historical conditions that shaped Alcott's xenophobia and understand how those attitudes had shifted over the course of a century, making immigration essential to the American story. Having been raised in the Midwest, Irish and German ancestry seemed quintessentially American to me. Who wasn't Irish on Saint Patrick's Day? Who didn't eat bratwurst and potato salad?

My own family history is unremarkable precisely for its conformity to major patterns of U.S. immigration. My father's family proudly traces its roots to Germany, having come to America in the eighteenth century, fought in the American Revolutionary War, and built lives in Pennsylvania. My mother's family fled anti-Jewish pogroms in eastern Europe to settle in New York City during the first decade of the twentieth century. As a child, these two versions of the American immigrant story—the Pennsylvania "Dutch" pioneer and the New York Jew—felt like paradigmatic examples of ethnic groups who managed to make better lives for themselves and their families in America. However, even within my own family's stories, it was apparent that the path toward upward mobility and cultural tolerance had been uneven, to say the least. Family oral history, as well as library research, further revealed that immigrants were both victims of discrimination by and perpetrators of discrimination toward other ethnic, racial, and religious minorities. And while religious intermarriage is now commonplace, it was a major obstacle in the way of my own parents' marriage forty-odd years ago.

Discovering these contradictions and complexities only fueled my curiosity for the messy turn-of-the-twentieth-century period when the United States underwent its most dramatic demographic transformations. Over the last two decades—first as an undergraduate, then as a graduate student writing a dissertation, and more recently as a professor teaching twentieth-century American literature—I have attempted to understand the changing meanings of "American" and the roles of immigrants and minorities in the national imaginary. The multicultural model for the United States (or even the world) became omnipresent in the late twentieth century, typified by advertisements for the United Colors of Benetton. While these images were seen as edgy and radical in the 1990s, they are now dismissed as mere hipster aestheticizations and appropriations of racial difference. Yet what kind of historical erasure does that dismissal effect? What potentially radical history might be forgotten? This book is my attempt to answer that question by tracing the roots of multiculturalism in the United States, which I found in late nineteenth- and early twentieth-century fictions depicting the nation as a kind of multiethnic or multiracial family. As Jo March declares at the end of *Little Women*, "I do think that families are the most beautiful things in all the world!" When the family became a model for racial integration in the nation and the world, new things were made possible.

Acknowledgments

This project has been nourished by many sources. I am indebted to friends and colleagues who have generously given their time and talents to make this book better. I am humbled by and grateful for their contributions.

At the University of Virginia, Eric Lott, Caroline Rody, and Susan Fraiman encouraged my intellectual exploration of the fascinating turn-of-the-twentieth-century period, while demanding rigor and clarity. Scott Saul first planted the idea that I should, and indeed could, write the book that I wanted to read. Sarah Hagelin and Jill Rappoport continue to teach me about friendship as a form of intellectual engagement. Their enthusiasm and astute critiques can be found on every page. Others who enriched this project include Stephen Arata, Cindy Aron, Alison Booth, Sylvia Chong, Barry Cushman, Stephen Cushman, Michael Genovese, Paul Gaffney, Justin Gifford, Grace Hale, Pensri Ho, Michael Lewis, Michael Lundblad, Rei Magosaki, Victoria Olwell, Hallie Smith Richmond, Jayme Schwartzberg, and Jordan Taylor.

At Bowling Green State University, I have had the great good fortune to work with Kristine Blair, the chair of the English Department and a champion of junior faculty. I am grateful for terrific colleagues in the English Department and across the university—many of whom are affiliated with the American Culture Studies program and the Institute for the Study of Culture and Society (ICS)—who have contributed to the book: Bill Albertini, Candace Archer, Ellen Berry, Francisco Cabanillas, Amílcar Challú, Kimberly Coates, Ellen Gorsevski, Beatrice Guenther,

Julie Haught, Emily Lutenski, Don McQuarie, Lee Nickoson, John Kaiser Ortiz, Vicki Patraka, Susana Peña, Pedro Porben, Amy Robinson, and Maisha Wester. I am especially indebted to Scott Magelssen, Clayton Rosati, and Allie Terry-Fritsch of the Visual and Cultural Studies Writing Group; their thoughtful readings of many chapters at multiple stages improved this book immeasurably. In addition, my undergraduate and master's students at BGSU have been a continual source of energy, enthusiasm, and creativity. Ashlie Dabbs and Patrice Whitney provided assiduous research assistance.

This book was supported by an English Department research grant to visit the Hull-House archives at the University of Illinois at Chicago, by an English Department grant for image reproduction rights, and by a semester-long ICS Scholar-in-Residence fellowship. I would like to thank Joshua Clark and Valerie Harris at the University of Illinois at Chicago Library, Stefanie Hunker at the Browne Popular Culture Library at BGSU, and Jessica Wade of the BGSU English Department for their assistance obtaining the images that appear in the book.

Much of this book was first worked out at conferences, in particular the American Studies Association, Association for Asian American Studies, and Dartmouth Futures of American Studies Institute. These fertile intellectual hubs, full of smart people who are passionate about U.S. culture, always renewed my excitement about the project and redoubled my commitment to make it better. I am especially appreciative of Colleen Glenney Boggs, Leslie Bow, Anna Brickhouse, Jean Lee Cole, Hamilton Carroll, Elizabeth Maddock Dillon, Cindi Katz, Eric Lott, Anita Mannur, Donald Pease, Cathy Schlund-Vials, Laura Wexler, and Robyn Wiegman for welcoming me into conversations about the meanings of American culture.

I am grateful to Anne Cheng, Sylvia Chong, David Eng, Franny Nudelman, and Beth Piatote for their invaluable feedback on and advice about various parts of the book. Sarah E. Chinn deserves special thanks for her comprehensive and trenchant commentary on the manuscript. I also wish to thank Katie Keeran at Rutgers University Press for tending this project to completion.

An earlier version of chapter 2 appeared in the *Journal of Asian American Studies* 13.1 (February 2010) as "'Citizen Sure Thing' or 'Jus' Foreigner'?: Half-Caste Citizenship and the Family Romance in Onoto Watanna's Orientalist Fiction." I wish to acknowledge the *Journal of Asian American Studies* for allowing me to reprint the material here.

Monica Schneider's countless commiserations have brought levity to long writing days. Rick and Ilene Sheffer, Garrett Sheffer, and Nicole Merlo have been indefatigable cheerleaders. George and Louise McInnis have provided an endless supply of cheerful snail mail and good sense. This book is dedicated to Daniel McInnis, who is fluent in the languages of my head and heart. He has taught me a new appreciation for and a deeper understanding of beauty, romance, and kinship. I am a better person for sharing my life with him, and this is a better book for his influence and insights.

Introduction

In a variety of popular fictions published in the United States around the turn of the twentieth century by authors who share no obvious ethnic/racial, literary, or personal ties, certain conventions appear again and again: mixed-race protagonists (mulatto/a, mestizo/a, half-caste, and half-breed), caught between two cultural "worlds," struggle to find their place, a dilemma illustrated through their romantic attachments. These mixed-race heroes, and especially heroines, are the product of previous generations of interracial romance or conquest between privileged and mobile white men (slave owners, missionaries, businessmen, sailors, and other fortune-seekers) and the racialized women with whom they came into contact. Whereas the relationship of the parents of the mulatto or half-caste reflected the historical inequalities between white men and racialized women, the romantic attachments of the mixed-race heroine in the present represent an imagined future in which equality is possible.

In Charles Chesnutt's short story "The Wife of His Youth" (1899), the self-serving Mr. Ryder justifies his preference for the exclusive company of educated and cultured light-skinned African Americans over the larger community of African Americans by using the language of Abraham Lincoln and Herbert Spencer: "'I have no race prejudice,' he would say, 'but we people of mixed blood are ground between the upper and the nether millstone. Our fate lies between absorption by the white race and extinction in the black. The one doesn't want us yet, but may take us in time. The other would welcome us, but it would be for us a backward step. 'With malice toward none, with charity for all, we must do the best we can for ourselves and those who are to follow us. Self-preservation is the first law of nature.'"[1] At the story's end, his beliefs are put to the test when he is faced with a choice between marrying the nearly white Mrs. Dixon (and thereby continuing his social ascension) or acknowledging 'Liza Jane, the "very black" wife he left behind on a plantation more than twenty-five years ago.[2] His decision to publicly recognize the "wife of his youth" marks his belated acknowledgment of the shared history of African Americans of all hues and socioeconomic classes. Chesnutt's story thus represents a binary choice facing Americans of mixed-race: between racial disloyalty and solidarity.

However, in much of the fiction of the period, particularly those works by minority women writer-activists, a mixed-race heroine's choice of husband does not so simply imply a choice between white assimilation or minority identification. For example, in Mourning Dove's *Cogewea* (written in 1916, published in 1927), the eponymous heroine is a place-less, mixed-race subject, despised by whites and distrusted by Indians. Cogewea explains her plight: "Yes, we are between two fires, the Red and the White. Our Caucasian brothers criticize us as a shiftless class, while the Indians disown us as abandoning our own race. We are maligned and traduced as no one but we of the despised 'breeds' can know. If permitted, I would prefer living the white man's way to that of the reservation Indian, but he hampers me. I appreciate my meager education, but I will *never* disown my mother's blood. Why should I do so? Though my skin is of the tawny hue, I am not ashamed."[3] Despite the novel's reiteration of racial binaries, *Cogewea*'s resolution is more ambivalent than in Chesnutt's story. After falling for a charming but ruthless white man who swindles and abandons her, Cogewea eventually marries her adoptive brother, Jim, a fellow "half-breed." Though this incestuous return to like-ness appears to be a rejection of white assimilation, Cogewea and Jim live comfortably together on a ranch with her two sisters, who are married to immigrant homesteaders. The three couples effectively create a new family of mixed-race subjects. In *Cogewea,* the half-breed heroines find acceptance in the American West without either sacrificing their racial identities as Indians or rejecting all white men as agents of exploitation.

Cogewea is just one of a multitude of popular American romances of the late nineteenth and early twentieth centuries in which the mixed-race hero(ine) is a stock-in-trade that provokes serious reflection over the nation's changing demographics and its history of inequality. These racial romances serve two main functions: (1) they reveal a history of exploitation of racialized women by between white men; and (2) they offer a multiracial model of national identity that promises a more egalitarian future for minorities in the United States or those affected by its imperial reach. Racial romances, particularly those written by authors who were themselves women of mixed race, make their political claims by illustrating the familial ties that bind people of various races into one nation. To underscore the familiality of racial difference, in these works, miscegenation is repeatedly linked to incest (that has already occurred or that threatens to occur) or incestuous eroticism (such as between non–blood relatives who treat each other like siblings). For example, in *Cogewea,* the adoptive brother is transformed into a romantic partner, blurring the line between endogamy (incest) and exogamy (marriage outside the family, including miscegenation). In other stories and novels, literal incest signifies a secret history of interracial romance, and especially of racialized women's exploitation at the hands of white men. For example, in several stories by Onoto Watanna (the faux-Japanese pen name of Winnifred Eaton), the "half-caste" heroine's suitor is revealed to be her long-lost brother or father, thus exposing white man's history of seducing and abandoning Japanese women while on business abroad (see chapter 2 of this volume). In Pauline Hopkins's novel *Of One Blood* (1902–3), two light-skinned African Americans passing as white fall in love and marry, aided by the husband's best friend, a wealthy white southerner, who soon plots the murder of the husband and the seduction of his wife (see chapter 1). The revelation of this treachery is complicated by the even more shocking discovery that all three—the husband, his wife, and his friend/enemy—are full siblings, the products of generations of miscegenation and incest under slavery and Jim Crow segregation. In these fictions, miscegenation and incest are inseparable acts, linked by a history of racial and gender oppression.

The miscegenation-incest scenario also appears in American literature focused on racial hierarchies throughout the Americas. As I discuss in chapter 3, the Mexican American writer María Cristina Mena deploys the racial romance in short stories illustrating changing social codes in a revolutionary-era Mexico transformed in previous generations by Spanish colonialism and in the present by U.S. capitalism. In the story "Doña Rita's Rivals," a young, aristocratic Mexican man is moved by two great passions: his love for a lower-class mestiza and the revolutionary politics of Pancho Villa. His domineering and incestuous Mexican Catholic mother breaks off the affair, resulting in the mestiza's suicide and her son's hysterical illness. The mother procures the dead girl's twin sister to minister to her sick son, who grows stronger as the substitute paramour becomes his adopted sibling; the sister transforms his interracial, cross-class romance into fraternal revolutionary fervor. In this Pan-American version of the racial romance, the fraternal erotics of the Mexican Revolution are a healthier alternative to the pathological incest of Spanish colonialism and U.S.-influenced neo-imperialism, which die along with the mother.

In every case, romance provides a model—either a positive or negative example—of the familial ties binding people of different races in the United States and/or its relationships with other nations. All of these plots were written between 1898 and 1916, and all feature young racially and/ or culturally mixed heroes and heroines caught between the "foreign" and the familiar, racially minoritarian and white hegemonic identities. They feature melodramatic plot twists: surprising revelations, shocking betrayals, madness, and death. They are titillating and sexually provocative, with their depictions of forbidden romances and taboo desires. Yet they are also familiar, even old-fashioned, in their reliance on the generic conventions of romance, orientalism, the gothic tale, the tragic-mulatta plot, and the captivity narrative. These are messy, overstuffed plots that merge conventional and radical, conservative and progressive politics. Yet these fictions share the central conceit that the nation is like a family, one that is racially, culturally, and biologically mixed. These stories allegorize the nation through depictions of queer or "deviant" families, representing the hope for (and sometimes fear of) a more egalitarian racial and political order. Merging anxieties and fantasies about racial mixing and the nation's changing demographics, racial romances offer a model of the nation as always already multiracial and multicultural.

The writers I discuss in the following chapters—Pauline Hopkins, Onoto Watanna (Winnifred Eaton), María Cristina Mena, Mourning Dove (Christine Quintasket),[4] and Jane Addams—wrote from a range of racial, social, and political positions, but they all sought a wide audience. Writing in English for the mass market was central to their efforts to gain fame, fortune, and influence. I focus mostly on fictional texts because these imaginative works capture the fantasies of the population (both their authors' and readers') and allow for a space of possibility often not realizable in the contemporary world. Popular fiction does important cultural work, offering imaginative alternatives to current social problems or calling attention to untold histories. Werner Sollors argues that allegorical romance in racial and ethnic fiction may not be "'realistically' convincing, but it is the result of a certain aesthetic strategy" that imagines an ideal response.[5] I am suggesting that the oft-repeated story of interracial incest—whether embraced, averted, belatedly recognized, or transformed into conventional romance—can be read as an imagined resolution to U.S. racial and sexual inequalities. Racial romances demanded that readers acknowledge the nation's history of injustice and imagine a more egalitarian future. In these ways, familial fictions helped to change social attitudes over time. As ideas gained popularity, they proliferated in mainstream fiction published in magazines and novels. That which was imaginable in fiction could become possible in fact.

These plots set the terms for more recent and familiar images of the nation as a mixed-race, incestuous family. From William Faulkner's *Absalom, Absalom!* (1936) to Lynn Riggs's plays (1930s–1940s), from Cherríe Moraga's *Loving in the War Years* (1983) to Carolivia Herron's *Thereafter Johnnie* (1991), from John Sayles's film *Lone Star* (1995) to Gish Jen's *The Love Wife* (2004), the racial romance continues to be a reliable trope in U.S. literature.[6] With its capacity for continual updating to reflect current debates over the constitution of national identity, the racial romance has become a familiar genre of American literature. Turn-of-the-twentieth-century women writers are part of this American literary history, and deserve credit for challenging political and social exclusion on the basis of racial difference vis-à-vis their kinship and romance plots.

This book shows how, despite a long tradition of nativism and racist legal and social policies, the United States became a multicultural melting pot, the quintessential model of a multiracial nation for the world. I posit a genealogy for multiculturalism as it was embodied in the language of the mixed-race family, or "mongrel nation." Those odd and oddly compelling turn-of-the-twentieth-century racial romances are the missing link, providing a window to a more radical prehistory of modern multiculturalism than we currently acknowledge. *The Romance of Race* argues that the multicultural myth developed in the late nineteenth and early twentieth centuries through the mainstream cultural productions of minority women writers. This ideology, while frequently contradicted in practice, nevertheless came to dominate the United States' national self-identity in the twentieth century.

The familial model is politically powerful and culturally meaningful, at least in part because it functions at a deep-seated level that resonates with psychoanalytic concepts of the family romance, the Oedipus complex, and identification. By the early twentieth century, Sigmund Freud's theories had begun to shape the nation's collective unconscious, initially through the elite milieu of Harvard's psychology and philosophy departments.[7] William James, the renowned psychologist, philosopher, and brother of the novelist Henry James, was an early advocate, publishing an overview of Freud's work with Joseph Breuer on hysteria for the inaugural issue of the *Psychological Review* (1894). Freud's theories quickly began to shape ideas about the self and Other, inviting analogy with national issues of immigration and cultural identity. In the early twentieth century, popular writers in the United States sought to make sense of—as well as shape—attitudes toward the nation's increasing racial diversity. One way to do this was through the analogy of the nation as a family. Over time, the mixed-race family fantasy came to supplement and displace (even if it did not completely replace) the Anglo-Saxon model of U.S. racial identity that had predominated in the nineteenth century.

In a nation transformed by mass immigration, the Civil War, Reconstruction and Jim Crow, western expansion, and imperial ambition, a multiracial imagination served a variety of interests. For millions of new Americans, it offered a more capacious model of national identity. For politicians, the image of the United States of America as a mixed-race family was a powerful public relations tool, differentiating the United States from European nationalist and colonialist traditions. The nation-as-family was a decidedly national fantasy, not simply the product of a particular literary tradition, minority experience, or individual psychology. Such imagery was repeatable and translatable, even co-opted to illustrate the United States' relationship with neighboring countries and foreign trading partners.

The rhetoric of the nation (and world) as a mixed-race family is entirely compatible with American ideals of freedom and equality—think only of Thomas Jefferson's promise of "life, liberty, and the pursuit of happiness" in the Declaration of Independence. Yet, as Jefferson's romance with his slave Sally Hemings ought to remind us, even within families, all members are not necessarily equal. The works I discuss feature the racial romance plot—which combines incest and miscegenation—to highlight the racial and sexual inequalities that treat "black," "red," "yellow," "brown," and even "white ethnic" Americans as second-class citizens, yet they also suggest more egalitarian family formations. However, like Leo Tolstoy's description of unhappy families, every racial romance functions in its own way. Each works out the particular histories of its racial subjects and offers distinct solutions. The combined incest-and-miscegenation scenario is therefore flexible, capable of metaphorizing a variety of alternative or queer family models of all races as fundamentally American.

A Genealogy of Multiculturalism

By the turn of the twentieth century, politicians and popular writers alike were publicly responding to the dramatic changes to the nation's demographics over the last half century, and their effect on national identity. In "True Americanism" (1894), Theodore Roosevelt argued that the United States had been, since its founding, a land of immigrants: "We were then already, what we are now, a people of mixed blood."[8] However, Roosevelt's notion of "mixed blood" referred exclusively to European immigrants—from sixteenth-century French Huguenots and Dutch settlers to nineteenth-century German and Irish immigrants—and he demanded that new citizens "heartily and in good faith throw in their lot with us" by learning the language, customs, and "spirit" of America. Roosevelt's model of inclusion was limited and coercive, applicable only to immigrants from Europe and requiring their assimilation to Anglo-Saxon "virtues." Roosevelt could not conceive of the incorporation of the African American offspring of slaves, Chinese "coolie" laborers, Native American "savages," Mexican American "greasers," or other minorities whose racial identities and histories differed so markedly from those settlers who had colonized the United States.

However, by the early twentieth century, public intellectuals began making broader claims about the changing national culture. Not everyone shared Roosevelt's conviction that inclusion required assimilation—particularly those who were themselves part of the "immigrant hordes." In a 1915 article in the *Nation*, the Jewish American philosopher Horace Kallen decried the "melting pot" model of American identity in favor of the more heterogeneous model of "democracy," which he compares to an orchestra. Kallen describes the similarities among white ethnics—"Anglo-Saxons, Irish, Jews, Germans, Italians, and so on"—as "one of place and institution, acquired, not inherited, and hence not transmitted. Each generation has, in fact, to become 'Americanized' afresh."[9] For Kallen, the nation's constituents need not transform themselves (melt) so much as learn to play in harmony. Like Kallen, the Progressive Randolph Bourne emphasized cultural pluralism, arguing for a new understanding of U.S. culture as "trans-national" or "cosmopolitan."[10] Bourne describes America in exceptional terms, as "a novel international nation, the first the world has seen."[11] While none of these critics explicitly compares the nation to a (mixed-race) family, Bourne comes closest to articulating U.S. *culture* as fundamentally hybrid—transformed by the admixture of races, nations, and religions. Such a model of multiculturalism *avant la lettre* came to dominate the United States' sense of itself as a nation, unique in the world.[12]

Roosevelt's and Kallen's focus on European immigrants culminated in a national expansion of the category of "whiteness" to include Americans of German, Irish, Italian, Jewish, Polish, and Russian descent. As a small army of cultural critics and historians have shown, during the turn-of-the-twentieth-century period these ethnic groups "became white folks."[13] However, as "white" became a more inclusive category, other racial lines grew more intractable. After decades of retrenchment from Reconstruction advances, including Jim Crow laws across the American South, the Supreme Court's ruling in *Plessy v. Ferguson* (1896) made "separate but equal" the nation's official policy, guaranteeing the second-class citizenship status of African Americans.[14] The hardening of racial lines also affected Asian immigrants, who found themselves the target of discrimination and terrorism. The Chinese Exclusion Act (1882) was the first race-based limitation on immigration in the United States; this legislation was also notable for denying naturalized citizenship to Chinese immigrants. Before long, Japanese and Korean immigrants also came under attack, culminating in the Immigration Act of 1917, which created the "Asiatic Barred Zone" excluding immigrants from the entire continent.[15] In the bizarre logic of racism, the turn of the twentieth century saw a new era in Native American policy that emphasized miscegenation and assimilation as the solution to racial difference. I will discuss this complex history in more detail in the next section. Here, I want to highlight the way that these racial lines of inclusion and exclusion provoked imaginative responses from progressives who rejected nativism, racism, and xenophobia. Popular writers of the period effectively combined Roosevelt's language of "mixed blood" with Bourne's transnational cosmopolitanism to create stories of mixed-race, multicultural families that function as microcosms of the nation. Incorporating the nonwhite races that politicians and public intellectuals neglected or rejected, these women writers challenged the white hegemonic definition of U.S. culture, yet did so stealthily, in popular fiction using familiar romantic conventions.

When cultural critics discuss multiculturalism, they typically refer to its mainstream popularization in media—television and advertising, in particular—during the Clinton era. The 1990s were the apex and nadir of multiculturalism. Multiculturalism promised to be the culmination of 1960s radicalism, transforming U.S. culture into a society where all people were equal, regardless of color, religion, or gender. David Theo

Goldberg defines multiculturalism as an attempt at "incorporation" that "seeks to undermine and alter from within the dominant, controlling, confining, and periphractic values of the cultural dominant."[16] Such a model of "strong multiculturalism" asserts that changing power relationships will have political consequences, and that representations have the power to move hearts and minds.

Yet, by the late 1990s, multiculturalism had become a tool of neoliberalism, useful to sell products from clothing to fast food.[17] Even more troubling, the acceptance of "multiculturalism" as a national value could, paradoxically, be used for socially conservative ends, to argue for the end of affirmative action programs by declaring them policies of "reverse racism." "Multiculturalism" became a bad word, a familiar shorthand for style over substance, for easy rhetoric and failed politics—what the performance artist Coco Fusco derisively refers to as "happy multiculturalism."[18]

My purpose is not to defend multiculturalism at the end of the twentieth century, as epitomized by advertisements for United Colors of Benetton (although I discuss the aesthetics and politics of these images in my conclusion). Instead, I am interested in how the trope of the multiracial nation-family that is so familiar today was popularized a century before. The familiar aesthetics, which is to say the erotics, of multiculturalism began long before the civil rights and Third World movements of the 1960s, and can be traced to popular mixed-race romances of the turn of the century. I want to recover this more radical history of multiculturalism. If we take seriously the mixed-race fictions of the previous century (and I think we must), then we might have to rethink what we know about multiculturalism today, or how it might yet be revitalized in the future. Turn-of-the-century racial romances were messy, strange, conflicted stories about the nation's past, present, and future. Blending radical politics and conventional literary forms, these fictions demanded that their readers *see* the United States and its people in new ways, as well as *feel* differently about its racial identity. Turn-of-the-century racial romances imagined the nation as already a mixed-race family, with incest both threatening and beckoning as proof of the primacy of those interracial ties. Blending the familiar and the strange, the familial and the foreign, these fictions were hugely popular and thoroughly mainstream, reflecting, as well as subtly altering, the affective policies (and politics) of the nation.

Historicizing the Nation as Family

Women writer-reformers such as Jane Addams, Pauline Hopkins, Onoto Watanna, María Cristina Mena, and Mourning Dove embraced the image of the United States and increasingly the world as a mixed-race, incestuous family. In allegorical novels, short stories, essays, and a museum, miscegenation is revealed to be the precondition of modern national and global identity. In these texts, incest and familial eroticism occur in order to explain and naturalize the bonds between seemingly distinct races of people.

For centuries, home and family have served as essential metonyms for national concerns; issues ranging from regional economic policies to minority rights are commonly characterized as "domestic issues," in contrast to "foreign affairs." Such language implicitly privatizes political concerns, marking those within its purview as lying outside the jurisdiction or intervention of other nations.[19] The language of domestic policy also feminizes those affected (immigrants, minorities, even "foreigners" newly made into colonial subjects), marking them as the responsibility of the patriarchal nation, akin to wives, sisters, or dependent children. Accordingly, when, in 1831, the Supreme Court voted to strip Native American tribes of their autonomy and treaty-making authority, it did so by redefining them as "domestic dependent nations" whose "relation to the United States resembles that of a ward to his guardian."[20]

By the end of the nineteenth century, the United States had become a truly global power, expanding the geographic range and demographics of its "domestic" concerns through a series of military conquests: the end of the Mexican-American War (1845–48) resulted in the United States gaining half of Mexican territory; the defeat of the Spanish in the Spanish-American War (1898) resulted in the acquisition of the Philippines, Puerto Rico, Cuba, and Guam; and the annexation of Hawaii and defeat of the Hawaiian independence movement (1898–1900) ensured the U.S. naval presence in the Pacific. With the Roosevelt Corollary to the Monroe Doctrine (1904), the United States positioned itself as a "big brother" to other nations throughout the Americas, intent on securing economic and political stability as a means to serve the United States' interests.[21] In the same historical period, the United States underwent dramatic social transformations within its traditional borders, as millions of African American men gained citizenship rights as a result of the Civil War, becoming participating members of the national family.[22]

Similarly, Native American populations, though comparatively small, experienced a considerable shift in government policy during the turn-of-the-century period. Once distinct "nations" with sovereignty and treaty-making authority, and then "domestic, dependent" wards, Native American tribes became the object of assimilationist government policy. The Dawes Act, or the General Allotment Act of 1887, required the privatization of tribal lands and the assimilation of Indians. The effect, over the course of several decades, was the loss of more than half of tribal-held lands. On the cultural front, public intellectuals, educators, and missionaries urged intermarriage with whites in order to "dilute" Indian blood, and promoted assimilation, particularly through sending Indian children to boarding schools.[23] The goal, in the infamous and oft-quoted formulation of Richard Henry Pratt, the founder of the Carlisle Indian Industrial School, was to "kill the Indian, and save the man." In practice, both official government policy and private-sector educational efforts sought miscegenation—cultural and biological assimilation—as Native Americans' path toward Americanization. To become full members of the "national family," according to these authorities, Native Americans had to give up their tribal customs. Despite these legislative and cultural efforts, tribal identification remained strong, so in 1924 the United States completed its end run around Indian sovereignty by declaring that Native Americans were U.S. citizens, despite the fact that few desired that designation.

Meanwhile, some 23 million immigrants, mostly from eastern and southern Europe, and overwhelmingly Jewish, Catholic, and Orthodox, arrived in the United States in the period between 1890 and 1920, challenging the white Anglo-Saxon Protestant (WASP) majority.[24] Such "infusions of alien blood," in turn-of-the-twentieth-century parlance, transformed U.S. national identity, but (as with Native American assimilation efforts) did not fundamentally challenge white hegemony; rather, European ethnics soon became, at least nominally, part of the "white" majority. Other immigrant populations, however, proved more problematic. On the west coast, several hundred thousand immigrants from China, Japan, Korea, and later the Philippines entered the United States, provoking fears over "coolie" labor and proving an even more profound challenge to the national imaginary with regard to citizenship.[25] Politicians responded to public fears by limiting immigration based on race and national origin: paranoia about the perceived inability of the Chinese to assimilate resulted in the Chinese Exclusion Act of 1882, the nation's first race-based bar to citizenship and entry. Similar laws targeting immigration from Japan, and then from all of Asia, followed over the next few decades.[26] Eventually, anti-immigration sentiment affected eastern and southern European immigrants as well. The Johnson-Reed Act (also known as the Immigration Act of 1924) established strict national quotas in an effort to undo much of the demographic change of the previous decades.

The nation's southern border, first redefined by the United States' annexation of Mexican territory and the Treaty of Guadalupe Hidalgo (1848), was challenged anew by immigration resulting from the Mexican Revolution (1910–17). Nearly a million Mexicans entered the United States in this period to escape the violence and political uncertainty in Mexico. Long the object of popular contempt in the Southwest—where white homesteaders displaced Mexican ranchers and Native American populations, despite the fact that Mexicans outnumbered white residents—Mexicans continued to be denigrated in the U.S. press as "greasers," "the mongrel breed," and "a people unfit for American citizenship."[27] Nevertheless, with the end of cheap labor from Asia, and the passing of the Johnson-Reed Act, Mexican immigrants become the nation's new low-wage workers on railroads and in agriculture.

Despite—or rather, as evidenced by—the nativist legislation of the Johnson-Reed Act two decades later, by the turn of the twentieth century, the United States had dramatically expanded its role across the globe and increased the racial diversity of its citizenry. Whether its citizens liked it or not, the United States *had* become a more diverse nation; it would take another several decades for the nation to popularly embrace its new identity as a "nation of immigrants." In the meantime, "foreign" groups were incorporated through familial language, their relationship to the United States naturalized by metaphors of kinship. For example, after the Mexican-American War, the U.S. press dubbed Mexico "Our Sister Republic," reframing the United States' southern neighbor as a familial responsibility rather than a former military enemy or contemporary trading partner.[28] Likewise, after the acquisition of the Philippines, William Howard Taft reportedly described Filipinos as "our little brown brothers," who were in need of up to a century's worth of "close supervision" by the United States.[29] This discourse of family may seem at odds with the xenophobia and racism of the era, during which non-Western nations and cultures were deemed "backward" barbarians compared to Western civilization and American culture.[30] Yet familial rhetoric circulated widely, not despite racial difference, but because of it. The language of familial ties—of sisters and brothers—served to justify American superiority to other nations, as well as to naturalize U.S. policies (slavery, Indian removal, imperial conquest) toward diverse peoples. In a time of great social anxiety resulting from demographic and geographic change, these family metaphors made the foreign feel familiar and manageable.

While political leaders like Theodore Roosevelt and William Taft used the language of the family to justify U.S. imperialism, other mainstream authors and reformers used familial language toward very different ends. Conservative cultural agents in the U.S. government sought to manage and respond to the nation's changing identity by controlling the amount of "foreign" culture. In contrast, many minority and women authors deployed the racial romance as a more progressive, even politically radical, cultural response that insisted "otherness" was a form of "likeness." By conjoining miscegenation (exogamy) with incest (endogamy), racial romances turned the discourse of kinship into a roadmap to a multicultural future.

Politically and socially progressive women writers, particularly minority women writers and reformers, doubtless were drawn to the discourse of family likeness by literary tradition. Women have a long history of allegorizing the nation via the family for politically radical ends, notably in nineteenth-century abolitionist and African American discourse.[31] Authors such as Lydia Maria Child and Frances E. W. Harper developed distinctly American versions of various literary genres—the domestic novel, blood melodrama, and tragic-mulatta tale—that allegorized the nation as an interracial family in order to illustrate the inequalities and injustices faced by the nation's black "brothers" and "sisters."[32] In particular, women writers disproportionately contributed to an American subset of the nation-as-family allegory, featuring miscegenation and incest as linked sexual practices under slavery.

Under the "peculiar institution" of slavery, miscegenation and incest did occur in tandem, creating a doubly forbidden (and hidden) family history. Slaves were property, not people, allowing white masters unlimited access to black bodies for manual and sexual labor. The children of enslaved women followed the "condition" of the mother, while legally being fatherless. The result was an ongoing cycle of slave labor to fuel the U.S. economy, as well as endless opportunities for white slave owners and their "legitimate" children to sexually exploit their illegitimate, increasingly mixed-race children and siblings.[33] The slave's fundamental lack of control over his/her own body (including all "bodily issue") produces what Hortense Spillers terms a pathological *syntax*—a "vestibular cultural formation where 'kinship' loses meaning, since it can be invaded at any given and arbitrary moment by the property relations."[34] This crisis over kinship was both figurative (family ties threatened by the laws of property) and literal (multigenerational acts of incest corroding the boundaries between inside and outside the family). African American writers sought to reestablish the primacy of blood and family ties through literature.

Miscegenation, incest, and the exploitation of minority women were thus essential features of the "sexually libertarian regime" that was slavery.[35] Miscegenation remained the ultimate social taboo in the South, even as its evidence was written on the faces and bodies of its enslaved population.[36] The long, ugly history of lynching after the end of slavery, throughout the Jim Crow era, is testament to the power and peril of interracial sex and familial ties in the popular imagination. The realities of the slave economy fueled a fantasy world where power relationships were reversed, in which black men threatened white women, as in D. W. Griffith's repugnant masterpiece *The Birth of a Nation* (1915). This inverse relationship between fantasy and reality, anxiety and eroticism, would be exploited in popular fictions intended to expose the hidden reality of the United States' racial history.

Emerging out of the abolitionist miscegenation-begets-incest literary tradition, and responding to contemporary U.S. foreign and domestic policies, turn-of-the-twentieth-century women authors of various racial backgrounds modified the interracial incest story to demand the inclusion of Asian Americans, Mexican Americans, Native Americans, and European immigrants. Beginning with antislavery fictions featuring "mulattos," the racial romance grew to include "half-castes," "mestizos," "half-breeds," "half-bloods," and other multiracial, "mongrel" identities.[37] The familial imagination thus functioned within the United States as a microcosm of the multiracial character of its citizens and culture as it was being transformed from without and within. Doris Sommer describes national allegories as "construct[ing] Eros and Polis upon each other."[38] Within the U.S. context, racial romances—my term for the miscegenation and/as incest plot—highlighted the erotic and political ties already binding the nation's diverse constituencies into a single family. The ongoing obsession with, and particular fantasies about, race and sexuality in the United States reveal a nation in a state of arrested development, unable as yet to reconcile the mixed-up, mixed-race world as it is with the binary order—white/black, us/them, civilized/barbaric—that the West has touted since the Enlightenment.

Incest and Miscegenation

In his *Treatise on Sociology: Theoretical and Practical* (1854), Henry Hughes infamously declares miscegenation to be a crime against nature. He explains, in baroque terms, that "the preservation and progress of a race, is a moral duty of the races. Degeneration is evil. It is a sin. That sin is extreme. Hybridism is heinous. Impurity of races is against the law of nature. Mulattoes are monsters. The law of nature is the law of God. The same law which forbids consanguineous amalgamation forbids ethnical amalgamation. Both are incestuous. Amalgamation is incest."[39] Hughes's conflation of "amalgamation" (also called "mongrelism" or miscegenation) and incest ("consanguineous amalgamation") has been widely discussed in critical discourse about nineteenth- and twentieth-century racial ideology, cited as evidence of either the incoherence of antimiscegenation discourse or of its structural logic.[40] But what does it mean to conflate the taboos against interracial and intrafamilial sex?[41] Hughes's central point was that interracial sex was an abomination, a crime against the nineteenth-century "scientific" order that defined the races as different species.[42] According to Hughes's logic, just as sex with one's mother or father, brother or sister, son or daughter was an unforgivable breach of community laws, so too was sex across the color line. Interracial sex was an unnatural transgression of social norms, which Hughes dramatized in the inviolable, and here inseparable, languages of science and religion: "The law of nature is the law of God."

Throughout the nineteenth century, incest and miscegenation were further linked by their assumed weakening effect on the genetic stock—the former through hereditary birth defects and the latter through "dilution" of racial qualities—both of which threatened white dominance. For this reason, prominent scientists and public intellectuals favored "dilution" and "extermination" of nonwhite minorities in order to maintain the "Anglo-Saxon" character of the nation. In 1898, Dr. Aleš Hrdlička, a prominent anthropologist who would become the first curator of physical anthropology of the United States National Museum (now the Smithsonian Institution National Museum of Natural History), suggested that the government should "scatter the negroes in the South over the whole United States and the recent acquisitions in the West Indies and the Orient."[43] No less a personage than Charles Francis Adams Jr.—great-grandson of U.S. President John Adams, grandson of President John Quincy Adams, and son of the diplomat Charles Francis Adams—endorsed the United States' history of "unchristian, brutal, exterminating" treatment of minority populations as necessary to prevent the United States from becoming "a nation of half-breeds."[44] Progressive reformers had to offer compelling, alterative perspectives to these popular nativist and eugenicist arguments.

Nativist pseudoscientific discourse inconsistently shifted between treating incest and miscegenation as equivalent or as mutually exclusive terms. Such confusion is especially peculiar since miscegenation is commonly understood as sexual relations outside of one's racial "family" (exogamy), while incest refers to sexuality within a kinship community (endogamy). The two terms seem intrinsically at odds. A variety of contemporary literary critics have attempted to parse the relationship between these taboos in literature of the nineteenth and twentieth centuries. For example, Leslie Fiedler argues that antimiscegenation fears are fueled by incestuous and homoerotic desires,[45] while Walter Benn Michaels insists that incest and miscegenation are mutually exclusive, with white folks choosing incest (a kind of family murder/suicide) over miscegenation (race suicide).[46] More recently, Gillian Harkins explains that "incest was used to figure a nation whose family matters were in crisis, whose racial and territorial boundaries were perceived to be terrorized by dangers from within and without."[47] These critics reveal the centrality of incest and miscegenation in the American imaginary as an index of racial anxieties. They do little, however, to examine how the incest/miscegenation conflation has been mobilized as an antiracist strategy.

While racial romances traded in exoticization, orientalism, and stereotypes, they were also politically radical, illustrating that the true threat to the nation was not miscegenation, but rather: (*a*) the failure to recognize existing interracial family ties, and (*b*) the social hierarchies on which those kinship bonds were based. In racial romances, certain forms of incest occur as the result of historical racial inequalities, while other forms of incest represent a model of hoped-for inclusion and equality. In order to understand their meanings in American literature, one must first understand the conflict and common ground between incest and miscegenation, endogamy and exogamy.

Kinship rules depend upon a delicate balance between endogamy and exogamy, between familiarity and difference. In large, complex societies, the laws of exogamy require members of one family to find partners outside their immediate kinship network. Exogamous marriage creates new families, incorporating those who were previously exterior into a new interior. Yet typically the pull of endogamy limits options to others within the same clan (or racial, ethnic, religious, or socioeconomic) group. Modern rules regarding marriage function to ensure both genetic diversity and social cohesion. In order to achieve the latter, social customs tend to prohibit certain alliances and promote others. In the United States, as Claude Lévi-Strauss explained in 1949, "modern American society combines a family exogamy, which is rigid for the first degree but flexible for the second or third degrees onwards, with a racial endogamy, which is rigid or flexible according to the particular State."[48] These rules varied widely according to race, by geography, over time, and asymmetrically by gender.[49] In some states, marriages between first cousins were prohibited as incestuous, while not in others; some states even applied incest laws to non–blood relatives, such as stepparents, stepsiblings, and in-laws.[50] For example, in Alaska territory in 1897, incest was defined broadly as marriage, cohabitation, or sexual intercourse knowingly committed between "any person related to another person within and not including the fourth degree of consanguinity," and punishable by three to fifteen years in prison.[51]

Historically, antimiscegenation rules were similarly variable. As of 1949, twenty-nine states had laws prohibiting some form of interracial marriage. Southern states prohibited marriages between whites and blacks, while western states passed antimiscegenation statutes prohibiting marriages between whites and Chinese, Japanese, and Filipino residents.[52] In each area of the country the color line varied, as did the quasi-anthropological classification systems upon which courts relied to justify their exclusions. Thus, in Alabama in 1867, black meant a "descendent of any negro, to the third generation," while in Virginia in 1924, a "colored person" was anyone with at least one-sixteenth Negro blood. An 1850 California law that prohibited "all marriages of white persons with negroes or mulattos" was emended in 1880 to similarly prohibit intermarriage with "Mongolians" (Chinese); the law was revised again in 1905, adding "Malays," after the courts found that Filipinos were not categorizable as "Mongolians." Indeed, antimiscegenation laws often grew progressively stricter in response to changing social mores, which tended toward love across the color line. Not until *Loving v. Virginia* (1967) did the U.S. Supreme Court invalidate all antimiscegenation laws as unconstitutional. As all of these laws reveal, exogamy and endogamy are most certainly *not* universal concepts with unequivocal definitions.

The antihegemonic model of the nation as interracial, incestuous family vividly refutes typical representations of the U.S. nation as a racially "pure," nonincestuous, and unequivocally heterosexual family promoted by Hughes and his ilk. The fantasy of pure national origins is contradicted by historic realities; indeed, that familiar national fantasy occludes the social conditions that have historically made racialized women the pawns of white men. Intersecting the racial hierarchy structuring American life and culture, then, is a sexual hierarchy that privileges men and heterosexual romance. The historical inequalities experienced by racialized citizens have, in turn, led to a host of "queer" family formations, from the matriarchal black household to the extended immigrant clan to the incestuous, interracial family.[53] Judith Butler argues that incest and miscegenation taboos, and the marriage laws that prohibit such unions, presume the heterosexuality of the family, in turn disguising the conditions of white male privilege and raced female abjection upon which the nation (and its identity) was built.[54] All of these alternative family formations, which nativists and racists have depicted as external threats to the American national family, have been the product of *internal* power asymmetries.

Turn-of-the-twentieth-century "racial romances" offered alternative models of the nation, as a mixed-race, incestuous, and frequently female-headed family. In so doing, they created the imaginative conditions for twentieth-century multiculturalism, with its foundation in the fantasy of the nation as an interracial family, where all the diverse members are truly, in Pauline Hopkins's biblical phrasing, "of one blood." From Winnifred Eaton's scenes of familial incestuous desire as a welcome alternative to military and capitalist conquest to Pauline Hopkins's revelations of black-white kinship and incest, from María Cristina Mena's rejection of Oedipal desire in favor of platonic sibling equality to Mourning Dove's equation of tribal/familial kinship with immigrant homesteading, to Jane Addams's multicultural museum featuring a family of immigrant mothers and Americanized daughters, these women writers challenged dominant discourse to imagine a more inclusive future for the nation's "mongrels" and outcasts.

Theoretical Stakes of the Family Romance

In titling this book *The Romance of Race,* I refer to the tradition of historical romances by women, and to the particular racial dimensions that they possess in the United States, as well as to Sigmund Freud's theory of the "family romance," the identification fantasy underlying individual psychology in the West.[55] According to Freud, the child fantasizes an alternative origin story, imagining that his "real parents" were of a higher social class.[56] This fantasy of alternative parentage, in which the alternative mother and father are somehow different from and better than the ones raising the child, marks the individual's struggle for identity after the failure of Oedipal desires. I wish to suggest that American culture exhibits a particular pattern of identity-formation that manifests itself in the interracial, incestuous romance. The racial romance can be read as both Oedipal and post-Oedipal, as Freudian and as revising Freud's familiar theses. These American identification fantasies focus around familial relationships that are always already interracial and incestuous. Instead of substituting one's "real" parents for a fantasy pair who are of noble birth, American racial romances are like national folktales, revealing a common identification with racial Otherness through plots featuring mixed-race children reuniting with (or rejecting) long-lost parents, grandparents, or siblings. In fictions featuring mixed-race sons and daughters seeking sibling or quasi-sibling romantic partners, as well as discovering long-lost parents, American multicultural romances emphasize both unspoken interracial histories and potential incestuous futures. These stories work to erase the line between biological and adoptive families, and between racial and cultural identities, further transforming racial Others into members of the Oedipal family.

The psychoanalyst Alain de Mijolla describes identification fantasies as the product not only of one's own familial environment, but also of one's parents' environment, which is communicated in myriad subtle ways through family lore; these multigenerational family stories are unconsciously incorporated into the subject's psyche.[57] Viewed in this light, racial romances should be understood as national identification scenarios that provide a window into the collective unconscious. Built on generations of stories that have been passed down, racial romances continue to shape the U.S. cultural imagination. They function as compensatory identification fantasies of an alternative social order, a desire for an "Otherness" that is actually likeness, typified in melodrama as the *voix du sang,* or "the voice of blood." These racial romances reveal a deep desire for racial integration beneath the surface of a racist society.

In addition to evoking this psychoanalytic meaning, "romance" indicates an entire spectrum of intense emotion and erotic attraction. Following Eve Sedgwick, I regard "desire" as "the affective or social force, the glue, even when its manifestation is hostility or hatred or something less emotively charged, that shapes an important relationship."[58] For my purposes, "romance" thus includes an array of erotic configurations and libidinal trajectories. The interracial romance includes scenes of desire both overtly sexual and covertly erotic, between same-sex and opposite-sex couples, and among and between generations (fathers and daughters, mothers and daughters, mothers and sons, sisters and brothers, twins). In racial romances, erotic energies run in many different directions to express forbidden desires and reveal hidden histories. Through their depictions of incestuous, interracial romances, the women authors of this study challenge the status quo of white supremacy and patriarchy.

Some of the depicted erotic arrangements are avowedly deviant, in order to show how contemporary social, political, and economic inequalities are pathological. For example, a white father attempts to seduce his half-caste daughter in Onoto Watanna's "A Half Caste" (see chapter 2); a Mexican mother is so (incestuously) overinvested in her son's romantic life that she renders him a hysterical invalid in María Cristina Mena's "Doña Rita's Rivals" (see chapter 3); and, in Pauline Hopkins's *Of One Blood,* a mixed-race southerner whose racial/familial history has been withheld from him seduces his sister and attempts to murder his brother (see chapter 1). In other cases, racial romances offer egalitarian options outside of traditional (heterosexual, intraracial) marriage: an orphan girl in Japan marries her adopted half-caste brother rather than a Japanese or an American suitor (Onoto Watanna, *The Heart of Hyacinth*); a "half-breed" Indian woman marries her childhood companion, her half-breed "brother," and creates an extended family of mixed-race couples with her two sisters and their European immigrant husbands (Mourning Dove, *Cogewea*); renewed mother-daughter bonds strengthen immigrant communities and reproduce ethnic culture, absent of men and sociosexual ills like prostitution and incest (Jane Addams's Hull-House Labor Museum). Racial romances thus function as parables for the nation and its citizens—warning against current inequalities and imagining future resolutions.

The term "romance" is, of course, problematic, since contemporary usage commonly implies consensual erotic attraction.[59] In the mixed-race fictions I study, the authors emphasize the profound inequalities structuring interracial relationships. Turn-of-the-twentieth-century racial romances are frequently anything but "romantic" in the conventional sense, featuring, as they do, coercion and exploitation, rape and death, misrecognition and thwarted unions. These domestic allegories question the possibility of mutuality and consent, even as they affirm the deep-seated desire structuring interracial sexuality. In this way, racial romance connotes a literary and psychological form in which eroticism functions at a deep, unconscious level, providing a window into a nation's fantasies and fears.

In titling the book, I also wish to problematize the meaning of "interracial" in "interracial romance." In "real-life" as in popular literature of the period, racial identity and identification are not monolithic. While the majority of my texts center on "mixed-race" men and women, I am also concerned with depictions of mixed cultures; in the following chapters I discuss the meanings of works featuring, for example, a white girl raised as Japanese, a "black" man raised to be a "white" slave owner, a Mexican creole who identifies with the revolutionary proletariat, and children of immigrants taught to serve as a bridge between the Old World and the New. The texts create an increasingly complex portrait of American genealogy, challenging any claims to racial or cultural "purity," instead pointing unswervingly toward a hybrid model of national identity.

In its elegant, substitutive simplicity ("insert mulatto, mestizo, half-caste, or half-breed here") and iconic, metaphoric function, the interracial, incestuous romance functions as a "scenario," Diana Taylor's term for "culturally specific imaginaries—sets of possibilities, ways of conceiving conflict, crisis, or resolution."[60] The racial romance imaginatively resolves intractable social conflict through the inviolable language of shared blood—to transform exogamy into endogamy, Them into Us, the Other into the Self. As *The Romance of Race* shows, throughout the long twentieth century, the miscegenated, incestuous national family was a recognizable, predictable, formulaic, and repeatable trope for popular writers attempting to challenge contemporary depictions of American racial and sexual regimes. By showing how the racial romance emerged as a scenario in African American, Asian American, Chicano/Latino, Native American, and white ethnic literary traditions, this book reveals deep structural continuities among works too often examined only within a single racial or ethnic context. In its fusion of two social taboos (incest and miscegenation), the racial romance underscores the deep psychological level at which national fantasies work, and are worked out.

This book focuses on women writers at the turn of the twentieth century because they wrote romances, the generic basis for allegories of the nation as a family. The world of popular domestic fiction was dominated by women authors throughout the nineteenth century and into the twentieth.[61] Women writers had long relied upon so-called "female" and feminized discourses to make more socially acceptable political engagement with issues of race and belonging. At the turn of the twentieth century, minority and reformist women emphasized "feminine" subject matter (like marriage, romance, family relationships, and domesticity) and utilized "female" narrative strategies (allegorical romance, sentimentalism), even as they wrote in and for the public sphere. The authors I study were part of no single social group, literary circle, or political movement, although each engaged in social activism. Yet all of these women used familiar generic conventions—the romance, the mystery, the gothic, the museum display—and borrowed contemporary intellectual thought— from anthropology, psychology, archaeology, and sociology—in order to urge their audiences into more sympathetic attitudes toward minority subjects in the United States.

This generation of women authors, when taken collectively, represents a profound shift in the popular representation of minorities in the United States. Their influence is hard to trace directly, but it clearly lives on in the celebration of the melting-pot myth, particularly in the late twentieth-century version of multiculturalism that imagines racial minorities as members of a common national family. The mixed-race cosmopolitanism of the contemporary era was made possible and desirable by their work.[62]

The Romance of Race focuses on texts primarily created for mainstream (read: white, middle-class) audiences in order to illustrate just how widely and deeply the nation-as-family scenario traveled through the currents of popular imagination—not only within works aimed at niche or minority audiences. The nation-as-family scenario was a decidedly national fantasy, and authors who employed its generic conventions did so deliberately, as part of a recognizable literary and political tradition.

Chapter 1 focuses on a new figuration of the mulatto as model of miscegenated America in Pauline Hopkins's serialized novel *Of One Blood* (1902–3). Hopkins, a highly influential African American writer, editor, and activist in the period, imagines the possibility of a new national identity founded on racial and psychic integration. Hopkins psychologizes U.S. history and politics, representing the mutual dependence of white and black at two levels: the family and the psyche. Just as incest indicates the expression of repressed (and inappropriately directed) desire, psychological illness (melancholia) and parapsychological phenomena (mesmerism, animal magnetism, ESP, and automatic writing) erupt in the novel as expressions of the nation's racial divisions. Hopkins's novel asserts that these expressions of the collective unconscious will continue until the dominant race recognizes its inviolable blood ties to its black brothers, sisters, sons, and daughters. Drawing on familiar slavery narratives as well as contemporary psychoanalytic concepts, Hopkins's novel features three miscegenated, incestuous siblings, representing the past, present, and future of race relations in the United States. Two of these siblings die, doomed by the nation's history of racial oppression and female abjection. The third sibling, however, offers hope of an alternative future. Hopkins's hero, Reuel Briggs, represents the future unification of black and white, Africa and America, mysticism and empiricism, the id and the ego. I argue that in *Of One Blood,* the revelation of generations of miscegenation and incest thus signifies the possibility of a binary world order coming together to form both a healthier nation and a kind of cosmic consciousness.

The second chapter contrasts father-daughter and brother-sister romance in the wildly popular orientalist fiction of the Anglo-Chinese-Canadian-American writer Winnifred Eaton. Revising John Luther Long's influential *Madame Butterfly* (1898), Eaton focuses on the half-caste, the mixed-race offspring of an earlier "temporary marriage" or "Japanese marriage" between a white American man and a Japanese woman. In a variety of short stories and novels published between 1899 and 1904, Eaton depicts lecherous white American fathers lusting after their mixed-blood offspring, thereby revealing the white man's longing for reconciliation with (and recognition of) his racialized offspring. Whereas the prospect of father-daughter incest indicates inequitable power relations, sibling eroticism in Eaton's fiction represents an egalitarian solution offering social recognition for shared blood *and* culture. In addition to its revision of familial dynamics, this chapter reveals the global relevance of the U.S. national family, as Eaton's heroines are "half-castes"—daughters of American businessmen and Japanese women—whose racial ambiguity marginalizes them in both Japan and America. I argue that Eaton deploys incest in these popular romances in order to highlight the economic and social imbalances occasioned by U.S. economic imperialism, as well as to offer an alternative model of race relations. Through the revelation and recognition of mixed blood and culture, Eaton imagines new, and surprising, formations of inclusion.

Chapter 3 highlights the communicability and intertextuality of the discourses of miscegenation, cross-class romance, and revolutionary politics as they traverse national borders. In María Cristina Mena's short stories, written in English and published in the United States throughout 1914 in *Century* magazine, the melting-pot imaginary of turn-of-the-twentieth-century U.S. culture finds its double in the mestizo, symbol of a new multiracial Mexican nationalism that arose in the wake of the Mexican Revolution of 1910–17. Mena's stories depict the United States and Mexico as multiethnic mirrors for each other; her mestizo, like Winnifred Eaton's half-caste and Pauline Hopkins's mulatto, is a member of an increasingly multiracial and multicultural national family. In Mena's fiction, Mexico has been freed from Spanish colonialism but is being transformed anew by U.S. imperialism and capitalism. I argue that Mena personifies and domesticates the political sphere in her stories featuring domineering aristocratic Mexican Catholic mothers, invalid sons, and the sons' forbidden objects of desire: women of other races, classes, and/ or nationalities. In her short stories, the modern Mexican (American) man regains his virility, potency, and political authority by symbolically killing his castrating mother, whose incestuous love threatens his (and his nation's) health, and instead mixing blood with the mestiza, his platonic sibling in revolutionary politics. In Mena's fiction, national and hemispheric debates are transformed into familial and psychological dramas of sex and death.

Chapter 4 looks at the case of the half-breed in Mourning Dove's novel *Cogewea* (written in 1912, published in 1927). Like the mulatto, the half-caste, and the mestizo, the half-breed is caught between two worlds. Like the "half-caste" in particular, interracial romance for the half-breed represents both historical inequalities (the tradition of the temporary "Indian marriage" between callow white men and vulnerable Native American women) and possibilities for future harmony. *Cogewea* rejects the popular image of the Vanishing Indian, which imagined Native American identity as permanently historical and atavistic, having no future in modern America. Instead, *Cogewea* shows Native Americans becoming members of the U.S. nation by identifying with—that is, by symbolically becoming—immigrants, through marriage and homesteading. After being courted, swindled, and abandoned by an unscrupulous Canadian fortune-hunter who sought a temporary marriage, the eponymous heroine marries her quasi-brother (a fellow half-breed), while her sisters marry recent European immigrants. The novel imaginatively reverses the legal situation in 1924, when Indians were granted U.S. citizenship (Indian Citizenship Act) and immigrants faced race-based quotas (Johnson-Reed Act) limiting their entry.[63] Miscegenation and quasi-incestuous marriage become parallel paths to incorporation, modeling a cultural (rather than biological) definition of kinship, tribal affiliation, and national identity.

Chapter 5 focuses on Jane Addams's Hull-House Labor Museum, which displayed live immigrant actors in ethnic costume performing women's domestic labor. In text and layout, the museum situated

European immigrants as members of the U.S. national family, but this inclusion came at the expense of other groups deemed inassimilable: African Americans, Asian Americans, and Mexican Americans. Accordingly, the Hull-House Labor Museum is in many ways the most conservative of the incest/miscegenation scenarios I describe; nevertheless, Addams's museum effectively countered nativist fears of immigrants by modeling the United States as a multicultural family-nation. Furthermore, the Labor Museum refuted public anxieties about ethnic women's sexuality through its homosocial fantasy of European immigrant mothers and Americanized daughters—a model of ethnic culture outside of sexual reproduction. Accordingly, miscegenation in Addams's museum is not literal; rather, it becomes a figurative act of cross-ethnic identification, as visitors to the museum were encouraged to interact with immigrant women and their domestic arts. Similarly, incest is transformed into a figurative act of intergenerational, homosocial identification between first-generation and second-generation immigrant women. Addams's Progressive inclusion of European immigrants relied upon a particularly paradoxical, and fictional, relationship to Native American identity: within the museum, immigrant children were asked to participate in American culture by weaving a Navajo-style blanket, yet real Native Americans were vanished in this transformation of immigrants into Americans. The Hull-House Labor Museum thus combined progressive and conservative politics, inclusive and exclusionary aims, and "real" and fictional representational practices. In so doing, it reveals the limits of the nation-as-family scenario as a universalizing strategy of inclusion.

As these chapters illustrate, turn-of-the-twentieth-century writers applied the model of the miscegenated, incestuous national family to incorporate European immigrants, African Americans, Asian Americans, Mexican Americans, and Native Americans. In popular literature and culture, these real-life excluded groups were reimagined as members of the national family. In the late nineteenth and early twentieth centuries, such maligned categories as the mulatto, mestizo, half-caste, and half-breed were reclaimed as symbols of cultural pluralism and resistance to racism and nativism. The figure of the incestuous mixed-blood, caught between two worlds, represents the failure of a binary racial system to represent an increasing multicultural world. Mixed-race fictions of the early twentieth century depict a nation in crisis, forced to reckon with the consequences of imperialism and racism. These texts also attempt to work through national anxieties about race and sex, imagining new forms of community through shared blood and culture.[64]

The women writers who created these fictions highlight the way that gender continually shaped interracial relationships. These authors depict the blood bonds that link racial and ethnic minorities to their white relatives, and the particular burdens placed on mixed-race women, as evidence of the asymmetrical power relations that historically structured interracial romance. In the works of these Progressive Era women authors—most of whom were mixed-race themselves—the racial romance has both political and literary significance, and through this literary device, mixed-race women challenge exploitation, exoticization, and patriarchal privilege.

1 / Mulattos, Mysticism, and Marriage: African American Identity and Psychic Integration

In this chapter, I analyze a figure whose revision of the conventions of race and romance marks a crucial moment in the transformation of American models of national identity. Pauline Hopkins was arguably the most influential African American woman writing during the first decade of the twentieth century. Her novel *Of One Blood* presents miscegenation and incest to be the very basis of American politics, economics, and society. Coupling the incest plot with such fantastical elements as ghosts, suspended animation, animal magnetism, and a lost African civilization, Hopkins imagines the United States as a national family in denial of its interracial roots and a national psyche in need of integration. Rejecting the ontology of "separate but equal" legitimated by the U.S. Supreme Court's decision in *Plessy v. Ferguson* (1896), Hopkins shows the inviolable connections and profound inequalities between black and white. Linking body and mind, blood and spirit, Hopkins articulates turn-of-the-twentieth-century American identity as racially divided to its core, causing extraordinary phenomena to erupt into ordinary life. Extending the tragic-mulatto trope into the realm of psychoanalysis, *Of One Blood* shows the profound physical and psychic symptoms of the social illnesses of slavery and Jim Crow.

By the turn of the twentieth century, psychology and psychoanalysis had gained a great deal of attention in popular media. In France, Jean-Martin Charcot led the study of hysteria and hypnosis, followed by figures like Alfred Binet and Pierre Marie Félix Janet. Sigmund Freud had briefly studied with Charcot at the Salpêtrière hospital in 1885, before embarking on his career in Austria. In the United States, the Harvard psychologist William James, scion of one of America's first families, avidly followed the works of these researchers and brought European theories into American society. In his influential work *The Principles of Psychology* (1890), James posited his own theories of the intimate relationship between the body and the mind, rejecting mind-body dualism and embracing the notion that truth is subjective.[1] In 1895, Sigmund Freud published *Studies in Hysteria* (with Joseph Breuer), followed by *The Interpretation of Dreams* (1900) and *The Psychopathology of Everyday Life* (1901). Although not translated into English until 1909, his work was widely read in German by American intellectuals. That same year, Freud made his first trip to the United States, lecturing at and receiving an honorary doctorate of law from Clark University in nearby Worcester, Massachusetts. On this trip, Freud was accompanied by the Swiss psychiatrist (and his later rival) Carl Jung and the Hungarian psychoanalyst Sándor Ferenczi. At the turn of the twentieth century, Boston was the epicenter of American psychological research, a vibrant hub of activity devoted to discussing the emerging science of psychology and psychoanalysis.

Pauline Hopkins was a Boston intellectual of the black bourgeoisie who shared James's fascination with the mysteries of the mind and its effect on the body. Her writings reveal a deep familiarity with contemporary theories of the mind-body connection, as well as her own idiosyncratic, yet profound, understanding of human behavior and mental processes. She brought the language of psychology and parapsychology—not yet distinct fields—to her criticism of American racism and gender bias. Her essays and novels illustrate the psychological, as well as physical, effects of social inequality on the nation's mixed-race citizens. Whereas Freud and most of his contemporaries associated hysteria with femininity and irrationality, in *Of One Blood* (1902–3) Hopkins focused on the social factors that cause women's, and especially African American women's, psychosomatic illness.[2] In this powerful and wonderfully strange book, Hopkins depicts a psychic split within the mulatto, a condition shared by the U.S. nation's citizenry, and perhaps the entire world. A dystopian vision of American racial history and its effect on the present, *Of One Blood* offers a utopian vision of an egalitarian world where black and white, African and American, feminine and masculine, body and mind, are (re)united into a seamless, healthy whole. Hopkins's formulation is a provocative precursor to the later twentieth-century language of multiculturalism, and an important literary application of

Freud's acknowledgment of the relationship between individual pathology and social patterns.

Hopkins was a novelist, activist, lecturer, journalist, and editor of the *Colored American Magazine*, the first mass-market publication for the black middle class.[3] Founded in 1900, the *Colored American Magazine* published celebratory portraits of African American leaders, articles about race and political action, and serialized novels.[4] During her tenure as editor (1900–1904), Hopkins was also its most significant contributor, publishing countless articles and serializing three novels, *Hagar's Daughter: A Story of Southern Caste Prejudice* (1901), *Winona: A Tale of Negro Life in the South and Southwest* (1902), and *Of One Blood; or, The Hidden Self* (1902–3), in its pages.[5] Her best-known novel, *Contending Forces* (1900), was published by the Colored Co-operative Publishing Company, parent company to the *Colored American Magazine*, and made available to subscribers of the magazine.

Like many of the other women in this study who achieved literary and political success in the early twentieth century, Hopkins's fame and influence were significant, but short-lived. After writing for the magazine the *Voice of the Negro* from 1904 to 1905, she disappeared from public view until 1916, when she briefly reemerged to edit *New Era Magazine*.[6] She never published another story or article, working as a stenographer until her death in 1930. Recovered by African American and feminist scholars in the 1970s, she has since been granted serious critical attention.[7] However, scholars overwhelmingly favor *Contending Forces*, which fits neatly within the literary tradition of what Claudia Tate calls "the domestic novel of ideal black family formation," especially the tragic-mulatto theme.[8] The tragic-mulatto/a motif, which consists of "the typically tragic, antebellum story of interracial love between the beautiful mulatta and her white husband," was particularly effective at illustrating slavery's effect on the national family via its impact on individual families in fiction.[9] In this light, Hopkins's serial novels follow in the tradition of such interracial dramas as William Wells Brown's *Clotel* (1853), Harriet Wilson's *Our Nig* (1859), Frances E. W. Harper's *Iola Leroy, or Shadows Uplifted* (1892), and Charles Chesnutt's *The House Behind the Cedars* (1900). The nineteenth-century plot of idealized domesticity offered an antidote to slavery's destruction of the African American family. Within the logic of the genre, the tragic mulatto or mulatta stands as the unacknowledged American citizen, the raced body denied his or her right to "life, liberty, and the pursuit of happiness." The mulatto/a is "tragic" because his/her fate is sealed as a result of the previous generation's sins and silences. A product of slavery-sanctioned rape, the tragic mulatto bears the privileges of light skin but the burdens of ostracism and alienation for being "not black enough." The mulatta's marriage, often cast as a choice between a white and a black suitor, represents both an act of identification and a return to social visibility through domesticity. In *Conjugal Union: The Body, the House, and the Black American*, Robert Reid-Pharr argues that black American literature only truly emerges out of black bodies in all-black households. In this sense, then, the long tradition of interracial familial melodramas is an expression of the adulterated, adulterous, and incestuous household. Following this logic, the mulatta typically avoids her "tragic" fate (only) by marrying a dark-skinned black man, and thereby returning to African American domesticity and pigmentation (see Harper's *Iola Leroy*). Such plots end up reifying the logic of blood, preferring intraracial endogamy to interracial exogamy.

By the early twentieth century, American writers treating this theme began emphasizing not only slavery's elision of family ties, but also the corruption of the family through the threat of incest. For when human beings are treated as chattel, familial relationships are obscured and sexual taboos are ignored, resulting in the twin transgressions of incest and miscegenation. Hopkins's last novel, *Of One Blood*, marks a significant shift toward a new iteration of the tragic-mulatto trope.[10] Combining the antebellum tragic-mulatto plot with the twentieth-century theme of incest, *Of One Blood* reveals the gendered forms of slavery and racism and their psychological costs. Moreover, *Of One Blood* depicts the consequence of continued racism in psychological (not to mention international) terms. *Of One Blood* asserts that America's "white" citizens are also of mixed blood, and are themselves damaged by the legacy of racism and sexism. Imagining the nation's citizens as part of a kind of cosmic consciousness, Hopkins brings out the political applicability of psychoanalysis, and also adds her own African American feminist spin on white, bourgeois psychoanalytic concepts.

Hopkins should be understood as an essential precursor to major authors of the twentieth century who focus on the national traumas of miscegenation and incest, and their psychological effects. Writers including William Faulkner, Ralph Ellison, Toni Morrison, and Alice Walker all, in various ways, deploy incest as evidence of slavery's corruption of the American nation, its families, and its citizens' sanity.[11] While the tragic mulatto serves as public evidence of private violations—of antimiscegenation codes and black women's bodies—incest threatens the entire social fabric. As these novels reveal, slavery is not simply a historic institution that allowed such sins to occur in the distant past; its legacy of exploitation and domination, desire and disgust, continues well after slavery's legal end. Indeed, in both the North and South, slavery's crimes are multiplied: incest is liable to occur in the next generation between "black" and "white" siblings ignorant of their consanguinity, while white men continue to exert power over black men and women, if now through racist ideologies and psychological manipulation more than physical violence. In antebellum black domestic novels, citizenship commonly is defined by participation in marriage and motherhood. Within the tragic-mulatto incest tale, however, the family no longer represents the ideal model of the nation, but rather its distorted reality.

Unfortunately, critical studies of Hopkins that prioritize her participation in the domestic novel tradition tend to overlook her more radical and innovative contributions.[12] Critics consistently neglect the incest trope, except as evidence of white supremacy and denial of responsibility. Hopkins's last and most challenging novel, *Of One Blood*, has been misunderstood, widely dismissed as "patently escapist fiction" due to its eccentricities and seeming excesses.[13] Critics of the novel deride its investment in both the paranormal (mesmerism, animal magnetism, suspended animation, and ghostly visitations) and Africa (a lost African civilization miraculously revealed after thousands of years) as fantastical and therefore apolitical. Only recently have scholars begun to appreciate the complex political message of this novel, and a growing body of criticism reveals the relevance and realism of this "science fiction" text.[14] As Dana Luciano, one of the most nuanced critics of the novel, rightly argues, "The novel's revisionary deployment of sensationalist and Gothic conventions represents not an antirealist digression but a protorealist intervention" that articulates "the psychology of racism and the psychic effects it produces."[15] According to Susan Gillman, Gothic racial melodramas like *Of One Blood* are "a history of excess or, put another way, excess in and as history."[16] Instead of marking a break from realism, then, *Of One Blood* should be understood as continuing the work of the earlier domestic novels, but pushing the allegory of the national family into new territory.[17] Where earlier African American novels work within the sentimental tradition to call attention to slavery's destruction of families, with *Of One Blood* Hopkins expands her critique, calling attention to the psychological consequences of racism and gender discrimination. Yet I believe that the novel goes even further in its critique than is usually thought. In its combination of history, anthropology, psychology, and the occult, *Of One Blood* does nothing less than offer a model for a national psyche, offering a holistic alternative to the Manichean binaries of black and white and enacting its own concern with the repressed, denied, and unrecognized half of American cultural life. In short, I argue that Hopkins's novel relies upon the scenario of the nation as a multicultural family, but then extends that metaphor to depict the entire world as consisting of two racial halves in need of integration both racial and psychic. In its evocative illustration of the psychological consequences of social injury, *Of One Blood* makes clear the continued relevance and importance of psychoanalysis to women's literature and minority literature.

Of One Blood is a remarkably complicated and convoluted novel, drawing its three main characters into a dense tangle of relationships, events, and unexplained phenomena. Due to its unusual complexity, I include here an extended plot summary. The novel opens with our protagonist contemplating suicide, alluding to popular associations of miscegenation with melancholia: Reuel Briggs, a solitary medical student at Harvard, is characterized by "broad nostrils," "powerful long white teeth," "an almost sallow color which is a mark of strong, melancholic temperaments," and a "passionate, nervous temperament" (3).[18] Such characteristics (which echo Onoto Watanna's descriptions of the Amerasian half-caste in the following chapter) convey to the savvy reader that Reuel is a tragic-mulatto figure who is successfully "passing" as white.[19] His white friends and colleagues, ignorant of such clues, assume him to be exotically, but not threateningly, ethnic: either Italian or Japanese (4). In Thomas J. Otten's pithy formulation, "Reuel is not quite white enough to pass unnoticed, but white enough to pass inspection."[20] Reuel, as his melancholic complexion forecasts, is haunted by thoughts of suicide, but he is saved by two things: first, a book about mysticism entitled *The Unclassified Residuum*, which seems to offer proof of his own beliefs in the paranormal; and second, a vision he has of a beautiful, golden-haired woman on whose lips he sees "an expression of wistful entreaty" (5). His will to live is reignited by the promise of recognition of his manhood through science, heroism, and heterosexual romance. Later that evening, at a concert by the Fisk University Jubilee Singers, Reuel becomes entranced by the lead soprano, Dianthe Lusk, whom he recognizes as the woman from his vision.[21] The novel thus combines realist details (like the Fisk University chorus, which did perform African American spirituals for northern audiences) with paranormal events.[22] The result is a novel depicting the psychological foundation of racial dramas for recognition and equal rights.

After another spectral visit from Dianthe, Reuel is asked by Aubrey Livingston, his wealthy white friend and fellow medical student, to consult on a mysterious case at the hospital—a woman appears dead from a train wreck, but shows no sign of injury. Because of his studies in psychology and the occult, Reuel recognizes a case of suspended animation and successfully reawakens the woman, who is none other than Dianthe. Since she suffers from amnesia, the two men collude to hide her African American heritage in hopes of keeping her within their circle of (white) friends. Dianthe is then rechristened Felice Adams and comes to live with Molly Vance, Aubrey's fiancée, and Molly's brother Charlie. Before long, Reuel has fallen in love with Dianthe, and the two become engaged. However, Reuel does not have the means to support them since his job prospects have suddenly dried up (presumably because his racial identity has been revealed to would-be employers). Aubrey, who has himself become obsessed with Dianthe, tells Reuel of a lucrative but dangerous expedition to Africa in search of archaeological artifacts. With no other means of income, Reuel agrees to leave on the day of his wedding, accompanied by Charlie Vance and Aubrey's loyal servant Jim Titus, apparently postponing the consummation of his marriage until his return.

During Reuel's absence, Dianthe's memory returns and Aubrey blackmails her into becoming his mistress by threatening to reveal her racial heritage to Reuel, whom she believes is ignorant of this information. Dianthe receives a ghostly visit from Mira, a slave woman whom Aubrey's father, Dr. Livingston Sr., often hypnotized for the entertainment of his friends. Mira cryptically warns Dianthe that "there is nothing covered that shall not be revealed" (73). Shortly thereafter Aubrey stages a boating accident in which Molly drowns and he and Dianthe are presumed dead. Aubrey abducts Dianthe to his ancestral plantation, where, through his own mesmeric powers, he forces her to marry him. Meanwhile, Aubrey has arranged for Jim Titus to murder Reuel in Africa, but Reuel is saved by Mira's ghost, who warns him of the murder plot.

Some weeks later, as the expedition reaches the ancient African city of Meroe, Reuel and Charlie (and we readers) learn from the expedition's professor-leader about the greatness of African civilization.[23] Despite his mounting excitement about the expedition, Reuel is devastated to learn of the boating accident back home. Believing Dianthe dead, Reuel runs off into the ruins to commit suicide. He is found by Ai, the prime minister of the hidden city of Telassar, which is home to the descendants of

Meroe. Ai shows Reuel the great city because, due to secret knowledge and his lotus-shaped birthmark, Ai has recognized Reuel as Ergamenes, "the long-looked-for king of Ethiopia, for whose reception this city was built!" (122). Before long, Reuel marries Candace, Telassar's virgin queen and Dianthe's darker-skinned double.[24] After their marriage, Reuel is initiated into the lost arts of reading the past, future, and present, at which time he learns that Dianthe is still alive and that Aubrey has betrayed him. Meanwhile, Charlie Vance enlists Jim Titus to help him search for his missing friend. Encountering the secret city of Telassar, Jim is fatally injured and the two men are brought before Reuel and Ai. On his deathbed, Jim confesses all, including the fact that Reuel and Dianthe are both the children of Mira and Dr. Livingston Sr., making them full siblings. Reuel returns home to confront Aubrey.

Meanwhile, at the Livingston plantation, Dianthe encounters old Aunt Hannah, a former slave and Mira's mother. Hannah reveals more knots in the tangle of family secrets: she switched Mira's child for Dr. Livingston Sr.'s "legitimate" heir, who died in infancy, meaning that Aubrey is in fact the full sibling of both Dianthe and Reuel. Three generations have seen Livingston men abuse black women: Aubrey's grandfather impregnated Hannah, producing Mira; Mira was victimized by Aubrey's father, her own half brother; and Aubrey has repeated the family pattern, this time with his full sibling, Dianthe. Hopkins here reveals miscegenation and incest, exogamy and endogamy, to be inseparable and indistinguishable. Moreover, under the peculiar logic of slavery and the gendered experiences of American racism, incestuous miscegenation is doomed to continue to recur in each generation. Indeed, such racial-familial crimes will only become more heinous with each succeeding generation unless something drastic occurs to transform the social order.

Mira appears once more to Dianthe, informing her that Reuel is alive and that Aubrey hired Jim to kill him. Seeking revenge, Dianthe attempts to poison Aubrey, but he forces her to drink the potion instead; she lives just long enough to die in Reuel's arms when he returns from Africa. Using telepathy, Ai hypnotizes Aubrey, forcing him to commit suicide, the punishment appropriate to princes of Telassar guilty of murder. Accompanied by Hannah, Reuel returns to Telassar, charged with leading the ancient city into the twentieth century.

One of my claims is that within the novel, incest has two distinct meanings. In the case of Aubrey's treatment of Dianthe, incest is the mark of depravity, the horrific consequence of generations of rape, racism, and exploitation. Aubrey's and his father's uses of hypnosis suggest the coercive nature of interracial sex, of the power inequalities that make it possible for white (or "white") men to treat black (or "black") women as sexual objects. Yet in its depiction of the mutually loving relationship between Reuel and Dianthe, *Of One Blood* also depicts the "good" incest of egalitarian romance, which is romantically sanctioned but must go unconsummated. One positive and one negative, both forms of incest are the result of national familiality. There is no such thing as racial purity in the novel, and as a result, incest is widespread and perhaps even inevitable. In *Of One Blood*, these family secrets are revealed and enabled by ghostly visitations, hypnotism, and unlikely coincidences. Through what Elizabeth Ammons calls its "literally incredible but symbolically accurate plot," the novel reveals the world of southern aristocratic privilege to be a cover for violent racism and sexism.[25] Slavery lives on in Reconstruction and Jim Crow policies, covered over by the discourse of civilization and "progress." As a result of this continued erasure of power relations, the trauma of slavery goes unrecognized, causing the next generation to replay its plots in a kind of hysterical, uncanny repetition.[26] To call slavery a traumatic event is to acknowledge its distortion of personhood and family, and to begin to consider how multiculturalism as a concept is structured around unacknowledged losses.

The gothic elements of the novel are realistic expressions of that traumatic history. As Kathleen Brogan explains, "As both presence and absence, the ghost stands as an emblem of historical loss as well as a vehicle of historical recovery."[27] *Of One Blood* highlights the ongoing repression of the reality of racial oppression and gender exploitation in America, resulting in a hysterical split between "black" and "white," "rational" and "irrational," consciousness and unconsciousness, and male and female. The truth of American history—and with it the possibility for change—emerges only when boundaries of life and death, waking and dreaming, past and present are crossed. In short, the uncanny features of the novel are expressions of cultural trauma and serve as a psychologically astute map for a path toward national psychic health: only by acknowledging the traumatic past can an alternative future emerge. In its conjunction of racial and psychological discourses, individual and community trauma, *Of One Blood* does more than model the national family as interracial and incestuous because fundamentally unequal; it imagines a national psyche in desperate need of integration.

Imagining a National Psyche

In *Of One Blood*, as in other turn-of-the-twentieth-century mixed-race fictions, incest (actual or prospective) reveals the mulatto/a's compulsion to reunite with his/her family and it results in white patriarchy's belated acknowledgment of its interracial family members. In this way, Pauline Hopkins's political fiction reveals the racial melancholia at the heart of African American literature, the blackness out of which whiteness is constituted, and the inseparability of white and black in American national identity. In Hopkins's novels, melancholia is an expression of the historical trauma of slavery, a trauma based in race, blood, and violence. Under slavery and Jim Crow, incest and miscegenation are inextricable acts that have always already occurred and are doomed to repeat in subsequent generations. These twin transgressions are based on inequitable power relations of race, gender, and capital, whereby people are treated as property. In this context, melancholia functions "as a symptom exposing the abject underside of American history," which is "less a pathology than a realistic response to racial conditions in the United States in the last part of the nineteenth century."[28] Rather than being merely the symptom of an individual's incomplete grieving process, melancholia is a suitable reaction to the continued denial of African American equality.

In *Of One Blood*, melancholia orients the reader to the emotional consequences of racism, and indicates the communal nature of the experience. As Jonathan Flatley explains in reference to Hopkins's contemporary Henry James, melancholia can bring together writer and reader, "facilitat[ing] the feeling that one is part of a collectivity"; such an "affective map helps to orient oneself emotionally: whom to blame, what situations to avoid, where to place one's anger, and with whom to form alliances."[29] Racial melancholia in particular is essential to the processes of psychological integration for a nation so long and so deeply divided. Even Hopkins's use of ghosts functions to emphasize the large-scale trauma shared by an entire population. Lois Parkinson Zamora defines magical realism as an expression of common experiences that cross the divide between individuals and communities; magical-realist texts "pulsate with proliferations and conflations of worlds, with appearances and disappearances and multiplications of selves and societies. . . . In magical realist fiction, [the] slippage from the individual to the collective to the cosmic is often signaled by spectral presences."[30] In this light, Hopkins's use of the supernatural is an extension of her critique of the political and cultural environment that subjugates black citizens.

Consistent with its disruption of binaries, the novel reveals realism and fantasy to be flip sides of the single coin of American racial history. With its strange and powerful narrative of families destroyed and reunited, murder and suicide, amnesia and extrasensory perception, medicine and mesmerism, hidden African cities and secret southern plantations, *Of One Blood* suggests that the "truth" of American history cannot be expressed in the official discourses of medical textbooks or national progress. An accurate history, Hopkins reminds us, requires attention to the violence, sex, and exploitation that have long been repressed and denied. The uncanny, as Freud tells us, "is in reality nothing new or alien, but something which is familiar and old-established in the mind and which has become alienated from it only through the process of repression."[31] The occult in Hopkins's novel erupts to expose the ignored and denied half of American life—racism, rape, and exploitation of black citizens. The novel's disruption of "realism" is the first step to transforming pathological social relations.[32] By bringing together normal and paranormal, black and white, the novel posits that black and white are part of a single, interdependent system. In this model, blackness and Africa are not the antitheses of American civilization and Western rationality; rather, Africa and America are mutually constitutive, even codependent. Failure to recognize the African half of the system, Hopkins suggests, will result in the perpetuation of a national split-personality disorder that threatens to destroy the national family through the recurrence of incest, fratricide, insanity, and female disempowerment in every generation.

Hopkins associates the unhealthy division between white and black to other binaries, such as rational and irrational, masculine and feminine. The relationship between all these categories is evident in the story of Dr. Aubrey Livingston Sr. and his concubine, the slave Mira (mother of Reuel, Dianthe, and Aubrey). In the novel, we learn that Livingston Sr. would hypnotize Mira so that she could "perform tricks of mind-reading for the amusement of visitors" (50). Livingston represents the dangers of white masculinity and medical authority akin to the figure of the husband-doctor in Charlotte Perkins Gilman's *The Yellow Wallpaper* (1892).[33] In contrast, Mira embodies the irrationality of the unconscious, mystical power, and black feminine passivity. The passive state of hypnotism symbolizes and exaggerates women's lack of power under slavery and Jim Crow. Like a marionette controlled by her puppet master, Mira performs at the will of her slavemaster, unable to access her powers for her own purposes. However, in her powerlessness, Mira reveals an independent personality and uncanny knowledge superior to that of her physician/owner/lover. She becomes "a gay, noisy, restless woman, full of irony and sharp jesting" who accurately predicts the coming civil war, informing the doctor's guests: "All the women will be widows and the men shall sleep in early graves.... Your houses shall burn, your fields be laid waste, and a downtrodden race shall rule in your land" (51). Through Mira and her trance-state predictions, Hopkins associates unconscious, prescient knowledge with blackness and femininity. Such mystical knowledge is denied, undesired, and unappreciated—so much so that Livingston later sells Mira. The sale of human beings as chattel is the ultimate act of domination, but it comes with a tremendous personal cost: he will eventually lose his plantation, child, and reputation.

Like Cassandra of Greek myth, Mira's predictions are disbelieved, ignored, and punished. Her powers of mind are treated as entertainment for the pleasure of her white master, an extension of her value as a sexual object and plantation commodity. Indeed, Livingston not only hypnotizes her, but (we later learn) impregnates her as well. Hypnosis here is an analogue for rape and pregnancy, with the master asserting his will over the woman's passive body. The slave woman is valuable for her reproductive capacity—that is, for her body, not her mind. Mira is doubly vulnerable due to her gender and race. Indeed, even the end of slavery will not end such exploitation, as Aubrey continues the Livingston legacy of controlling black women through blackmail and mind control. Aubrey uses and abuses Dianthe, reducing her, like her mother, to a performing, passive, and penetrable body. Aubrey's manipulation signals ongoing white privilege and female abjection, and his commission of incest with Dianthe marks the further distortion of familial ties.

Importantly, the black woman's mind and will are not only exploited by men like Livingston *père*. Reuel learns that, prior to Aubrey, Dianthe was first weakened by a white female mesmerist who hypnotized her in front of audiences as paid entertainment. This detail is significant. According to Cynthia Schrager, "Hopkins's choice of gender might be read as an indictment of white women's collusion with the abuses of the slave institution and, by analogy, with the widespread interlocking practices of lynching and rape of African American men and women in the post-Reconstruction era as an equally heinous form of social control."[34] Unlike Harriet Beecher Stowe's *Uncle Tom's Cabin*, which aligns white and black women together through the discourse of motherhood, Hopkins here shows womanhood to be no guarantee of virtue, since the female mesmerist is as capable of exploitation as the southern slave owner. The "solution" to the social problem of racism will not come through an alliance of white and colored women. The answer can only come through the complete restoration of family ties, which requires recognition of the repressed half of national identity. This fantasy of unification is Hopkins's contribution to the turn-of-the-twentieth-century nation-as-family scenario, with the mixed-race nation allegorized by the Livingston-Briggs-Lusk family as a kind of cosmic psyche.

While *Of One Blood* features three mixed-race siblings, it is the mixed-race woman who is the ultimate victim of the racial and patriarchal regime of the Old South. Whether on stage as a singer or as a hypnotist's dummy, Dianthe is always an aesthetic and sexual object. Even to Reuel, she appears as fragmented body parts, "tints of cream and rose and soft moist lips" (5). In keeping with this complete objectification that denies her personhood, Dianthe is infantilized, admired for her "rose-tinged baby lips" (5). She is repeatedly described as being "like a child" (34) or "a tired child" (35). Dianthe alone among the characters "los[es] her will-power" (69), to the female mesmerist and then to Aubrey; the first abuse leaves her more vulnerable to the second. Her treatment as a passive object without a will of her own obscures her identity so much that when Reuel treats her in the hospital after a train accident, the white physicians fail to recognize her as the acclaimed soprano from the concert: "Strangely enough, none of the men that had admired the colored artist who had enthralled their senses by her wonderful singing a few weeks before, recognized her in the hospital waif consecrated to the service of science. Her incognito was complete" (39). Outside of the performance hall, Dianthe simply does not exist. This social invisibility allows Aubrey and Reuel to transform black Dianthe Lusk into white Felice Adams. At the same time, the ease with which Dianthe can be made white highlights the incoherence of the one-drop rule, which refuses to admit the possibility of racial ambiguity. Dianthe is simultaneously invisible and embodied. The mixed-race woman thus represents the paradox of racialization: social invisibility is predicated on visible racialization.

The trance state functions in Hopkins's novel as an illustration of the forced abjection of black women under American racism and slavery. In addition to this political message of female disempowerment, Hopkins evokes contemporary medical/psychological formulations of femininity as pathological. Dianthe appears as a casebook hysteric: she is the survivor of a train accident, the classic traumatic scene. Her lethargy and amnesia echo Sigmund Freud and Joseph Breuer's catalogue of symptoms in *Studies in Hysteria*: "neuralgias as well as the different kind of anesthesias, often of years' duration, contractures and paralyses, hysterical attacks . . . , all kinds of visual disturbances, constantly recurring visual hallucinations, and similar affections."[35] Just as Reuel represents the melancholia of the half-caste or tragic mulatto, Dianthe represents the hysterical woman whose femininity is itself pathological. Indeed, there is a deep similarity between melancholia and hysteria (as we see with Reuel's own capacity to see and hear what others cannot); melancholia is a condition long associated with racial difference, while hysteria has been tied to sexual difference. According to the logic of white male supremacy, which informs both imperialism and medicine, all raced bodies are gendered female for their supposed inferiority. However, Hopkins shows us that black female bodies are especially at risk for physical and psychological exploitation. As Deborah Horvitz explains, the textbook nature of Dianthe's hysteria reveals its basis in social trauma, rather than psycho-biological weakness: Hopkins "interprets the behaviors and symptomatology of hysteria as expressions of the very specific trauma inherent in the political and familial histories of black women: rape and incest perpetrated by white men."[36] In *Of One Blood,* hysteria is the result of social trauma, not mental weakness. Pathology is made, not inborn.

Hopkins's interest in contemporary psychology is immediately apparent, as the novel opens with Reuel reading *The Unclassified Residuum* by "M. Binet," a book about advances in psychology related to trance states and extrasensory perception. Reuel and Aubrey share the belief "that the wonders of a material world cannot approach those of the undiscovered country within ourselves—the hidden self lying quiescent in every human soul" (7). Conjoining the languages of science and spiritualism, *The Unclassified Residuum* explicitly contrasts the "material world" of biology and medical science with the "hidden self" of the unconscious. The book Reuel reads thus speaks of "the hidden self" as a metaphor for psychological depth. In Hopkins's novel, however, "the hidden self" also refers to blood and racial amalgamation, which is the open secret of American genealogy. Reuel compliments Aubrey on his "greater gift of duality [mesmerism]," foreshadowing Aubrey's manipulation of Dianthe, which will "render her quiescent in his hands" (166). However, Reuel's observation also highlights the fact that, by comparison, Reuel will be better able to think nondualistically—that is, to think across the boundaries of race and psychology. Where Aubrey manipulates the spiritual realm for material, personal advantage, Reuel learns to unify the material and spiritual worlds for the greater good.

The Unclassified Residuum is a thinly veiled reference to an 1890 article by William James entitled "The Hidden Self," which is the subtitle of *Of One Blood*.[37] James details Pierre Janet's and Alfred Binet's findings on hysteria and hypnosis, arguing that "superstitions" or "mysticisms" are real phenomena of the mind that ought to be understood via the developing field of psychology. While clearly referencing these psychologists' work, Hopkins significantly revises their model of the unconscious to correlate racial segregation to hysterical disorders. In James's summary of Janet's and Binet's clinical research, the hysteric has a reduced capacity for holistic thinking, resulting in compartmentalized responses that disconnect the patient's physical sensations from emotional responses such as memories: "Our minds are all of them like vessels full of water, and taking in a new drop makes another drop fall out; only the hysteric mental vessel is preternaturally small. The unifying or synthesizing power which the Ego exerts over the manifold facts which are offered to it is insufficient to do its full amount of work, and an ingrained habit is formed of neglecting or overlooking certain determinate portions of the mass."[38] In *Of One Blood*, Hopkins revises James's psychological formulation of the hypnotic state to make a political point about the unhealthy divisions within the American *national* consciousness. Whereas James describes the hysteric as being handicapped by his/her condition, Hopkins portrays the hysterical trance state as powerful and potentially advantageous. If properly mobilized and controlled, hypnotic suggestibility signals a greater capacity to unify body and mind, normal and paranormal. Although Dianthe is weakened by her extended periods under hypnosis and does indeed experience amnesia and incapacitation, this should be seen as an expression of her abjection under the present social conditions. Reuel better embodies a balance between black and white, masculine and feminine, science and psychology, and he learns to manage his gifts of animal magnetism and mesmerism. Like the super-ego responsible for limiting the uncontrollable urges of the id, Reuel's nature is "deep and silent and self-suppressing" (75). The national narrative of the mixed-race family is transformed into an allegory of national psychology, providing a model for psychic and social healing.

Reuel possesses the capacity to balance black and white, masculine and feminine, body and mind. His role as powerful hybrid is contrasted with that of Aubrey, his traitorous friend, biological brother, and "white" double.[39] Like Aubrey, Reuel is physically powerful, with "superior physical endowments," a "vast breadth of shoulder," and a "strong throat" (3). Both men are intellectual medical students who read and practice contemporary psychology. But Reuel alone is capable of feeling and expressing emotion. He evidences "dog-like" devotion, "affection and worship" for his friend, whereas Aubrey is as cold and unfeeling as the statue of "a Greek God" he resembles (6). Following Reuel's confession of love for Dianthe, Aubrey Livingston reacts like living stone: "His face was like marble in its impassiveness. The other's [Reuel's] soft and tremulous tones, fearless yet moist eyes and broken sentences, appeared to awaken no response in his breast" (43). Reuel's openness to love as well as to the uncanny is described in the stereotypical language of femininity, his "soft tones" and "moist eyes" symbolizing his permeability and penetrability. It is precisely this openness of mind and heart that will make him a suitable king of Telassar, a leader capable of bridging the divide between Africa and America, the occult and the rational, femininity and masculinity. Reuel's collusion in creating Dianthe's new identity reveals his participation in the erasure of mixed-race female identity, while also highlighting Reuel's tenuous position due to his own secret black heritage. Only after Reuel abandons his allegiance to white power structures (including Harvard, Western medicine, and Aubrey) and accepts his own authority as a black man (including his occult powers) will he be worthy of the title of African king.

While Reuel's feminization is a sign of his capacity for synthetic thinking, it also marks a particular erotic relationship with Aubrey. Throughout the novel, Aubrey and Reuel seem locked in a fatal attraction of their own. Accordingly, in the first chapter Reuel "gazed admiringly at the handsome face" of his friend, looking "with soft caressing eyes" at Aubrey as the two discuss mesmerism (7).[40] The attraction is partly based on the unwitting pull of likeness, since the two men are in fact brothers. In addition, Aubrey's desire for Dianthe can be read as an expression of competition with Reuel, a classic example of Sedgwickian homoeroticism, with Dianthe literally positioned "between men" who seek her love. The overlapping desires—familial and romantic, homoerotic and heterosexual—are deliberately opaque, for the inequalities of slavery and American race relations create a gnarled family tree in which "love is not always legitimate" (66).

Ignorant of their shared blood, Aubrey is obsessed with his sister. According to Augusta Rohrbach, Aubrey's "lust for Dianthe is the primitive desire for incest not the racialized desire of white for black."[41] In this view, incest in Of One Blood is an expression of twisted psychology rather than the biological inheritance of race. While I agree that Hopkins is deeply invested in psychological drives, Rohrbach underestimates the way that personal psychology and social forces are inextricably linked through the peculiar racial history of the United States. Aubrey's desire may be an unconscious drive toward incest, one shared by his "black" brother Reuel, but it is also a conscious expression of his assumption of racial entitlement, which Reuel does not possess. Aubrey is, by blood, as black (and white) as Dianthe or Reuel, but he believes himself to a privileged white son of the South and uses that authority. At the same time, the irony is that he is truly "of one blood" with the two people he abuses. As a result of both his ignorance of his biological ties to Reuel and Dianthe and his feeling of white privilege, Aubrey commits "bad" incest; in contrast, Reuel's incestuous love for Dianthe is never consummated, and it emerges from Reuel's recognition of and identification with Dianthe's mixed-race heritage. These complicated sibling relationships reveal how slavery and post-Reconstruction racism create truly unhealthy divisions. Indeed, Aubrey's crimes against Dianthe might be said to result from his own role as a victim of slavery's obfuscation of family ties and trespassing of taboos.

The divides between black and white, material and spiritual realms are further illustrated in the geographies of Africa and America, West and East. Hopkins invents an archaeological expedition for Reuel in Africa as a contrast to the white urban intellectualism of Boston. The Africa in *Of One Blood* is based on historical African civilization and an invented mystical mythology. In the novel, Reuel and Charlie learn that Ethiopia is the true cradle of civilization, providing the foundation for Egyptian achievement in science and the arts, which in turn was the basis of Greek civilization and Western culture.[42] The consequence of this revisionist history is no less than the establishment of "the Negro as the most ancient source of all that you value in modern life" (87).[43] Instead of representing the antithesis of civilization and progress, the African becomes the progenitor of Western civilization, and the African American is its rightful heir. Hopkins redefines America's future as an interracial marriage, a mixed-race family and consciousness. The state of blacks in modern America, Hopkins suggests, reveals more about American racist practices than inherent racial aptitude. In keeping with the novel's association of Africa and blackness with the unconscious mind, Charlie jokingly but accurately predicts that the African city of Meroe will be entered via the "back door key of the sphinx' head [*sic*]" (97). Meroe and its modern incarnation Telassar function structurally as the hidden, repressed, and denied half of a national psychology. Reuel offers the possibility of bringing the repressed to light and ultimately unifying these halves. As Otten explains, the "protoanalytic structure" of Hopkins's novel reveals that "if race can be seen as a pathologically hidden side of the self, then it can also be therapeutically brought to the surface and refigured."[44] In her invention of a model for social and mental divisions, Hopkins echoes, and outstrips, contemporary theories of individual and group psychology to account for racial and gender differences.

The language of psychology and the hidden self is, for Hopkins, always an expression of racial dualism. There is an evocative interplay between the registers of race and psychology. In one of her trance states, Dianthe describes her mesmeric powers in language that echoes W.E.B. Du Bois's formulation of the color line from *The Souls of Black Folk* (1903): "I know much but as yet have not the power to express it: I see much clearly, much dimly, of the powers and influences behind the Veil, and yet I cannot name them. Some time the full power will be mine; and mine shall be thine" (40). According to the ontology of *Of One Blood*, the "Veil" refers to the line between the "real" world and the spirit realm, where ghosts speak and people have powers of mind control. While Schrager argues that Hopkins feminizes Du Bois's famous concept of double consciousness, I argue that Hopkins's revision is even more significant than gender alone.[45] Racialization, feminization, and the unconscious are all states of invisibility and untapped power.[46] Only when these hidden issues are brought to light, when they have moved into conscious awareness, can society be transformed.

Consistent with her representation of blackness, Hopkins feminizes Africa, describing Meroe as the "queenly city" of Ethiopia (94). Hopkins thus conjoins nineteenth-century imperialist discourses that represent Africa as savage, sexualized, and feminized with the twentieth-century psychological model of the unconscious as irrational (and thus feminine). Africa, femininity, and the unconscious are linked, contrasted to the masculine, "rational" model of the United States. As Valerie Rohy convincingly argues, "Hopkins' strategy in *Of One Blood* represents a sort of compromise, which reverses but does not abandon the binarisms of western philosophy."[47] The United States will have to learn to listen to its black/feminine half if the future is to be progressive, and not regressive.

Yet, there is a limitation to Hopkins's fantasy resolution, for she leaves out actual women like Mira and Dianthe, who are, in Deborah McDowell's phrase, "bodily vessels of history" rather than agents of change themselves.[48] Candace, the African queen, is a darker-skinned and more powerful version of Dianthe, yet she is not a person so much as a title that exists in relation to her king. She is Reuel's inferior, bowing to his male authority, sinking "upon the cushions at his feet that had served her for footstools" (137). Reuel's succession to the throne of Telassar offers a new chapter in world history in which an American black man is a powerful figure of authority. While the future of African American women remains uncertain, the novel is unambiguous about the ongoing power of kinship, miscegenation, and incest. Reuel's incestuous desire for Dianthe is not discharged so much as displaced onto her African double. In this way, we see that "bad" incest has been banished, while the desire for familial likeness returns, and is rewarded this time with legitimate marriage. *Of One Blood* reveals the familial imagination at the heart of contemporary racial fiction and the field of psychology. The family romance is as much a story of race relations as it is of the foundations of Western culture.

Psychology functions in *Of One Blood* as a metaphor for racial relations, but race turns out to reveal just as much about the field of psychology. In the work of James, Binet, Charcot, and Freud, psychoanalytic structures of mind are based in the familiar language of race and civilization. To be raced is to be atavistic, uncivilized, regressive. Hopkins's association of Africa with the unconscious is problematic since it threatens to relegate African Americans "to the position of the 'repressed unconscious' or 'secret self'" of white America, which "invokes racist connotations of Africans as 'inferior,' 'primitive,' 'irrational,' or 'uncivilized.'"[49] Hopkins's formulation calls to mind Freud's infamous claim that "the sexual life of adult women is a 'dark continent' for psychology."[50] Freud reveals the racialization of femininity in the popular (masculine) medical imagination, as well as the feminization of racial difference. As Mary Ann Doane explains, "Just as Africa was considered to be the continent without a history, European femininity represented a pure presence and timelessness (whose psychical history was held, by Freud, to be largely inaccessible)."[51] Hopkins does rely on turn-of-the-twentieth-century anthropological discourse that associates race with primitivism, such as was popularized in the 1893 World's Columbian Exhibition in Chicago (and on which Freud's theories of racial and sexual development rely). However, Hopkins also revises those racist assumptions, redefining African and African American primitivism and irrationality as *superior* knowledge, advanced civilization, and awesome mystical/ spiritual/psychic powers. Indeed, African technology supersedes American invention: Ai (homonym for "I," which is composed of conscious and unconscious states of mind, or what Freud would later identify as a tripartite structure of ego, superego, and id) teaches Reuel Telassaran methods of reading the future and seeing the past.

Hopkins's Telassar represents blackness as a source of wisdom both otherworldly and progressive, originary and advanced. In *Of One Blood*, Africa is a place of mystical knowledge and mesmeric powers, but it is also a land steeped in history, architecture, and art. Africa is not the absence of civilization and mental capacity, existing outside of consciousness; Africa and blackness instead function as the world's id, an untapped reservoir of knowledge and power. Reuel is like the superego, charged with bringing the id's power into consciousness and recognition.[52] He will put the ancient arts of Telassar into contact with the twentieth century, thereby uniting the spiritual and material worlds, Africa and America, black and white. As such, he is a figure of mulatto modernity, a world citizen and model of psychic and racial integration.[53] Hopkins mediates between racial stereotype and radical revisionism, just as Reuel is meant to balance white and black, masculinity and femininity, medicine and mysticism.

While Hopkins portrays Africa as the heart of enlightenment rather than darkness, a once-great civilization that will soon be great again, the United States in *Of One Blood* is a nation far less civilized than its white citizens would like to believe. In fact, Hopkins's America continually threatens to regress to the ethics and practices of slavery: once Reuel is gone, Aubrey manipulates Dianthe like his father controlled Mira, rendering her a passive black female body to be used for his sexual pleasure; he murders his fiancé Molly Vance; and he enlists his loyal servant Jim to kill Reuel in Africa.[54] Likewise, it is no accident that Aubrey takes Dianthe from elite, academic Boston back to his family's southern plantation. The America of the novel does not stand for modernity, progress, and enlightenment, but represents the savagery and barbarism of slavery that is always ready to reemerge. This "hidden self" is the white, masculine authority of brute force and sexual aggression.

Back to Africa: Freudian Fantasies and Displacements

Critics have long argued over the significance of *Of One Blood*'s geographic shift from America to Africa; most interpret Reuel's return to Africa as a mark of Hopkins's pessimism. Typical of this perspective, Susan Gillman argues that the novel forecloses positive change: "The novel concludes that for the protagonists there is no possibility for a happy ending in America or elsewhere: Reuel returns to Africa to rule with Queen Candace over an imagined Pan-African community that is already under threat."[55] Luciano, on the other hand, interprets the novel's open ending as "a kind of melancholic deferral of closure" that illustrates the cycle of denial and repression that produces (and reproduces) racial melancholia.[56] I argue that Hopkins's refusal of a facile happy ending must be understood as an act of social criticism, and not merely as an expression of personal psychology. Indeed, just as Hopkins shows the impossibility of distinguishing incest from miscegenation, endogamy from exogamy, she refuses to see the political and the personal as distinct realms, or as requiring different solutions. The novel's irresolution is deliberate, reflecting the incomplete integration of the national psychology. We as readers may feel dissatisfied that Reuel has not (yet) returned to the United States, that his brand of mystical/material communion is not (yet) universal, and we may crave vengeance like Dianthe, but this dissatisfaction highlights that the work of transforming American racial consciousness is not finished by having read a novel. The reader is charged with carrying forward the work of compensation and integration. The work of uniting history and fantasy, African mysticism and American culture remains an unfulfilled promise. Likewise, America's recognition of its darker half is incomplete, but not impossible.[57] Hopkins returns the reader to the situation of social unrest and segregation, implicitly demanding a real-life action plan.

Deborah McDowell argues that the novel's turn toward Africa is not an escape from American social life, but should be understood "as a version of Ralph Ellison's hero's cellar down below: as a hiatus of a kind or, in his narrator's words, 'a covert preparation for a more overt action.'"[58] In this light, Hopkins's "back to Africa" and supernatural plots function as parallel strategies for working out and revising American racial and gender discrimination. Hopkins does not offer her readers Africa as an alternative to transforming U.S. racial and gender relations. Rather, Africa in *Of One Blood* functions, to use the language of Freud's *On Dreams*, as a *displacement* and *condensation* of U.S. racial politics. Freud defines displacement as the projection of a particular psychological meaning onto another, unrelated object, often through inversion. Condensation appears as an overdetermination of symbolism, as in the dense web of ancient history, mythology, and occult practices Hopkins imagines for Telassar.[59] In the novel, I argue, the significance of race is heightened through displacement, such as by Hopkins's reversals of African backwardness and American progress. Africa is America's double, and

America is Africa's. Hopkins's Africa represents a rich history of black achievement that has been forgotten or denied; the retrieval or creation of such a history in America is left to her readers to fulfill.[60]

To underscore the ideological link between Africa and America, Hopkins continually returns the reader to the American scene throughout the African portion of the novel. Thus, after Reuel is proclaimed Ergamenes, ruler of Telassar, Hopkins informs her readers that this king of Africa responds to his lush new surroundings not as an African, but as the American he is: "But Reuel remembered the loathsome desert that stood in grim determination guarding the entrance to this paradise against all intrusion, and with an *American's practical common sense*, bewailed this waste of material" (134, emphasis mine). Reuel remains the quintessential pragmatist in the image of Ben Franklin or Thomas Paine, even in Africa. In turn, Hopkins's Africa reflects the contemporary United States, promising to be a new melting pot. Ai foretells, "The tide of immigration shall set in the early days of the twentieth century, toward Afric's shores, so long bound in the chains of barbarism and idolatry" (143). Africa is to be the new Promised Land, welcoming the huddled masses of darker-skinned people around the world who did not immigrate voluntarily to the United States and have not been treated as equal citizens since their arrival. Hopkins's Africa echoes the tenets of freedom and progress dear to American national identity, but transforms them to deliver to its black citizens the inclusion and progressive possibility promised in America's founding literature but denied in contemporary practice.

Time, Narration, and the Uncanny

Hopkins's reversal of stereotypes of African backwardness and American progress reveals Africa to be the source of civilization and America to be regressing toward savagery. Hopkins plays with polarities and linear temporality in the novel in order express the traumatic nature of African American history and shed new light on American values. For example, ghosts from the past intervene to change their ancestors' future; narration and point of view shift unexpectedly; and plot points are told out of chronological order. Taken together, these disruptions to conventional time and narration highlight the legacy of violence and oppression that, Hopkins implies, continues to imperil the U.S. nation. Secrets multiply when memory of previous abuses is repressed or denied. The novel's disorienting mode of narration, coupled with the novel's fantastical elements, marks the eruption of the uncanny, which is the result of American social and political inequality.

Mira is the most significant figure for the return of the repressed, representing the temporal disturbance caused by slavery. She continually appears to warn her descendents of their repetitions of the past. Thus, after Aubrey attempts to coerce Dianthe into becoming his mistress, Mira appears to Dianthe with a cryptic warning of secrets exposed. Mira's appearance is followed immediately by a shift in narration from past to present tense. This disruption of narration and temporality reveals young Aubrey's otherworldly power over Dianthe: "[Aubrey] turned from her and going to a distant part of the room, threw himself into a chair and covered his face with his hands. Against her will, better promptings and desires, the unfortunate girl *is drawn* by invisible influences across the room to the man's side. *Presently he holds her* in his eager, strong embrace, his face and tears hidden against her shoulder. *She does not struggle* in his clasp, only looks *into the future* with the hopeless agony of dumb despair. At length he broke the silence" (72, emphasis mine). In its shift from the measured, omnipotent past tense in which the entire novel is narrated ("He turned from her") to the present tense ("the unfortunate girl is drawn," "he holds her," "she does not struggle") and back to the past tense ("he broke the silence"), Hopkins enacts for her readers the trauma of the past returning in the present. The trauma theorist Cathy Caruth describes trauma as an event that "is experienced too soon, too unexpectedly, to be fully known and is therefore not available to consciousness until it imposes itself again, repeatedly, in the nightmares and repetitive actions of the survivor."[61] Hopkins's paranormal intrusions mark the traumatic past's return. Like her mother before her, Dianthe is powerless. Her speech is muted ("dumb despair"), and her body is enveloped in Aubrey's arms. Dianthe is thus rendered a passive object whose will is erased, and with it, her capacity for consent. She shares the family talent for hypnotic suggestion and seeing spirits, but she is as imprisoned within her receptivity as she is within Aubrey's embrace. In effect, she is a ghost—unseen, unheard, without the protection of family and friends. Like her mother, Mira, she is as good as dead. Such is the situation of mixed-race women in turn-of-the-twentieth-century America—utterly alone, without community, family, or friends.

These narrative disruptions reveal a cultural trauma of victimization that cannot be channeled into a progressive narrative. Yet Aubrey is similarly described as not being fully in control, as his role in the seduction is expressed in the passive voice (Dianthe "is drawn by invisible forces").

Notable, too, is the fact that Aubrey is here capable of emotion, that is, of producing tears; he is like Reuel and Dianthe, but he hides his vulnerability in order to get what he wants. The absence of clear agency alludes both to the mysteriousness of Aubrey's power over Dianthe and its intangibility. This use of the passive voice underscores the similarly naturalized, ubiquitous, and unchecked authority that Aubrey embodies through masculinity, visible whiteness, and medical science (hypnosis). His birthright has been his unlimited access to black women without impediment or penalty. Aubrey's control is so complete that his agency is submerged, his power naturalized. Within the novel's logic, Aubrey's secret biological claim to blackness is doubtless the source of his mystical power, but Aubrey's social claim to whiteness hides his abuse of that gift. Hopkins also suggests that Aubrey's actions are not entirely willful; "his face and tears" are hidden, leaving readers to wonder if he is actually master of his own aggression or if he is likewise compelled by the forces of traumatic national history. Social forces are inseparable from psychological ones.

Mira's appearance in the text always signals the past returning in the present, but the present also breaks through to affect the future, further revealing the need to change the status quo. Likewise, objects come to life to prevent continued abuses, such as a letter that mysteriously reveals itself to Dianthe in order to warn her of Aubrey's treachery: "Dianthe lay in long and silent meditation. . . . Dianthe's restlessness was soothed, and she began tracing the shadows on the carpet and weaving them into fantastic images of imagination. What *breaks* her reverie? The moonlight *gleams* on something white and square; it is a letter. She left the couch and picked it up" (168, emphasis mine). As Dianthe lies in a near-hypnotic state, secrets are revealed to her across time and distance. The heretofore hidden letter, written by Jim to Aubrey, reveals Aubrey's plan to murder Reuel in Egypt. This scene presents Dianthe for the first time as master of her own powers, which she uses in order to rescue Reuel. Dianthe ceases to be a passive object; she becomes the master of objects as the letter reveals itself to her, highlighting her powers of mind similar to those of her brothers. Just as Dianthe here manages briefly to be an active agent, time itself breaks free of linear chronology. The present interrupts the retrospective narration of the past ("was," "began," "breaks," "gleams," "left"). Such temporal disturbances call to mind Freud's formulation of the uncanny, when déjà-vu moments of the past reemerge and repeat in the present. In *Of One Blood*, time *will* be out of joint—with ghosts from the past intervening and the present breaking through past-tense narration—until African Americans receive recognition and redress for the history of slavery in the United States. Once again, the novel's social meanings are expressed through psychological events and discourse. As Claudia Tate describes in her study *Psychoanalysis and Black Novels*, "explicit, public, racial identifications" accompany "the implicit, private psychological effects of narrative subjectivity."[62] In Hopkins's last novel, the private has fully erupted into the public, and vice versa. The family's past is the nation's history and, like Morrison's ghost-baby Beloved decades later, it won't go away until the story has been told. Indeed, what I see as the novel's model for an integrated psyche functions as an example of the "latent wishes" or "unconscious discourses" that erupt in some black novels. Such eruptions in *Of One Blood* function as expressions of the American racial, social, and political landscape. The psychoanalytic critic Shoshana Felman describes the treatment for traumatized subjects as learning to "testify"—to narrate the traumatic events in order to regain a sense of agency, to rediscover "one's own proper name, one's signature."[63] "Fantastical" fiction like *Of One Blood* should properly be understood as an attempt to narrate that traumatic past to create an alternative future.

The message of the novel is that only when artificial, imposed Manichean binaries are integrated will the racial-cum-psychological truth of American life emerge. Only when the gifted biracial subject learns to unify black and white, unconsciousness and consciousness, science and mysticism, will the past cease interrupting the present. Until such time, unexplained phenomena promise to increase in intensity and frequency. Thus, while Reuel is in Africa but before he is initiated into the powerful secrets of Meroe (and while Aubrey is simultaneously committing rape, incest, and miscegenation), Reuel receives the mother of all visions. In an orgiastic crescendo of parapsychological revelation, Mira reveals to Reuel the villainy of Jim Titus and Aubrey, and then Reuel hears the spectral voice of Dianthe calling, "Reuel, Reuel, save me!" (90). Next, a lion roars nearby, "as of a human voice rising to heaven in passionate appeal for mercy, and dying away in sobbing and shuddering despair," and Charlie receives a message of his own: his sister Molly calling, "'Charlie, brother, save me!'" (91). This truly fantastical intervention combines auditory and visual visitations, animal and human messengers, life and death. Even the rather dull Charlie Vance is granted access to this mystical intervention. Struck dumb by this outpouring of mystical telephony, Reuel is temporarily incapable of mastering his powers of hypnosis in order to interpret the message. Finally, "after several ineffectual attempts to concentrate his powers,"

Reuel is able "to exercise the power" of clairvoyant sight to see the events that had occurred in the United States during his absence (91). This fantastical vision, with its dead black and white women crying from the afterlife and a lion wailing across the African desert, is as complete an expression of the alignment of the unconscious with the mystical and the feminine as anything in American literature. On account of its extreme Gothicism and surrealism, this vision eloquently speaks to the violent silencing of black and white women in American social life. Since Dianthe and Molly are already dead, their communication from the grave is less a cry for help than a demand for redress. What Hopkins's female characters demand is the "vast scheme of compensation and retribution" that Reuel reads about in the novel's opening scene (8).[64] The novel as a whole functions as an act of compensation, giving credit as it does to racial identity and its association with the unconscious, and of retribution, as it critiques and punishes Aubrey. The novel is itself a cry across the wilderness, calling attention to a long-denied history.

Just as Reuel and Charlie receive a message, so do readers. Hopkins warns that redress cannot be achieved through simple revenge. Indeed, Hopkins underscores this point by dramatically breaking the narration. After Dianthe considers poisoning Aubrey for his treachery, the narration shifts tense and addresses readers with a cautionary message: "We know we're tempted. The world is full of precedents, the air with impulses, society with men and spirit tempters. But what invites sin? Is it not something within ourselves? Are we not placed here with a sinful nature which the plan for salvation commands us to overcome? . . . When we conquer sin, we say were are virtuous, triumphant, and when we fall, we excuse our sins by saying, 'It is fate'" (171). Here the text speaks directly to its readers through the inclusive "we" and the interrogative mode. In this passage, the text's unconscious seems to speak, breaking the wall between character and reader, fiction and reality. Where the novel as form creates a reality for its readers, these unanswered questions open up that closed fictional world.[65] This message of social obligation and psychological justification is the only such utterance (save for the novel's last paragraph)[66] that is directed at the audience in order explicitly to extend the world of the text to the world of its readers. Hopkins breaks the narrative frame, shifting from the language of social obligation to the rhetoric of religion—temptation, sin, and salvation. The world of men takes credit for virtue but blames God for our failings.[67] Hopkins transforms the burden of history into the fallibilities of all men and women. Attributing the power of white patriarchy to the choices of ordinary people, the narrator tells us that sin is "something within ourselves"; sin, rather than blood, has become part of "the hidden self" that must be brought to light. Our mistakes, Hopkins tells us, cannot be excused on account of social norms or even, she implies, righteous anger. Dianthe's desire to kill her tormentor is criticized as a sin that "salvation" demands we combat.

Given this sudden turn, readers are forced to acknowledge that the crimes of rape and racism within the novel cannot simply be blamed on social norms; these are the crimes of individual men and women, and responsibility lies with the humans who commit them. Hopkins here explicitly contrasts novelistic inevitability—such as Aubrey's repetition of familial crimes and Dianthe's victimization—with personal responsibility in the real world. Far from being what Sundquist labels "escapist fiction," then, *Of One Blood* argues for the reality of fantasy and the rights and responsibilities of individuals amid powerful social forces.[68] *Of One Blood* is an indictment of contemporary power structures, but responsibility for changing those structures is placed squarely in its readers' hands. As in Winnifred Eaton's fictions discussed in the next chapter, Hopkins uses the fictional world of the mixed-race family to illustrate contemporary inequalities, demanding that readers take these lessons to heart in the outside world. Drawing from the sentimental tradition that demanded its readers' tears as evidence of sympathy, turn-of-the-twentieth-century ethnic women writers demand that their readers respond with anger, outrage, and a commitment to social action of some kind, however inchoately articulated.

The novel's various binaries—black and white, science and mysticism, Africa and America, past and future, personal psychology and social forces—all combine to imagine a unified psyche in a world beyond "caste prejudice" (129). The novel's last paragraphs situate Reuel in Telassar with old Aunt Hannah, where "he spends his days in teaching his people all that he has learned in years of contact with modern culture" (193). Once more the narration shifts to the present tense as Reuel stands at the threshold of a new century, doing the work of integrating the two halves of racial consciousness, two temporalities, and two types of civilization. Meanwhile, younger women are largely left out of the equation, too damaged by their experiences to participate in the work of cultural transformation. Hannah stands as a reminder of the *ancien régime* of slavery and concubinage. She is a mute witness to the past, not an agent of the future. Dianthe is dead. And while Candace represents physical and mystical powers superior to those of the American women, she has no personality or individuality; she remains a cipher rather than a citizen, under continual threat from the forces outside.

The future remains uncertain, with "the advance of mighty nations penetrating the dark, mysterious forests of his native land" (193). Hopkins again reminds her readers that such transformations may begin with books, but they can only be carried out in the contemporary world. Moreover, by claiming Telassar, not the United States, as Reuel's "native land," Hopkins once more links fantasy and reality, past and future, Africa and America in an endless Möbius strip. This embrace of Africa is a turn "toward defining the 'race problem' as global rather than merely domestic."[69] The novel finally moves from America and notion of divided national consciousness into a world community, through the acknowledgment of the neocolonial origins of the American nation. Once more, the reader is charged with ending gender and racial inequalities, although now on a world stage. The novel refuses to resolve these tensions.

Pauline Hopkins's novel *Of One Blood*, like the other works I study in this book, represents the United States through the metaphor of the family. Her fictional world of sibling rivalry, fratricide, rape, and incest is a microcosm of the slavery and race prejudice upon which U.S. national life is founded. Hopkins's novel dramatically transforms the rhetoric of the national family into a model of a national-cum-world consciousness equally comprised of black and white, mysticism and medicine, ancient and modern civilizations. Such a symbiotic relationship, however, is as fragile within the world of the novel as it is in the world of its readers: women's role in this future is uncertain, and black authority remains at risk of violent suppression. The novel fantastically imagines transformations in psychology, but translating that to social life must be realized by readers in real life.

2 /   Half-Caste Family Romances: Divergent Paths of Asian American Identity

In "A Contract" (1902), one of Winnifred Eaton's popular Orientalist romances published under the pen name Onoto Watanna, O-Kiku-san, a young Japanese woman, explains to her suitor, the Japanese-born but racially white businessman Masters, the difference between citizenship and belonging. She tells him, "You Japanese citizen sure thing . . . all the same you jus' foreigner, all the same" (55).[1] Masters protests, insisting: "You are trying to rob me of my birthright. Am I or am I not Japanese?" (56). Kiku's answer is unwavering: "Japanese citizen, yes. . . . Japanese man? No, naever" (56). Speaking as a full-blooded Japanese woman in Japan, Kiku articulates the vast gap between legal rights and social recognition, between being a "sure" citizen under the law while nevertheless ("all the same") being perceived as "jus' foreigner," one who is virtually indistinguishable from all other foreigners (as indicated by the repetition of "all the same"). In this scene, Masters wants to be recognized as Japanese, and the most effective means by which he imagines achieving recognition is to marry a Japanese woman, with the hope that "the next of our line possibly may be partly Japanese, and the next" (56). In this story, as throughout Eaton's body of work, those who look different on account of race—whether as a white man in Japan or a biracial woman in the United States—are perpetually seen as "jus'" foreigners. The white man's status as perpetual foreigner in Japan neatly reverses the far more common experience of Asians in early twentieth-century America, particularly since Kiku's judgment of Masters's foreignness is also based on his apparent failure to assimilate: he was educated in the West and lives in the English colony within Japan. Here, as throughout Eaton's fiction, mixed blood is the primary measure of and means to cultural acceptance, more powerful than the legal rights granted by citizenship and more persuasive than residency.

Eaton's formulation of the "citizen sure thing" who is nonetheless a perpetual foreigner complicates Lisa Lowe's paradigmatic account of the ways that "the American *citizen* has been defined over against the Asian *immigrant*, legally, economically, and culturally."[2] Again and again in Eaton's fiction, the route to recognition is imagined through romance, breeding, and familial ties, embodied by the figure of the "half-caste," the offspring of a white man and a Japanese woman. With her focus on the plight of the biracial figure born of the West's previous encounters with the East, Eaton's stories should be read as aggressive dramas of national belonging in which white men desire mixed-race women, and mixed-race children demand recognition in the U.S. family. In the story "A Half Caste" (1899) in particular, Eaton merges the interracial love story with a familial reunification plot in order to make the controversial claim that the threat of incest may be productive, serving as the means by which the half-caste can secure her rights as daughter and citizen. In Eaton's fiction, the moment of incestuous desire and its disclosure occasions recognition of the half-caste's rights as a member of the family and, by extension, as a citizen of the American "fatherland." By contrast, in Eaton's oeuvre, incestuous eroticism between siblings signifies a fantasy of equality and belonging, a unification of racial divisions, both within the half-caste's blood and with the culture(s) at large. In works like *The Heart of Hyacinth* (1903), identity is defined not only by blood, but also by cultural identification. The half-caste sibling romance is thus an alternative social order, where familiality is recognized as a product of mothers and fathers, motherlands and fatherlands, Japanese and white cultures.

The term "half-caste," which was invented to define the mixed-race children of European fathers and Indian mothers on the subcontinent, relies upon the entrenched gendering of raced bodies and the racialization of women.[3] In America as in Europe, masculinity and fatherhood have long been associated with the West, while femininity and motherhood have been aligned with racial and cultural Otherness. In the United States, ever since Commodore Matthew Perry "opened" Japan to American trade in 1853, American audiences have responded enthusiastically to the image of an American captain penetrating the mystical, oriental East via military and economic might—symbolized by the cannons extending from Commodore Perry's ships when he entered Tokyo

Bay. This "scenario" of Western political-sexual conquest, to use Diana Taylor's term for the "predictable, formulaic, hence repeatable" forms that tropes of encounter take, was particularly compelling, reiterating as it did long-standing Western belief in Western masculinity and Eastern feminization, while also providing a powerful image of the United States as a global power.[4] Popular literature and theatrical entertainments from the late nineteenth century replayed this scenario. From Lafcadio Hearn's nonfiction books about Japan to John Luther Long's short story "Madame Butterfly" (1898) to Giacomo Puccini's operatic version (1904), American audiences were fascinated by tales of a mysterious Japan and titillated by depictions of the pleasures and perils of interracial romance.[5]

Capitalizing on the public's interest in such dramas, Onoto Watanna made the romance between white American men and exotic Asian women her stock-in-trade.[6] Onoto Watanna was the pen name of Winnifred Eaton, the daughter of an English-educated Chinese woman and a British father. Born and raised in Canada, Eaton lived in and traveled across the United States for most of her adult life, but found fame and fortune writing popular romances set in Japan, a country she never visited.[7] Eaton chose a Japanese-sounding pen name, posed for publicity photographs in full Japanese dress, and created a fanciful new biography that matched her literary plots: "Onoto Watanna" claimed to be the daughter of a Japanese noblewoman and an English silk merchant.[8] Meanwhile, Eaton's elder sister, Edith, wrote sympathetic stories about Chinese immigrants for U.S. newspapers, which were published under her Chinese name, Sui Sin Far. Winnifred Eaton's exchange of her mother's Chinese ancestry for a fictional Japanese lineage followed the current of popular sentiment, which found (at least for a brief period at the turn of the twentieth century) Japanese heritage to be more exotically appealing and less threatening than Chinese ancestry. Despite—or rather, because of—their vital role in gold mining, the building of the transcontinental railroads, and the settlement of the western United States, by the late nineteenth century Chinese immigrants had become the target of public resentment. Increasingly associated with "coolie" labor and "Yellow Peril" fears, Chinese laborers were legally excluded from immigration and naturalization in 1882.[9] Meanwhile, the Japanese benefited from their nation's military success in the Sino-Japanese War (1894–95), which inspired widespread admiration for and fascination with the formerly closed nation.[10] Eaton's window of opportunity was sadly narrow, for public opinion would turn against the Japanese after the Russo-Japanese War (1904–5); Japan's military victory provoked

FIGURE 1. *Hyacinth*. Illustration by Kiyokichi Sano (signed EM-HMS) from
The Heart of Hyacinth.

U.S. anxieties about Japanese expansion, resulting in the "Gentlemen's Agreement" of 1907, which effectively extended the Chinese Exclusion Act to Japanese laborers.

In the context of shifting U.S. international policy, Winnifred Eaton's decision to focus on Japanese characters and settings was a canny one. Her half-caste romances rely on clichéd orientalist tropes to tell fabulous tales of love affairs in foreign lands, charmingly populated by geisha girls and samurai and decorated with rickshaws, samisen, tatami mats, and shoji screens. The feminization of an orientalized Asia was reinforced in the marketing of Eaton's novels, which were beautifully illustrated and embossed, and given such florid (and floral) titles as *The Wooing of Wystaria* (1902), *The Heart of Hyacinth* (1903), *The Love of Azalea* (1904), and *A Japanese Blossom* (1906); the "flowers" of the titles refer to the novels' plucky heroines, whose sexual appeal lies in their femininity and oriental exoticism.[11]

Due to her exoticization and reliance on generic romance plots, critics have tended to dismiss Eaton's Japanese settings as unreal and insignificant. Dominika Ferens argues that Eaton simply "removed her characters from the field of U.S. racial politics."[12] In another vein, Jean Lee Cole argues that Eaton's heroines remain exceptional cases; although she "was able to establish her readers' sympathy for [her half-caste heroine], she never asked or expected them to transfer that sympathy to Eurasians (or Asians) as a whole."[13] I argue, to the contrary, that Eaton used the East–West script in provocative and political ways to address concerns with citizenship, national identity, and cultural recognition. Susan Koshy contrasts the prohibition surrounding miscegenation at "home" in the United States with the widely sanctioned practice of interracial romance abroad; as she explains, "the extraterritorial represents the space identified with the forms of sexuality that had to be excluded from the moral order of the nation."[14] Like Koshy, I want to highlight the relationship between these two geographic spaces in the social imaginary when miscegenation and racial identity are at stake. Eaton's depictions of Japan are entirely dependent upon U.S. racial politics, if often illustrated through tactics of disguise, indirection, and reversal. Like Eaton's reinvention of herself by donning a kimono in publicity photos, her "Japanese" stories should be read less as about trying to "pass" than as a kind of drag performance, under which cover she could highlight the ambiguity of racial and cultural markers and demand inclusion of racialized citizens. Indeed, the "Japan" of her fiction is a screen for U.S. racial politics and economic practices on which she projected the nation's anxieties about and fantasies of racial mixing, as well as offered imaginative resolutions in which the nation's mixed-race offspring find their legitimate place.

By setting her novels and stories in a Japan made familiar (and feminine) by Western orientalism and imperialism generally, and by American racial and sexual codes in particular, Eaton exposes the gendered practices of American racism as well as the inequalities of global capitalism. The gendering of race, particularly the feminization of Asian men through Western orientalism, has been amply documented by critics such as Edward Said, Gary Okihiro, Frank Chin, and David Eng.[15] More recently, Leslie Bow has shown how Asian and Asian American women have served as "symbolic boundary markers for ethnic and national affiliations" through their sexuality, which is typically figured through the logic of loyalty and betrayal.[16] In light of Bow's formulation, Eaton's fiction highlights the ways that women's national identity and loyalty are secured through heterosexual romance or paternity, rather than by women's status as citizens. By paying attention to the role of the half-caste and romantic plots in Eaton's stories and novels, we can discern a critique of white American male hegemony and its treatment of Asian women through a field imaginary defined by race, recognition, and sexual appetite.

In their focus on the in-between space occupied by half-caste women, Eaton's stories and novels call attention to the gap between civic rights and social equality, the distance between one's self-perception vis-à-vis national identity (that is, as citizen) and the far more limited ways that the racialized and gendered body is read by the dominant culture in the United States (foreigner). Eaton's fictions show us an early moment in the construction of a multiethnic American identity, when the rights of citizenship are occluded due to narrow expectations of what constitutes the visible markers of U.S. cultural identity, especially by white men who see in the half-caste only a new form of feminine exoticism. The half-caste is a perpetual *foreigner-citizen*, a position marked by both presence and absence, hypervisibility and invisibility, possibility and lack. In Eaton's fictional universe, the full array of rights and privileges signified by citizenship can only be realized when white men acknowledge their abuse of racialized women by recognizing their mixed-race daughters. This recognition is occasioned by the incest scenario, in which a second generation of interracial romance is thwarted by the revelation of consanguinity. The interracial incest plot is a trope to which Eaton returns again and again, with incest threatening to occur as a result of political and economic inequalities between men and women, whites and Asians,

America and Japan. Eaton defines social belonging in the irrefutable language of shared blood, placing maternity, paternity, and interracial romance at the center of national identification.[17]

Variations of this incest-recognition plot abound in Eaton's oeuvre, functioning to condemn the white father whose abandonment of his Japanese family renders the half-caste alienated and vulnerable, while also illustrating the links between blood, culture, and belonging. In the short story "A Half Caste" (1899), a father unwittingly attempts to seduce his long-lost Amerasian daughter. In "A Father" (1900), a young white man and the half-caste young woman he hopes to wed are dismayed to discover that they share the same father. In other stories, sibling eroticism is endorsed to mark a common love of the Japanese mother and motherland. Thus, in *The Heart of Hyacinth* (1903), a male half-caste falls in love with and marries his adopted white sister, while in "Miss Lily and Miss Chrysanthemum: The Love Story of Two Japanese Girls in Chicago" (1903), the most compelling romance is the homoerotic relationship between half-caste sisters (one raised in Japan by their mother and another raised in the United States by their father) who are reunited in adulthood.[18] Even in works where there is no incestuous desire, Eaton nonetheless offers a fantasy of familiarity and familial closeness through substitution, where a brother's best friend stands in for the brother himself: in *A Japanese Nightingale* (1901), the half-caste Yuki marries an American whose best friend turns out to be Yuki's brother. Like a musical motif with infinite variations, incest and incestuous eroticism recur to highlight the plight of the half-caste and her longing for a place within the nuclear national family.

While the revelation of the risk of incest halts the progress of the traditional romantic plot—in itself no insignificant detail for a writer of popular romances—it links half-caste children with their families across the divides of race and place, reuniting lost relatives from two continents. Notably, Eaton's stories typically begin with the aftermath of interracial seduction and abandonment, not with the initial interracial encounter, which often does end tragically, with a dead mother à la *Madame Butterfly*. Her tales gain force and political weight from this modification of the familiar interracial romance plot. The Japan of Eaton's fiction is populated with half-caste daughters who have been orphaned by their mothers' deaths and abandoned by their fathers. In the context of incest, the bond of shared blood occasions the white father's belated recognition of his civic and familial responsibilities, while the shared cultural experience of siblings offers a vision of a hybrid future.

The Romance of Recognition

Eaton's white male characters are radically mobile missionaries, businessmen, and sailors—paradigms of Western freedom, privilege, and conquest. They are captivated by the exotic women of Japan, especially the half-caste girls and women whose bodies and faces are ambiguously marked. In contrast to the cosmopolitanism of her male characters, these women lack mobility, financial security, and familial or communal bonds, rendering them vulnerable to exploitation. Eaton's stories imply that without clear ties to a single racial or national—and perhaps most important, familial—community, they are at greater risk of being treated as aesthetic and sexual objects by the white men who pursue them. Echoing the plots of African American gothic romances that turn on denied paternity, "A Half Caste" asks, if a father doesn't acknowledge his own daughter, what is to stop him from seducing her as he did her mother? Importantly, though, while incest threatens, in Eaton's work it also beckons, for the revelation of the blood tie occasions the father's belated recognition of his outcast child, as well as offers hope for an egalitarian partnership among siblings.

The most explicit and cynical of Eaton's incestuous interracial stories is "A Half Caste." The story begins in typical Eatonian fashion, with a white man headed for an adventure in Japan, but takes a sharp turn toward the incest scenario. Norman Hilton is Eaton's emblematic white male who, years earlier, "had married a Japanese girl—in Japanese fashion" but had "left her in American fashion" (3). The Japanese wife had a child, and the story opens with Hilton's return to Japan to find the child he abandoned fifteen years earlier; this sense of purpose falters, however, when he falls in love with a young geisha girl named Kiku (that is, Chrysanthemum, yet another flower girl). Hilton's desire for Kiku is first excited by her difference from the other young women at the teahouse; he admires her "red cheeks, large eyes and white skin" (4), physical attributes at odds with orientalist expectations of "narrow" eyes and "yellow" skin. And yet white skin and red cheeks may be cultivated through elaborate makeup, particularly the exaggerated whiteness of powder and the rosiness of rouge.[19] Eaton is playing with visual markers of racial difference and the contradictory ways those features can be interpreted.

Kiku's speech similarly indicates both her connection to the West and her distance from it. To Hilton, "her broken English was prettier than anything he had ever heard" (6). Kiku's lack of fluency is charming insofar as it marks her fragility, femininity, and exoticism. Like Commodore

Perry before him, Hilton clearly hopes to penetrate what he perceives to be an oriental mystery. Hilton's emphasis on Kiku's "broken English" also reveals a desire for likeness-in-difference: she speaks English he understands, but with an accent that renders it delightfully defamiliarized. Just as her body can be read as both familiar and foreign, so can her speech. Here as elsewhere in Eaton's work, the half-caste's body and speech are marked simultaneously by whiteness and Asianness. Hilton chooses to hear her accent rather than emphasize her fluency.

Although Hilton tries to fit her into a familiar orientalist script, Kiku is neither a "modern" American girl nor a typically demure Japanese maiden. Instead, the narration informs us: "She said things that no American girl would say, and that few Japanese girls would understand, and in spite of this she was a charming individual. . . . She was unlike any Japanese woman he had ever known—unlike any woman he had met" (7). As Hilton here seems to acknowledge, Kiku lives in a marginal state between two recognizable national and racial identities. Kiku's difference from every other woman serves the reader as evidence of her biraciality and, therefore, her structural relation to Hilton, the self-proclaimed father of an Amerasian child. However, Hilton's sexual desire for Kiku in the present blinds him to the consequences and evidence of his past conquests. The revelation of biological relation finally occurs when Kiku speaks back, refusing to be passively read as an exotic and sexual text any longer. She demands of him: "'You thing I loog lig Japanese girl?' She suddenly loosened her hair, and it fell down around her in thick, shining brown curls. 'Thad lig Japanese girl?—thad?—thad?—thad? Thad?' She pushed back the sleeves and showed him the white purity of her arms" (10). Eaton emphasizes the physical markers of Kiku's racial identity: hair that is brown and curly, skin that is "white" and "pure." The use of "purity" is complicated here. In eugenicist terms, half-castes were "half-breeds" whose racial traits were corrupted and weakened by intermarriage. Eaton clearly relies on the ideology of white superiority to privilege Kiku's pale skin. However, in her insistence that Kiku is "pure"—that is, virtuous—in her rejection of Hilton's sexual advances, Eaton provides an ironic gloss on Kiku's racial "impurity," as well as decouples racial superiority from its association with moral superiority. As Peter Brooks explains, the melodramatic moment of recognition (of the blood tie between Kiku and Hilton) is fundamentally "a moment of ethical evidence and recognition" proving Kiku's virtue and worth.[20]

At the level of plot, the exotic geisha girl is revealed to be the long-lost daughter through a fortuitous coincidence that highlights Hilton's

pathological compulsion to return to the site/sight of his crimes. Such a
seemingly unrealistic moment of melodramatic recognition reveals literature as a means to resolve a larger social crisis. As Werner Sollors argues,
the surprise ending in racial and ethnic fiction may not be "'realistically'
convincing, but is the result of a certain aesthetic strategy" that imagines
an ideal response; such an idealized response features a character claiming a previously disavowed ethnic-racial identity, whereas a naturalistic
ending would have the character continue to deny identification with
the denigrated group.[21] The story of incest averted is therefore both a
cautionary tale and an almost-happy ending. With her direct speech and
attention to her physical body—to the signs of whiteness in her brown
hair and fair skin—Kiku demands that her flesh be properly read and
interpreted as a text inscribed by the sins of a callow white father. The
coincidence that brings father and daughter together is thus an "idealized" conclusion wherein the interracial tie is finally acknowledged. And
in its links to very real historical patterns of white male conquest in the
East, the moment of recognition is also a "realistic" conclusion.

Kiku's hysterical repetition of "that?—that?—that? That?" rendered
in a pidgin accent can be read as an example of what Evelyn Ch'ien
describes as "a conscious appropriation of hybridity" in which "appeals
for community are embedded in the writing."[22] Kiku's speech highlights
the fact that her hybridity should have been evident all along.[23] Moreover, her hysterical insistence on the legibility of her body is a form of
self-objectification by means of which she calls attention to Hilton's
objectification of her and his denial of her subjectivity. The white father's
refusal to recognize his daughter in the sexualized body before him is a
kind of psychological injury that demands a response, and an embodied
one at that. As Diana Fuss explains, "The hysteric speaks through her
symptom, transforming the body into a textual utterance."[24] In "A Half
Caste," Kiku's hysterical response to Hilton's seduction is quite literally
a demand that Hilton read her body in order to recognize her as biracial
and, consequently, his own child.

Importantly, while virtually every Eaton story and novel features
a half-caste heroine, these women rarely encounter other women like
themselves; in "A Half-Caste," this makes Hilton's failure to recognize
Kiku all the more striking. In this way, Eaton's choice of an indefinite
article in the title ("A Half Caste") indicates that though Kiku is unique,
she is not unusual or exceptional in her biraciality. Hilton's ignorance
regarding his mixed-race daughter is thus more accurately described
as a sustained act of denial. Kiku's brown curls and pale skin render

her whiteness legible to anyone willing to see, but Hilton has seen only what he wishes to see: an exotic young woman available to his sexual advances.[25] Because so much energy is oriented toward establishing the legitimacy of and demanding social recognition for the half-caste, it makes perfect sense that *sight*—the viewing of physically embodied evidence—is what forces Hilton to acknowledge the truth before him.

Eaton's emphasis on skin color is clearly problematic. Eaton seems to want to transform the rhetoric of race as bodily contaminant—the "one-drop" epistemology of race in America—into a positive identity. But this new visual schema depends upon the recognition of her heroine's inherent whiteness.[26] Seeing is believing in ideologies of racial and sexual difference. As such, the moment in which Hilton recognizes his daughter can be read as the moment when the half-caste effectively "becomes white." Racial Otherness occasions the recognition of familiality, which, in turn, grants the recognition of shared whiteness. Eaton's emphasis on the legibility of whiteness benefits those who are part white and look it, but its applicability to less visible forms of hybridity is uncertain. However, it would be a mistake to simply dismiss Eaton's work on account of racial preferences. Kiku's performance calls attention to the subjective nature of such phenotypologies. Kiku points to her own body to prove her whiteness, but Norman Hilton has heretofore stared at this same body and seen only difference. In truth, she is equally white and Japanese, and Eaton refuses to have Kiku relinquish one racial/national tie for another. Both sets of racial characteristics are always present, but the (white male) viewer has seen only what he wants to see: Otherness. In this way, Eaton's work serves as an example of the essentialist belief that race is legible on the body and simultaneously offers a critique of that assumption. Hilton learns to recognize Kiku's relationship to himself only when he is offered a different vantage point from which to look. As readers, we are likewise demanded to acknowledge our racial blindness and recognize mixed-race members of the national family and, by extension, our own cultural miscegenation.

Paternal Appetite and Object Relations

Hilton's belated recognition of his daughter occasions an entirely new kind of vision than the gaze of romantic desire. The "new eyes" with which Hilton is forced to perceive Kiku differ greatly from his previous glances (and speech), which have been endlessly devouring. As the narration informs us, Kiku-san "was the prettiest thing he had ever seen, far prettier than all the other geisha girls. If she would not dance for him he would not insist. In fact, he was content simply to look at her" (5). Hilton may not "insist" that she obey his will, but his gaze is acquisitive and voyeuristic. Hilton's language reveals Kiku's status as object to him—she is a "thing" to be admired and observed. Indeed, his desire for the geisha girl is best expressed as rapacious sexual desire: "By evening he was seized with a fit of unconquerable restlessness and blues. He was awake the entire night, tossing restlessly from side to side. . . . [He goes to see her.] The man was intoxicated with his hunger for her, and caught her in his arms with all his pent-up love and passion" (8). Here, the language of conquest is explicitly tied to his sexual desire for the young woman through the language of appetite. His "intoxicating hunger" points to the compulsive desire to possess, incorporate, and even ingest the exotic, sexualized Other.

Further revealing the voraciousness of his gaze, Hilton compliments her by telling her she "looks like a Japanese sunbeam" when she smiles. This orientalized image of beauty is abstract and insubstantial: a sunbeam has no corporeality to repel his advances, while the racial specificity (the perceived "Japaneseness") of her body is what makes her the object of his penetrative gaze. Hilton's compliment relies on a gendered and racialized portrait of femininity that assumes Kiku's availability in relation to her apparent exoticism.[27] Moreover, Eaton emphasizes the repulsive acquisitiveness of this orientalist appreciation: "'Now you look like a Japanese sunbeam,' he told her, softly, looking *unutterable things* at her out of his deep gray eyes" (6, emphasis mine). The synesthetic relationship between "unutterable" things that are communicated through the eyes is noteworthy, foreshadowing the revelation that his desire is in fact unspeakable, taboo.[28]

Despite Hilton's self-proclaimed desire to rectify past sins, he even speaks of reconciliation in the language of conquest, possession, and obsession. He declares at the beginning of the story: "There was a child. I want it" (4). Lest readers assume this pronoun choice is a result of not knowing the sex of his child, a sentence later Hilton explains that "it" was a girl. From the beginning of the story, then, Eaton emphasizes the object status that children, the Japanese, and perhaps all women hold for privileged white men like Hilton. This object status is reinforced with the third-person limited narration describing Hilton's motivation to find his daughter: "At the age of forty, Hilton found himself altogether alone in the world, with a strange weariness of his own companionship and an *unconquerable* longing to have someone with him who actually *belonged* to him. . . . He was suddenly keenly alive to the fact that he was a father; that he owed his first duty in life to the one being in the world who *belonged* to him—his little Japanese daughter, whom he had never seen" (4, emphasis mine). Through Hilton's speech and Eaton's narrative description, we see that the cosmopolitan man speaks of love and duty in the rhetoric of domination and ownership. The language of possession is common to both sexual conquest and parental longing, creating a troubling correspondence between these desires. In short, Hilton's paternal longing sounds suspiciously like perverse sexual desire. Kiku's extreme youth highlights white Western assumptions about Asian female sexual precocity and availability: she is only fifteen. When Hilton asks her age, she first claims that she is twenty-two. His response is, "You look like a child" (7). That this does not minimize his desire for her is, I believe, intended to disturb and disgust the reader. Incest in this story serves to exaggerate Hilton's greed—for women, power, mobility, and the oriental Other. This appetite for exotic women is sanctioned by common practice within the world of Eaton's romances: Norman Hilton is only too "normal" a man in his casual wooing and abandonment of Japanese and half-caste women. But these appetites are finally exposed as monstrous when he attempts to seduce his own daughter. The revelation that the sexual exotic actually *is* the lost daughter-object highlights the pathological psychology of the white man's appetite.

Melanie Klein's theory of object relations is relevant here, for Hilton's greedy glances can be read as an expression of his immature development. As Klein explains, "As a child (or an adult) identifies himself more fully with a good object [such as the breast], the libidinal urges increase; he develops a greedy love and desire to devour this object and the mechanism of introjection is reinforced."[29] Like an infant, Hilton expresses his idea of love through the language of hunger, appetite, and orality. He cannot see Kiku as a whole-object, a woman with a history and desires of her own. His solipsism and ethnocentrism cause him to treat her as an aesthetic and sexual partial-object. Paradoxically, only by recognizing her as his daughter (as a person related to himself, sharing his blood) can he see her as a distinct person. Psychoanalysis usefully illuminates the primitive drives underlying Eaton's fiction, but it also provides a model for the connection between object relations to race.

As discussed in the previous chapter, incest has long served as a plot device marking miscegenation as a peculiarly American condition based in the "peculiar institution" of slavery.[30] Antebellum antislavery novels depict the vulnerability of black women to their white male masters who frequently are also their fathers or brothers. Throughout the nineteenth century, the dysfunctional family unit has served as a microcosm for the nation, with the probability of incest (endogamy) intertwined with the history of white male privilege and miscegenation (exogamy). The power of incest as a rhetorical device lies in its secrecy. As Hortense Spillers explains, the "unsayable" act of incest actually gains force from its unspeakability. As a result, according to Spillers, "fictions about incest provide an enclosure, a sort of confessional space . . . and in a very real sense it is only in fiction . . . that incest as dramatic enactment and sexual economy can take place at all."[31] Incest functions as the literary test limit for white male privilege and racialized female abjection, since what could more graphically illustrate the dangers of male conquest and female victimization than the horror of father-daughter incest? In African American fiction, the act of incest marks the utter destruction of human, familial, and legal ties under slavery. In the context of Asian American identity as seen through Eaton's half-caste tales, the possibility of incest marks the West's dangerous denial of its responsibilities, while offering a last-chance opportunity to make good on its earlier promises. In "A Half-Caste," Hilton's recognition of the blood tie averts the family-destroying act of incest. His failure to continue the seduction is an acknowledgment of the structural relationship between white and Asian identities, and of the white, patriarchal privilege that previously allowed him to see all women as sex objects. Eaton holds out the promise that the white father's sexual desire for the foreign girl-woman might be rewritten as a familial desire for his own half-Japanese blood relative. "A Half Caste" thus warns readers that the nation's failure to acknowledge its interracial history (and the inequalities that underlie it) threatens the basic unit of society: the nuclear family.

In her focus on the half-caste, Eaton moves the miscegenation plot beyond the black-white divide. Moreover, in her fiction, incest simultaneously serves as an indictment of white male privilege and its objectification of raced female bodies *and* functions as a positive step toward the acknowledgment and recognition of the nation's miscegenated children. Redefining the "problem" of racial admixture as the denial of familial and social bonds, not the fact of its occurrence, Eaton's fiction posits miscegenation as the precondition for a multiracial national identity. The threat of incest paradoxically facilitates the Amerasian's social recognition as a member of that family. The half-caste's desire for recognition as American is accomplished only through recognition by her white father of their biological tie. The father's failure to act on his incestuous desire marks the first recognition that the half-caste is a member of the family, for the taboo against incest only exists if consanguinity is acknowledged. To be belatedly recognized as a daughter is to have (finally) a social place, a validated identity. In this way, incest remains repulsive, a taboo not to be broken, but its threat exposes the fact that East and West, America and Asia, are already mixed.

As in the African American context, the incest plot functions in Eaton's fiction as a kind of shock tactic that forces the reader to recognize an overlooked threat to social order (white male power in its domination of nonwhite Others) and redefine the racialized woman as victim, rather than vixen. In Eaton's fictions, consent is coerced, rather than resulting from brute force, in accordance with the social relations that structure East/West contact. Eaton's plots are consistently propelled by privileged white males' attempts to seduce, woo, and/or marry exotic women.[32] For all Hilton's salacious glances, what he wants above all is for Kiku to desire him back. Like the 1907 "Gentlemen's Agreement" that curtailed Japanese immigration to the United States under the pretext of equality and consent, romantic relationships between white American men and Asian women in Eaton's works are determined by American economic, cultural, and political dominance at the turn of the twentieth century. Incest in these stories and novels is not an act of physical violence with the knowledge of probable blood affinity; it is a result of the coercive nature of American imperial power at home and abroad.

To return to the relationship between psychology and race, just as object relations are founded in the individual psyche, race and racism are expressions of similar power structures at the level of culture and society. Hilton's desire to possess Kiku reveals the role of race in both social relations and object relations, with Hilton a melancholic subject searching for a beloved lost object, his half-caste daughter. Anne Cheng insightfully draws out the racial melancholia that constitutes all American identities—white or racialized—but which is particularly inflected for Asian American subjects who fall outside the American chiaroscuro of black and white. Racial melancholia functions as a kind of double consciousness, whereby race is the unacknowledged heart of national identity. As Cheng explains, "Racialization in America may be said to operate through the institutional process of producing a dominant, standard, white national ideal, which is sustained by the exclusion-yet-retention of racialized others."[33] Karen Shimikawa presents a similar formulation of Asian American identity as "abject" in relation to mainstream American identity; Asian American identity is characterized by "its constantly shifting relation to Americanness, a movement between visibility and invisibility, foreignness and domestication/assimilation."[34] In the context of abjection and the melancholic desire for recognition, the incest scenario is an expression of the psychoanalytic roots of racial formation.[35]

Racial melancholia and object relations take on added resonance in the context of half-caste identity. Popular literature linked the half-caste with the mulatto, depicting both as afflicted with melancholia, hysteria, and other mental and physical disorders as a consequence of their divided (and doubled) racial identities.[36] Eaton reinforces the association of biraciality with weakness and melancholia in her "nonfiction" essay entitled "The Half Caste," which was published a year before the fictional story with the nearly identical name (but for the indefinite article).[37] In the quasi-sociological account, Eaton describes the peculiar psychological characteristics of all half-castes: "The Japanese half breeds are wonderfully precocious," "extremely erratic and moody," "nervous, highly strung, jealous, conceited, yet humble and self-deprecating and overly modest at times, sarcastic, skeptical, generous and impulsive. It is hard to analyze their natures, because they are so changeable." Importantly, Eaton's depiction of the collective precocity and melancholia of the half-caste is tempered by an emphasis on the social factors contributing to those psychological characteristics. Their sensitivity, Eaton implies, is a result of the fact that "from their earliest childhood, whether *in this country, Europe, or Japan*, they are made to feel that they are different from those about them.... From constantly being called names and shunned, they become morose, bitter and harsh in their judgments" (149–52, emphasis mine). The half-caste suffers for not fitting into existing racial and national boundaries, although Eaton also indicates the anger of those denied their birthright as part white: "In this country or in England they are accused of being 'niggers,' 'Chinese,' etc." (149–50). Through this repetition of the gap between geography, nationality, and race, Eaton depicts her half-caste desiring the privileges of whiteness, in part, I argue, because whiteness confers national identity. In her desire to distinguish the half-caste from other ostracized groups, Eaton reflects the racial hierarchies of her time and place. Yet this ought not blind us to the psychological truths she expresses.

Accordingly, as in the story of Kiku and Norman Hilton, Eaton again articulates the importance of racial-cum-familial recognition. Further psychoanalyzing the half-caste personality in terms of family ties, she explains: "The Japanese half breeds seldom make good sons or daughters, nor do they have that great reverence and love for the parents which is common among children of ordinary parentages. I do not know why this is so, unless it lies in the fact that the same love and care that are given by most good parents to their children are withheld from them. . . . Usually the Japanese half breed does not know the counsel, and the dearly-to-be-desired strict guidance of a father, or the watchful, tender loving care of a mother" (151). Again yoking desire and discipline, fathers are "dearly-to-be-desired" figures of authority. However, in the short story "A Half Caste," the longed-for father figure is not only absent but lacks the very moral fiber upon which the paternal role is ideally based. Norman Hilton is deficient as a father and a man; his belated recognition of his daughter is not enough to grant him moral authority. Rather, Kiku performs her own moral authority through her rejection of Hilton. Reading Eaton's "nonfiction" piece "The Half Caste" alongside her story "A Half Caste" emphasizes the link between nationality, race, and familial recognition in both works.

To return to her avowedly fictional world of the half-caste romance, in "A Half Caste" incest is the mechanism that reveals the danger of unacknowledged miscegenation as well as the fantasy of familial and psychological wholeness. In virtually all of Eaton's stories, the half-caste heroine is melancholic in her desire for recognition, for reconciliation, and, more problematically, for whiteness. And yet that's only half the story, for the hegemonic white man is melancholic, too. His orientalism turns out to be a form of egotism: the desire for the exotic (exogamy) is actually a desire for likeness (endogamy). Indeed, what Hilton desires is not merely whiteness, but familial blood and, by extension, the Otherness that constitutes his own identity and against (and through) which his whiteness is defined. The melancholic nature that is the burden of the half-caste is suspiciously similar to the restless, capricious, and acquisitive nature of the absent white father. In her "nonfiction" piece, Eaton tells us that typical half-castes are "very pretty" and "generally enjoy fine physical constitutions, through they are nervous, highly strung, jealous"; in the story "A Half Caste," Norman Hilton is described in nearly identical terms—he is "extremely handsome" with "a keen, clever face" and "fine athletic figure," although he is lost in "a moody dream" and answers questions "nervously" in the story's opening scene (3–4). In her fiction, Eaton thus shows the white man sharing the half-caste's fantasy of recognition, reconciliation, and wholeness, perhaps being even more obsessed with the racialized Other than the half-caste is with him.[38] Racial melancholia is a shared condition arising from the dialectical relationship between whiteness and racial difference. In the context of the half-caste, that bond is psychic, social, and biological—in a word, undeniable.

The "unconquerable" aspect of Hilton's desires takes on new meaning in the context of the infinite deferral of melancholia. His desires are unfulfillable because they are within himself, and therefore, self-consuming. In "A Contract," the story with which I opened this chapter, Masters wants to produce a mixed-race lineage to ensure his place as a white minority in Japan; Hilton's return to the site of his earlier romance occasions the reunion with the half-caste child, thus assuring *her* recognition in the American cultural context. In both stories, the half-caste is the ultimate melancholic lost object (as well as being the fantasized good partial-object). The insatiability of racial melancholia finds its ultimate expression in incestuous desire, which can never be fulfilled, because to do so would be to pervert the very tie that makes it desirable. Moreover, the incest plot shows us that Hilton's orientalist sexual fantasy is predicated on his refusal to recognize Kiku's own subjectivity and desires.

Eaton seems aware of the role of fantasy and its unfulfillability in the relationship between the privileged white man and his half-caste daughter, for she forecloses the happy ending of the family reunion. In the moment of mutual recognition, Kiku rebuffs Hilton: "She pushed back the sleeves and showed him the white purity of her arms. Then she turned and left him with the same still look of despair on his face and the pitiless sun beating on the golden fields" (10). Kiku, formerly Hilton's insubstantial fantasy of a "Japanese sunbeam," has become a "pitiless sun" powerful enough to scorch her father with her disdain. Kiku effectively abandons the father who abandoned her mother and herself fifteen years earlier, becoming an independent entity in her own right. Moreover, as a "pitiless sun," she homonymically becomes a "pitiless son" who Oedipally desires to kill the father, representative of fatherland and the Law of the Father, to better love the mother, and by extension, motherland and mother tongue. The gendering of this substitution is telling, for as a daughter, her power to castrate her father is achieved only on the linguistic level; she remains physically vulnerable to his predations. Moreover, by ending with Kiku's rejection of her father, Eaton refuses to transform Hilton's deviant sexual desire into parental solicitude. Hilton's sexual and paternal desires are left unsatisfied, with the result that the desire for recognition and the work of achieving that recognition is transferred to the white father.

Despite, or perhaps because of, the unhappy ending, "A Half Caste" offers a kind of imaginative resolution by implicitly demanding the restructuring of social and sexual relations. The revelation of paternity is a radical recognition of racial abjection. The definition of the national family has expanded, with the desire and demand for recognition occurring in both directions. Incest is averted, and Hilton's sexual desire is exposed as socially unacceptable. In the context of racial identity, the nightmare of near-incest is transformed into a fantasy of future reunion. Incest may "ruin" the romance plot, but it becomes the means to imagine a representational solution to the problems of gender and race that are impediments to a sense of belonging for "half-castes" in America. The problem of being a "citizen sure thing" who is nonetheless considered a "foreigner" is negotiated through the revelation of shared blood and mutual melancholia. In its focus on the interracial family as model of American imperialism in Asia, Eaton's fiction expands the notion of American citizenship and national identification beyond the boundaries of the exceptional body, and places the burdens of recognition squarely in the laps of its wayward white fathers. Yet, while the bilateral revelation of likeness turns a family reunion into a national drama of recognition, the ending remains uncertain. We do not know what happens next. Will Kiku eventually reconcile with her father? Will she stay in Japan or go to America? Will she find a social place by creating a family of her own? The future remains outside the story's horizon, and Eaton leaves it to her readers to determine the resolution—both in her fictional world and in the real world it reflects.

Equality through Sibling Eroticism

Eaton's interest in the familial romance as an allegory of national identity extends beyond such literal threats of incest between father and daughter. Indeed, Eaton returns to the family romance with a pair of works published in 1903 that focus on sibling relationships as a means for half-castes to gain equality and social recognition. Both "Miss Lily and Miss Chrysanthemum: The Love Story of Two Japanese Girls in Chicago" and *The Heart of Hyacinth* portray eroticized sibling affection as an egalitarian alternative to sexual conquest and paternal appetite. Instead of foreclosing romantic resolutions, these two works imagine romanticized and eroticized sibling love as a reciprocal answer to the problem of racial recognition. Rather than looking for likeness through the recognition of shared biological whiteness based on patrilineage, Eaton's heroines in these works value cultural and familial ties associated with lost mothers and motherlands, which can be maintained or recovered through sibling relationships.

Eaton's half-castes may desire social recognition (including citizenship) from their white fathers, but they desire psychological wholeness and emotional identification through their longing for mother and motherland. Caroline Rody evocatively describes the mother-daughter reunion trope in African American and Caribbean literature as "the romance of a returning daughter and . . . the mother-of-history," which serves as an allegory of the author's "imaginative return . . . to her traumatic ancestral past."[39] In Eaton's fictions, Japanese mothers represent the trauma of exploitation and abandonment experienced by racialized women from white men. Though mothers are rarely alive in these fictions to literally comfort their half-caste daughters when the world (of men) threatens, Japanese mothers remain a palpable source of love and acceptance through living siblings. In this way, sibling eroticism offers the half-caste a social place through nurture and culture, in contrast to the masculine order of nature, blood, and racial identification.

We first see the way siblings substitute for the lost maternal source in "Miss Lily and Miss Chrysanthemum," a short story in which two half-caste sisters vie for the same young white suitor. This apparent love triangle masks the far more compelling erotic affair between the two women, a relationship based on a shared longing for a dead mother and an accepting "motherland." Indeed, the heterosexual romance functions primarily as a means to bring the divided Japanese American family together, spatially as well as through sanguinity. While both girls were born in Japan, Yuri, the "Lily" of the title, was raised in England and America with their white father, while Kiku (Chrysanthemum), remained with their Japanese mother. The two women are reunited in Chicago after the deaths of both parents, "For in this double orphanage, thousands and thousands of miles apart, the two had felt strangely drawn to each other" (67). Chicago, site of 1893 World's Columbian Exposition, is an important geography in which to set this story; the exposition was notable for its instantiation of new anthropological models of racial difference and technological advancement. The two women's likeness relies on the biological distinctions of racist anthropology, while their differences from each other represent the mitigating power of "culture" to affect destiny. By situating the reunion in Chicago, Eaton suggests the merging of nature and nurture, blood and culture, in the making of identity. The bond between the two women is familial, cultural, racial, and national.

Yet the world of fathers and racial identity represented by the United States is not entirely satisfying. For, rather than having Kiku join her in America, Yuri "would rather have gone *home* [to Japan] to her" (67, emphasis mine). Eaton here suggests that America can never feel like "home" so long as the half-caste is treated as an outsider. As a result of the perpetual rejection experienced by the half-caste in the United States, Japan is imagined to be a substitute for and synecdoche of the lost mother/land. Accordingly, Eaton writes that Yuri "had forgotten her mother tongue," when describing her inability to speak Japanese with her long-lost sister (67). In these works, as throughout Eaton's oeuvre, Japan is associated with the feminine realm of "home," mothers, motherhood, and language, representing a fantasy of psychological wholeness and national belonging. Yuri romanticizes and idealizes Japan as an alternative to the hard world of the United States. Yuri's longing for an unknown Japan where all her problems are solved is akin to psychoanalytic theories of infant identification with the mother, before the splitting of the partial-object (Klein), mirror stage (Lacan), or Oedipus complex (Freud). Yet this feminization and domestication of Japan is itself merely romanticized wishful thinking. As the narrator warns readers, "Perhaps she [Yuri] loved even more dearly than Kiku the home that she could not remember" (68). The maternal nostalgia Yuri feels toward Japan is an unrealizable fantasy of racial purity and female homosociality that must be transformed into interracial heterosexual romance. Nevertheless, the feminine cooperative of untroubled sisterhood and of mothers and daughters represents desire for a respite from the exclusion and alienation of American and English fathers and sons.

Yuri feels like an outsider in Chicago despite her long residency due to her racialized (and, less explicitly, gendered) body, which are a continual reminder of her difference from others. This feeling of ostracism is common to patriarchal white cultures on both sides of the Atlantic. Thus, Yuri also felt like an outsider as a child in England, where "she had never mixed with companions of her age, on account of the strange antipathy the English had shown to her in her childhood, because of her nationality; which prejudice, however, they had long outgrown. Yet it had had a rude effect on her life, making her supersensitive" (68). Apparently, England and its children have "outgrown" their racial prejudices, in contrast to the United States. Yet the victim has not forgotten her experiences of racism, which remain associated with white patriarchy. Yuri recalls: "From the time when the little schoolmates at the public school had called her 'nigger,' 'Chinee,' and other names . . . Yuri had distrusted, not them, but herself. That she was inferior to them she never for one moment thought, but that she was different from them, and one whom it would be impossible to understand, she firmly believed; hence her strange love for the home she had never known. Holding herself aloof from all whom she met, she had lived a lonely, isolated life ever since her father's death" (69). Despite Yuri's magnanimous claim that England's prejudices are a thing of the past, her visceral memory of the stings of ridicule reveals the ongoing power of stigmatized racial embodiment. Eaton's Yuri is seemingly haunted by the traumas of orientalization and racialization, traumas she associates with white fatherlands—England and the United States.

The racist Othering to which Yuri refers reveals her double alienation and her incomplete citizenship. While she is geographically tied to the United States and England, she remains outside the structures of power. She feels an intense affective tie to Japan, but this motherland is a place she does not know. Yuri's allegiance to each nation is incomplete, rendering her a foreigner on both soils. Just as the melancholic mourns the lost object, Yuri here endlessly grieves for and fantasizes about her lost mother(land). The link between mothers and motherlands is not so much "natural" or biological as psychological, in contrast to the white fatherlands that repeatedly deny her claims of belonging. Eaton's solution is not a physical return to the lost maternal homeland, but an act of substitution, whereby a mother is replaced by a sister. Wholeness may then be achieved by the two sisters' shared sense of doubleness—the hybridity of the "half-caste."

In this way, the absence Yuri feels is filled by her "Japanese" sister, Kiku. The half-caste from Japan is more delicate, fragile, and childlike than her American sister. While Yuri herself longs to have a mother and a motherland, she becomes the mother to her sister Kiku, and Kiku recognizes this solicitude, calling Yuri "liddle mozzer" (72). Furthermore, Kiku speaks of herself in the third person and in pidgin English, infantilizing the younger sister in ways akin to Hilton's orientalization of (the other) Kiku in "A Half Caste." The sororal blood tie clearly substitutes for the parent-child relationship.

Yet this substitution brings further complications. It is not possible to return to a fantasmatic (pre-Oedipal) Oneness with the lost maternal, and so Yuri's desire reveals Oedipal undertones of desire and jealousy. Yuri's maternal solicitude toward her sister is queer desire, expressed in erotically charged language that sounds suspiciously like incest:

"Is *this* lofe?" she [Kiku] asked wistfully.

"Love, love?" asked Yuri, shivering a trifle. "Why, little sis, what a great big question that is! Of course it is love, and such love as never was perhaps between two sisters."

Her voice was quite hushed as she kissed the upturned, question-ing face. Kiku's restlessness puzzled her.

"I fear you have been out too long," she said gravely; "come, sis-ter will undress you."

Kiku shook her head. "No! She said almost fretfully, "Kiku does not wish to go to bed yet. Kiku wants to hear about this—lofe."

Yuri laughed, the easy, good-natured laugh of an American-bred girl.

"Why, you absurd little goosie; what can I tell you, save that this is 'lofe,' as you call it?" And she bent down and kissed Kiku on the lips.

"Kiku shook her head impatiently.

"But *he* did not do that," she said with puzzled eyes.

"*He*! What do you mean?" said Yuri with a sudden fear at her heart. (72–73)

Yuri speaks as the experienced "American-bred" lover seducing the childlike, uninitiated Kiku. Kiku's innocent question, "Is *this* lofe?" causes Yuri to "shiver," the encounter thrilling for its possibility of offer-ing "such love as never was perhaps between two sisters." The stilted syntax of that sentence ("as never was perhaps"), with its abstraction and evasion, emphasizes a certain kind of unspeakability. In this linger-ing description, it is the American(ized) Yuri whose voice is "hushed" and "grave," and who kisses (twice), undresses, and feels jealousy over her beloved Kiku. Kiku, however, has thoughts only for Walter Palmer, the "pritty American gentleman" who lives in the same boardinghouse and with whom Kiku has discussed "lofe" (73). Eaton asks the reader to believe that Yuri is jealous of Walter, who actually loves *her*, and not her "Japanese" sister. But the energy of the story is so excessively oriented between the two women that Walter remains an outsider, an interloper intent on destroying their happy sorority. His intrusion marks a kind of fall from grace for Yuri, out of a circle of feminine love into a fraught and insecure world of white masculine authority.

These homoerotic tensions are ostensibly relieved by the plot machi-nations that would transform Yuri's desire for her sister into jealousy that Walter prefers her sister to herself. Thus, the narrator tells us that Yuri struggled with her jealousy: "That Kiku was as dear as, if not dearer than, the other to her she told herself repeatedly, calling up a pitiful resent-ment against the man" (73). Yet Yuri doth protest too much. As read-ers of the romance, Eaton expects us to accept the relationship between

Walter and Yuri as the real and appropriate love between adult man and adult woman, yet the affective force of the story lies in the highly charged sensuality Yuri feels for Kiku. This capitulation to patriarchy is central to the work of popular romances, as Janice Radway has shown in relationship to late twentieth-century romance novels. According to Radway, one of the appeals of the romance novel is its transformation of the "oppression and emotional abandonment suffered by women in real life" into a fantasy of masculine solicitude; thus, "romances provide a utopian vision in which female individuality and a sense of self are shown to be compatible with nurturance and care by another"—that is, in heterosexual marriage (55).

Given the queerness of Yuri's exchange with Kiku, Yuri's jealousy arises more plausibly from her desire for her "Japanese" sister's unalloyed loyalty and devotion. If, as the narrator tells us, "[Yuri's] great love for her sister made her sensitive on her account, and it was with apprehension and a good deal of bitterness that she thought of Palmer" (73), readers ought to understand Yuri's bitterness toward Walter Palmer as a result of the threat of his elopement with her sister, her own object of affection. Yuri's repeated emphasis on their tie of sisterhood—"sister," "little sis"—emphasizes the primacy of this bond. Yuri's passion for her sister is far more convincing than her interest in Walter, although the conventions of the heterosexual romance and of (white) American superiority demand the (mixed-race) endogamous circle be broken.

Walter, while young and "pretty," nevertheless represents a paternal domination that is at odds with the gentle homosocial world of the two sisters. We can see Walter Palmer's similarity to Norman Hilton in his behavior toward Kiku, which sets in motion the misunderstanding that serves as the plot of "Miss Lily and Miss Chrysanthemum." Despite having "been in love with Yuri-San for many days" (68), he gets caught up in the exoticism and naïveté he perceives in Kiku: "Her face in its mixed beauty intoxicated the man. He could not remove his eyes from it. He forgot Yuri. He thought only of the girl sitting opposite to him, with the sweet faced softened with the questioning that her innocent soul could not solve. With a sudden fierceness he reached over and caught her little soft hands in his, whispering huskily" (72). Such descriptions of his "intoxicat[ion]," "fierceness," and "husk[y]"-voiced confessions effectively repeat the gendered and racialized plot from "A Half Caste," with Walter positioned to fulfill the role of white father figure to Kiku's infantilized half-caste girl. The romantic and sexual tension works at two levels simultaneously: (1) in the familiar romance between the white man and half-caste woman; and (2) in the homosocial alternative. Yuri wishes to take Walter's place, and Eaton asks her readers to imagine Yuri as romantic partner. Indeed, Yuri's "seduction" of Kiku is more intimate, sympathetic, and detailed than any encounter either woman has with Walter. Implicitly, then, such sisterly affection functions as an endogamous solution to, and a retrenchment from, the racism and exploitation of American men. Yet, Yuri's adoration for her "Japanese" sister is not reciprocated. Kiku thinks only of the white man's attentions, leaving the other half-caste girl without a partner. Through Kiku's rejection of Yuri, Eaton exposes the desire for a Japanese motherland as a fantasy that cannot be fulfilled, an impossibility for half-castes adrift in the American landscape.

While the emotional force and sexual tension of the story is located between the sisters, such homoeroticism must be discharged in the familiar machinations of the interracial heterosexual romance. Quite literally, Yuri's anger and antipathy are transformed into romantic angst: "Of Palmer she would not think. His white face haunted her constantly, and she hated herself because the bitterness she had conjured up against him was slowly passing away, *to be replaced* with a feeling of pain and yearning and longing that the girl could not comprehend" (76, emphasis mine). Walter Palmer arrives to confess his love for Yuri, thereby returning the feminine alternative family to the familiar romance between a white man and a half-caste woman, while also firmly situating Yuri's story and its resolution within the American social context. This U.S.-based romantic conclusion rescues Yuri from a loveless marriage to a Japanese suitor who would have her move to Japan with him, but it also results in Kiku's return to Japan, alone. The Japanese sister is thus sacrificed to secure the American sister's social place in the United States. In "Miss Lily and Miss Chrysanthemum," Eaton highlights the ongoing struggle, as much psychological as social, for the half-caste to find a place in America.

Heterosexual romance is the necessary conclusion, yet it continues to come at the cost of maternal ties. Once more, the truly idealized conclusion, whereby familial and romantic ties are united in an egalitarian marriage, is deferred.

Adoption and Cultural Hybridity

Whereas in "Miss Lily and Miss Chrysanthemum" the heterosexual romance replaces and forecloses sibling eroticism (and with it, any remaining ties to mothers and motherland), the heterosexual romance finds its resolution in sibling incest (or, more accurately, quasi-incest) in *The Heart of Hyacinth*. In this novel, Eaton again transforms homosociality into heterosexual romance, but does so more convincingly and palatably by offering kinship and shared culture without actual shared blood (or homoeroticism). The novel begins as another tale of an absent white father, but ends with sibling marriage. The eponymous heroine is born in Japan to a dying white woman who has run away from her philandering American husband. The orphaned white child, Hyacinth, is taken in by Aoi Montrose, the Japanese widow of an English sailor. Hyacinth is raised as a sister to Aoi's own half-caste son, Komazawa (Koma), who is approximately eight years older than Hyacinth. After an idyllic childhood with his adopted sister, Koma is sent to England for education and to secure his father's estate. During his absence, Hyacinth is betrothed in an arranged marriage to a Japanese young man. Koma returns to stop the marriage, but finds a greater crisis: Hyacinth's biological father has returned to Japan to take her to America with him. Hyacinth must decide where and with whom her loyalty and love should lie; her dilemma is solved by Koma's confession of having fallen in love with her. Their impending marriage, with which the novel ends, saves Hyacinth from leaving the family on account either of outside marriage or her father's claim to biological and racial affinity. Technically unrelated by blood, but siblings by adoption, Hyacinth and Koma are drawn together by their shared cultural hybridity; they alone understand the ties of Japan and Japanese cultural identity represented by Aoi's maternal nurturance and domesticity, as well as the bond of paternity and whiteness.

As I will show, the novel reveals several important things about race, culture, and acceptance. First, Eaton emphasizes that racism is universal, common to the Japanese and Anglo-Americans alike. Second, the novel shows that identity is shaped by culture as much as by blood. Last, Eaton imaginatively resolves the "problem" of divided loyalties through Hyacinth and Koma's marriage, rejecting an unsatisfactory choice between either mother/land or father/land. Incest once again functions as a fantasy solution, a metaphor for the multiracial family whose "culture" is hybrid rather than singular; this shared culture is more meaningful and defining than the bond of shared racial identity. *The Heart of Hyacinth* reveals the Japanese mother to be the center of both children's affective ties; Hyacinth and Koma's marriage sacralizes the bond of maternity that the two children have with Aoi, regardless of biological parentage.

One of the most important features of Eaton's novel and its implicit political-social critique is its indictment of racism as a matter of (false) racial pride among the Japanese as well as among Anglo-Americans. When Koma first returns from his travels to England, Hyacinth is twelve years old and he is around twenty. Having lived abroad, he returns to teach her that her antiwhite, anti-West beliefs are wrong. Significantly, Hyacinth's racism mirrors that of Western orientalism, which views Japan and the East as uncivilized. Koma admonishes his sister, "No; the people in the west were not all savages and barbarians" (73). Aoi, too, reveals race prejudice when she tells Koma that she's tried to protect Hyacinth from knowing "of her peculiar physical misfortunes . . . the hair, eyes, skin— how strange, how unnatural" (77). Koma chastises her, saying, "Oh, my mother, you are growing backward. You are seeing all things from a narrowing point of view. Because Hyacinth is not like other Japanese children, she is not ugly. Why, the little one is beautiful, quite so, in her own way" (78). Aoi's assumption that Hyacinth's Caucasian features are defects highlights the cultural relativism of beauty, pointedly reversing the West's denigration of "yellow" skin and "slanted" eyes. Koma's statement that *just because* Hyacinth does not look Japanese does not make her ugly can also be read another way, indicating a causal relationship between racial difference and beauty; perhaps *because* Hyacinth is not like other children she is beautiful (exoticism = beauty). In either case, Koma represents the modern, enlightened perspective of cultural relativism, while Aoi reveals a provincialism that blinds her to her adopted daughter's physical charms. The Yamashiros, Hyacinth's future in-laws, are even more bigoted and backward, tolerating their son's betrothal to Hyacinth when they presume she is a half-caste but forbidding the marriage when they learn she has no biological claim to Japanese identity.

Such nationalist racism is equally evident among the U.S. nationals in Japan. The American lawyer Knowles, responsible for tracking down Hyacinth for her American father, urges her to go to the United States because "You belong to his home. It is some fatal and horrible miscarriage of fate that has cast your destiny among this alien people" (145). Knowles assumes that race determines belonging, a misguided assumption given Eaton's idealized representation of the Montrose household. Hyacinth responds by claiming possession of and by the Japanese nation: "Not alien! . . . *My* people—my—" (145). Language fails to adequately explain the ties that bind, particularly those outside of racial taxonomies; Hyacinth is reduced to the state of a child insisting on the status of her objects as "mine!" Even the more sympathetic young American attaché

Saunders had assumed the superiority of the West and of white blood, arranging the reunion of father and daughter with the intent "to render a splendid service to the little girl, yet now—well—I feel like a—criminal" (146). According to Eaton, to define identity exclusively on racial terms *is* a crime against the natural ties of brotherhood and sisterhood between racial groups who are equally part of a national family that is always already intermixed. *The Heart of Hyacinth* imagines a social space that is neither Japanese nor American but both. Koma and Hyacinth's marriage creates an alternative site of hybrid identity and multiple identifications.

Such hybridity is an epistemological problem for narrow-minded Japanese and Americans alike. Koma's half-caste status is unacceptable to the conservative Reverend Blount, who urges the Anglicization of Koma on the basis of racial phenotype. "'He is in fact one of us,' continued the minister. 'He has the physical appearance, somewhat of the training, and let us hope, the natural instincts of the Caucasian. It would be not only ludicrous but wicked for him to continue here in this isolated spot, where he is, may we say, an alien, and particularly when it is his duty to follow the wishes of his father as regards his English estate. Certainly this is not where Komazawa belongs'" (57). According to this reductive and essentialist logic, Koma must be educated in England in order to decrease the influence of his mother and motherland and increase the role of father and fatherland in Koma's identity.[40] Such attitudes reflect the racial binaries of Anglo-American culture, which demands the sacrifice of one identity for another. This form of American "inclusion" demands a disavowal of the feminine and racial Other represented by the Japanese mother and motherland. The hybrid hero or heroine seeks a way to claim both racial and cultural inheritances. Accordingly, Koma explains: "[Japan] is, indeed, my home. Do not, I beg you, be deceived in that matter. It is true that I am also Engleesh, but, ah, I am not so base to deny my other blood" (57). Koma defines identity as the product of essential racial difference ("blood") as well as nationality ("Engleesh"). Race and nation, biology and culture, are independent variables that *together* define identity.

Koma's insistence on his double racialization (through nationality) is echoed by Hyacinth, who has no biological claim to Japaneseness, but is nonetheless a hybrid subject like Koma. What this points to is the importance of adoption in this novel, both literally in terms of Hyacinth's parentage, and figuratively in that she claims her "authentic" identity through place and experience rather than biology and blood. Koma's hybridity is racial, while Hyacinth's is entirely cultural, based as it is in her experience growing up in Japan among the Japanese. In *The*

Heart of Hyacinth, the heroine's own sense of identity is seemingly determined solely by the Japanese culture in which she lives, complete with antiwhite, anti-Western bias. However, at a crucial moment, Hyacinth quite literally learns to recognize (in a mirror, no less) that her identity is also dependent on how she is *seen,* on her perceived racial characteristics such as eye and hair color. As discussed earlier in the chapter with regard to "A Half-Caste," identity is defined not only through a sense of self, but also through the melancholic relationship between self and other. Hyacinth learns the lesson of double consciousness—that her identity is based both on how she thinks of herself and how others perceive her. In this convoluted novel of biological and adoptive siblings, blood and culture, identification and recognition, identity is not reducible to either nature or nurture. The half-caste's exceptional status calls attention to the fact that blood and culture are two distinct facets of identity.

As another of Eaton's "Japanese romances," *The Heart of Hyacinth's* critique of racism and biological essentialism can be best understood through analysis of Hyacinth's options for romantic partnership. Each of Hyacinth's suitors represents a choice in her racial identification. Like a turn-of-the-twentieth-century Goldilocks, Hyacinth must decide who is too Japanese, who is too white, and who is just right. Hyacinth's first suitor, to whom she is betrothed as a child of thirteen, is Yoshido Yamashiro. He and his parents are Japanese supremacists, excessively patriarchal and materialistic. Yamashiro père is "imperious and lordly" (106), an Asian despot committed to capitalist "progress" at all costs, representing the worst of East and West. Yoshida follows in his father's footsteps, "save that he spent his restlessness upon the pleasures of youth . . . Yoshida frittered his way through life with the idle and rich young men of Sendai" (108). The Yamashiros break Hyacinth and Yoshida's engagement when they learn that both of her parents were white. Terrified of being forced to go to America with her biological father if Yoshido will not marry her, she begs him, "'If you will marry me," she said, "I will be Japanese altogether'" (237). Of course, Hyacinth cannot be "Japanese altogether," and so she must find another savior.

Hyacinth's second suitor is the American attaché Saunders, who is a double for her American father, Richard Lorrimer. Saunders literally brings father and daughter together, and in his mobility and faith in Western superiority he is an extension of Lorrimer. Saunders functions as little more than a straw man, a suitable romantic proxy for Lorrimer's attempt to win Hyacinth's affection and take her away to America. Like Norman Hilton in "A Half Caste," Lorrimer is an utterly inappropriate

FIGURE 2. *"Now come, little one: come, give me that welcome home."* Illustration by Kiyokichi Sano from *The Heart of Hyacinth*.

suitor who wants "to possess" his daughter (229). Characterized by vanity and vice, Lorrimer bears "the evidence of rich living in the somewhat reddened and bloated appearance of eyes and cheeks" (192). His new wife echoes his nationalism in her hope that "a few years in the West may make a great change in [Hyacinth]. Who knows, we may make quite a little civilized modern out of her yet" (235). The best these Americans can offer is further conquest and possession.

Clearly, for Eaton, racism and nationalism are extensions of patriarchal authority. While Eaton's description of the patriarchal Yamashiro clan invokes the American perceptions of the Japanese in the wake of the Sino-Japanese War (1894–95) as harsh, cruel, or brutal in their military dominance and intense nationalism, she also is highlighting the similarities between American and Japanese fathers. Both Japanese and American men value materialism and superficiality; Yoshida is a playboy like Lorrimer in his prime. Similarly, both Anglo-American and Japanese cultures seem to treat women as chattel, the course of their lives determined by their male relatives. With Hyacinth already engaged to Yoshida, her autonomy is further undermined by the white missionary Reverend Mr. Blount, who is so outraged by the arranged marriage that he sets out to find her biological father. To avoid being a pawn to Lorrimer's demands in turn, Hyacinth still has no choice but marriage. The romance plot in *The Heart of Hyacinth* thus functions to highlight that marriage is the only alternative to patriarchal authority, and it may not be an escape at all.

Given the racist and sexist attitudes that both American and Japanese men assume toward Hyacinth, none of the aforementioned suitors are appropriate. Eaton offers Hyacinth's brother, Koma, as a more suitable alternative. Neither too American nor too Japanese, Koma navigates both cultures, yet without cultivating the patriarchal and nationalistic will to power exhibited by Blount, Lorrimer, or the Yamashiros. Indeed, instead of deploying the language of brute force and conquest, Koma's admission of love is a demand for reciprocity.

> "Confess to me . . ." "I will not try to urge you to stay here—with me—unless—"
> "I—I cannot speak," she said. "I know not what to say."
> "Then I will speak," he said. "I love you, I love you, Hyacinth; with all the life that throbs within me, I love you. . . . I want you for my own. . . ." (249)

Koma's confession asks Hyacinth for an admission of her own. He wants her to "confess" her love: he will not ask her to stay with him in

Japan until and "unless" she willingly accepts his advances. In this way, Koma's confession offers a legitimate alternative to exile in America. However, the language of possession remains, albeit at a lower frequency: Koma "wants [her] for his own" and speaks over her silences. The language of confession places Koma in the role of priest (a better version of Blount), indicating authority and power, while discharging those obligations to a higher power (the spiritual power of love). Clearly, there is something odd about this romantic coupling, but we are asked to accept their union as a fitting conclusion to the novel. By the logic of the popular romance, this marriage is a romantic ideal, not a simple pragmatic solution—thus Koma insists that life and love "throb" within him.

Once again, familial bond is the solution to the divided loyalties and pressures of half-caste status. Moreover, the sibling bond is quite clearly presented as more egalitarian than the paternalism and sexism exhibited by traditional Japanese culture (the Yamashiros and the practice of arranged marriage), white patrician authority (Lorrimer and Reverend Blount), or modern American cultural imperialism (Saunders). Sibling equality is constituted by cultural equality, as both Hyacinth and Koma are "half-castes." The fact that the two share exactly the same childhood domestic experience makes their union truly equal. Moreover, this partnership effectively reverses the Freudian family romance by revealing Hyacinth's "real" parents to be morally, if not socially, inferior to her adopted Japanese mother. Eaton reveals the psychological fantasy of alternate parentage to be a nightmare of white dissipation and possessiveness. Hyacinth represents the truth that home is defined by where the heart is, not where one may be granted citizenship.

The novel offers the union of Koma and Hyacinth as a harmonious blend of East and West, nurture and nature, femininity and masculinity. Marrying Koma legitimizes Hyacinth's connection to Aoi and the motherland of Japan. In this way, *The Heart of Hyacinth* is also (or instead) a story of love between women, with Koma serving as the bridge between mother/land and daughter. Arguably, the "heart" of the title belongs as much to Aoi as to Koma. At the novel's close, as Koma and Hyacinth walk together toward marriage, they offer prayers to "the Goddess of Mercy" and Kuannon, "the Heavenly Lady" (250). Once their allegiance has been paid to the orientalized feminine power of Japanese religion, they head to Blount's mission house, where, Koma explains, "now we will turn to the God of our fathers" (251). In this ending, Eaton imagines an alternative romance that does not demand the sacrifice of feminine

FIGURE 3. *"He knelt in a rapt silence beside her."* Illustration by Kiyokichi Sano from *The Heart of Hyacinth*.

power and authority, but rather combines feminine and masculine, Japanese and American, nature and nurture.

In *The Heart of Hyacinth*, Eaton imagines new possibilities for national belonging. That which constitutes likeness has expanded from race to shared culture, and thus from miscegenation toward hybridity. By attempting to dehierarchize the West and emphasize multiple identifications, Eaton offers a new egalitarianism in gender and sexual relations. Just as Koma and Hyacinth redefine sibling relationships from blood to culture, so too do they redefine the meaning of East and West, sibling and lover. In *The Heart of Hyacinth*, neither Koma nor Hyacinth has to sacrifice his or her identification with Japan, Japanese culture, or mother Aoi. Eaton thus solves the problem of racial and gendered inequality through the sibling marriage that technically is not incest. However, such a resolution through heterosexual romance makes the solution fundamentally private and domestic, rather than public and national. Eaton presages Lauren Berlant's description of "the privatization of citizenship" in the late twentieth century, notable for "the Reaganite view that the intimacy of citizenship is something scarce and sacred, private and proper, and only for members of families."[41] Eaton's turn toward marriage is a form of enclosure that removes the exceptional body from public view. Yet as familial identification turns toward the heterosexual conservatism of the romance genre, there remains something undeniably unsettling about this incestuous resolution.

There is a remainder, an excess that is not contained within the neat plot twist of the East-meets-West sibling-love solution. Eaton betrays the terror inspired by masculine lovemaking. Koma says he had to return to Japan to learn the meaning of love. "'Yet you have been back but a day,' she said, tremulously. 'And love is born in a moment,' he whispered, and took her hand softly in his own. She withdrew it quickly, and turned from him in a sudden panic of incomprehensible fear, the morning had wrought such a change in her" (216). Hyacinth's "sudden panic of incomprehensible fear" reveals a discomfort at the heart of Eaton's conventional marriage plot: perhaps Hyacinth recognizes that romance threatens female autonomy. Her "panic" is that of a half-caste girl who fears that there is no such thing as acceptance and equality, even among siblings, in a world where men and women are not treated as equal. Eaton can imagine a racially egalitarian solution through the union of two different kinds of "half-castes," but the problem of gender inequality cannot be so easily solved.

On a larger scale, the balance of East and West, masculinity and femininity apotheosized in *The Heart of Hyacinth* was similarly tenuous. Japanese military conquests in China and Korea made American politicians and the American public increasingly nervous. In the United States, the public grew more nativist and isolationist leading up to the First World War. The interest in East-West romances declined as anti-Asian attitudes spread across the United State. These political shifts toward isolationism and suspicion of "alien" races curbed Eaton's ability to sell the interracial romances that had made her famous. Rising anti-Asian sentiment would result in the creation in 1917 of the Asiatic Barred Zone, preventing immigration and naturalization for those arriving from the entire continent. This racial barrier to citizenship remained in place until the 1950s, when communism became the new bogeyman.

Eaton's use of the trope of the half-caste is frequently read as merely a reflection of her identification with whiteness and a desire to claim its cultural authority. Yet her stories and novels exceed such reductive readings. The figure of the half-caste serves a reminder of the long-standing interrelationship between East and West. Eaton's fictions criticize the unequal power dynamic that grants white men cultural, economic, and political authority over their consorts, a state of affairs that places racialized women at risk of double exploitation—first as wives/lovers and again as daughters. Yet Eaton's heroines are never passive victims. They are spunky, independent young women who successfully navigate the treacherous waters of courtship and paternity by confronting their errant fathers-cum-lovers and demanding acknowledgment and equality. They speak the unspeakable and, in so doing, legitimate their own status as representative of a miscegenated nation. In this way, the half-caste stands in as a paradigmatic representative of a potentially multiethnic America, whose eventual recognition would signal the achievement of U.S. rhetoric of freedom and equality. While the turn-of-the-twentieth-century period was a time of limited opportunities for Asian Americans, Eaton's fictions create an entire world in which the national family was undeniably mixed-race and culturally hybrid. Drawing on the African American literary tradition, Eaton expanded the mixed-race model of national identity to include Japanese Americans, and by extension the entire continent of Asia. Although legal equality would not occur for decades, the cultural work of her popular romances lingered in the mainstream imagination, gestating for decades until American policy caught up with American popular fiction. Winnifred Eaton should be understood as an important early figure who attempted to redefine American citizenship at the turn of the twentieth century through the provocative language of incest. At the turn of the next century, we can see her legacy in the novels of Ruth Ozeki and Gish Jen, who once again see the United States as a kind of family, defined equally by blood and culture.

3 / The Mexican Mestizo/a in the Mexican American Imaginary

In the previous two chapters, I showed how the racial romance traveled from African American literature featuring the "mulatto/a" to Winnifred Eaton's "half-castes," doing important cultural work to imagine a multicultural, mixed-race nation. In the early twentieth century, the racial romance also came to apply to *mestizos,* the national figure of mixed-race Mexico and Mexican America. Like Winnifred Eaton's fictionalization of U.S. militarism and economic involvement in Japan, the Mexican American writer María Cristina Mena shows how U.S. trade in the nineteenth and twentieth centuries permanently transformed Mexico. Mena further suggests that the Mexican Revolution of 1910—in which rebels sought to break free of the legacy of Spanish colonialism, U.S. imperialism, and the homegrown corruption of Porfirio Díaz's regime—might offer lessons to the United States about the possibilities for a more multiracial and egalitarian national identity. In the following pages, I read Mena as a crucial figure for understanding the range and scope of the racial romance in turn-of-the-twentieth-century U.S. and North American culture. Mena's fictions highlight the transnational implications of miscegenation, incestuous desire, and kinship in this period. In her stories of interracial, cross-class desire and generational conflict, Mena separates the incest narrative from the miscegenation narrative, aligning the former with Mexico's colonial history and the latter with its postrevolutionary future.

The Mexico of Mena's stories must throw off its aristocratic, colonial Spanish heritage, illustrated by a parasitic and incestuous family model:

a castrating mother whose obsessive love threatens her son's health and happiness. Failure to do so will result in a body politic that is hysterical, incestuous, and in a state of arrested development. Yet Mena's Mexico must simultaneously redefine its relationship with the United States in the age of empire, as illustrated by the imbalanced romance between a young Mexican man and his seductive American guest. Mena thus depicts Spanish colonialism as a system of racial/class endogamy that is claustrophobic and detrimental to the nation's development. She also distinguishes the neo-imperial discourse of transnational capitalism from the genuine exogamic multiculturalism of the Mexican Revolution. Mena thus shows a nation going through a civil war to assert its independence from colonial and neo-imperial bullies, rejecting endogamy (incestuous, elitist) in favor of exogamy (multiracial, cross-class, egalitarian). The mestizo emerges as the revolutionary figure that is racially marked by prior colonial encounters, yet embodies new multicultural ideals.

Mexico and the United States have a complex, intertwined history that has long been metaphorized through the language of familial ties. From at least the end of the Mexican-American War (1845–48) through the Mexican Revolution (1910–17), Mexico was continually referred to in U.S. newspapers, travel books, and political speeches as "Our Sister Republic." Invoking the familial metaphor of sibling relationship, this phrase situated Mexico as intimately connected to the United States, if also paternalistically—or, better yet, fraternalistically—in need of guidance and protection. In a typical example, a foreign correspondent for the *New York Times* explained in 1899, "Mexico is our sister, older in years though far younger in her present form of successful Government."[1] Mena takes up this familial relationship, both directly and obliquely, in order to highlight the kinship bonds and ideological commerce between the two nations.

Mena's stories illustrate *mestizaje* as a multicultural alternative to the progressive, evolutionary model of U.S. racialization that depicts immigration as a Spencerian struggle for dominance, and "white" ethnics as more capable of evolution and adaptation into normative whiteness. Yet Mena also rejects the racism inherent in creole authority within Mexico, which privileges those of Spanish blood over indigenous and mixed-race citizens. Unlike imperialist and colonialist forms of domination, which operate hegemonically from the top down, Mena's Mexican American *mestizaje* works in multiple directions, creating a new culture out of diverse influences—the United States and Mexico, indigenous and imported, elite and proletarian, familiar and exotic, endogamous and exogamous. In fictions written during and after the Mexican Revolution of 1910, Mena shows the two nations functioning as doubles for each other, each a distorted reflection of the rules of race, class, and gender relations at "home." María Cristina Mena's Mexico is a fully realized place being transformed from within (by class, racial, and religious revolutions) and without (by U.S. capitalism and popular culture); it is an alternative to the U.S. racial regime as well as a reflection of the effect of contemporary U.S. imperialism on Mexican culture.

Throughout the nineteenth century, the United States had expanded its role in the politics of its political neighbors, particularly Mexico. The Monroe Doctrine (1823) established the "principle" that the Americas were closed to European colonization, situating the United States as a "big brother" in charge of protecting and/or controlling its Latin American neighbors.[2] This policy deprived Latin America of European assistance for its independence movements (which the United States had received during its own Revolutionary War), as well opened it to U.S. annexation. Indeed, just two decades later, the United States invaded Mexico; with the Treaty of Guadalupe Hidalgo (1848) ending the Mexican-American War, the United States gained more than half of Mexican territory.[3]

A new stage of paternalism/fraternalism emerged in 1904, with the Roosevelt Corollary to the Monroe Doctrine, which threatened U.S. intervention in Caribbean and Central American nations that failed to satisfactorily guarantee order, stability, and prosperity. Theodore Roosevelt's Corollary was an unambiguously imperialist maneuver that defined national "stability" in economic terms—that is, as it affected U.S. markets and creditors.[4] Gretchen Murphy describes how popular U.S. fictions at the turn of the twentieth century link "commerce and democracy as forces of progress that the United States was bound to protect through paternal control of a racially inferior Latin America."[5] Mena's fiction criticizes such greed and paternalism, whether it appears under the banner of Mexican aristocracy or U.S. democracy.

In Mexico in the early twentieth century, the Roosevelt Corollary resulted in the United States providing military aid and even invading its southern neighbor in order to ensure economic and political stability during the Mexican Revolution. After decades of despotism, as well as modernization and U.S. investment, under Porfirio Díaz (president from 1876 to 1880 and 1884 to 1911), a coup against his successor Francisco Madero (president from 1911 to 1913) led to an armed uprising among various factions, including new president General Victoriano Huerta,

Venustiano Carranza (who became president in 1914 and ratified a new constitution in 1917), and famed guerilla leaders Emiliano Zapata and Francisco "Pancho" Villa. In 1913, Woodrow Wilson's administration provided arms to President Huerta. After it became clear that Huerta was not capable of subduing the other factions, the United States established an arms embargo against him, invading the port of Veracruz in order to provide weapons to Carranza and members of the "Constitutional-ist" faction. In 1916, Wilson sent twelve thousand troops under Brigadier General John J. Pershing into the Mexican interior in an unsuccessful attempt to capture Pancho Villa.[6] Following this embarrassing failure, the United States backed off of its military involvement in the Mexican civil war, although U.S. politicians, media, and readers continued avidly to follow the political drama occurring to the south.

Amid the chaotic political environment of the Mexican Revolution, María Cristina Mena was arguably the most prominent and significant public figure in the United States to fictionalize the relationship between the two nations, as well as represent a transformation of Mexican iden-tity in the twentieth century. Mena was born in Mexico City in 1893, immigrating to New York City in 1907 in advance of the looming Mexi-can Revolution. As a young woman in the United States, Mena embarked on a literary career, publishing in mainstream English-language maga-zines such as *American Magazine,* the *Monthly Criterion* (edited by T. S. Eliot), *Cosmopolitan,* and *Household Magazine.* In 1914 and 1915, Mena wrote a series of stories on Mexican American life for *Century* magazine. As a result of this exposure, Mena was later touted as "the foremost inter-preter of Mexican life."[7] Simultaneously a successful American writer and publicly declared a Mexican native informant, Mena straddled two geographic "homes"—her birthplace of Mexico and her adopted home, the United States. In later life, she befriended D. H. Lawrence and wrote children's stories based on Mexican history and Aztec mythology.

Like the other women I discuss in this book, Mena was a popular writer as well as a reformer, a canny woman who used her marginal sta-tus for maximum personal benefit and political clout. Her magazine fic-tion remains her most important legacy, written for an educated middle-class American audience for whom she served as a cultural interpreter, mediator, and bridge between Mexican and U.S. life. Her depictions of the complex cultural legacies of both Spanish conquest and U.S. eco-nomic imperialism are contemporary political statements, even as they sometimes rely upon entrenched U.S. attitudes toward Mexico and its people. Like Hopkins's mulattos and Eaton's half-castes, Mena's mestizo characters challenge racist depictions of mixed-race citizens by identifying the historical causes for contemporary Mexican class relations and offering more egalitarian political alternatives. Although Mena's stories are mostly set in Mexico, they were written in English for U.S. audiences, and they are overwhelmingly concerned with modern national identity in the age of transnational flows throughout the Americas. As such, her stories reveal at least as much about U.S. attitudes toward Mexico as they do about Mexico itself.[8] Indeed, Mena holds a mirror to the United States, daring her readers to recognize themselves in what they see of Mexico.

The "Mestizo" in Mexican History

By 1914, when Mena's stories appeared in *Century* magazine, the mestizo had become a powerful symbol of democratic nationhood in Mexico, distinct from, but running parallel with, the works of U.S. writers who deployed mixed-blood heroes and heroines as symbols for twentieth-century national identity. The figure of the mestizo in Latin America has a long and complex history that is beyond the scope of this book. However, I will give a brief outline in order to situate Mena's usage of the trope in the Mexican American context. As the *Oxford English Dictionary* explains, a mestizo refers to "a person of mixed European (esp. Spanish or Portuguese) and non-European parentage; *spec.* (originally) a man with a Spanish father and an American Indian mother; (later) a person of mixed American Spanish and American Indian descent."[9] Like the term "half-caste," "mestizo" originally was defined by particular racial, class, and gender relations—white European men consorting with native women—but eventually came to apply to a range of interracial unions.

Despite the linguistic capaciousness of the term "mestizo," within the Spanish colonial context, all interracial unions most certainly were not equal. In addition to marriages between European colonists and indigenous subjects, mixed-race offspring resulted from unions with African former slaves, as well as with other mixed-race subjects. An elaborate categorization system (and racial/class hierarchy) emerged, documented in casta paintings commissioned by the Spanish court.[10] The initial racial categories, in descending order of privilege, were (1) Peninsular, referring to Spaniards born in Spain; (2) Criollo/Criolla, for one of Spanish descent born in the Americas; (3) Indio/India, for a person indigenous to the Americas; and (4) Negro/Negra, a person of African slave descent. These four categories, in turn, combined to illustrate a dozen more categories, including "mestizo," the offspring of a Spaniard and an Indio/a.[11]

(These secondary terms, in turn, gave way to dozens of further combinations, each defined and ranked, although not with any reliable consistency.) By the end of the eighteenth century, the classification system had been greatly simplified, largely subsuming the mestizo into the broad category of *castas* (mixed-race peoples).[12]

Despite these shifts, among the many terms for mixed-race subjects coined in the Americas, "mestizo" has had the greatest longevity and range of meanings, periodically reemerging as a symbolic identity for the nation.[13] According to Ilan Stavans, in sixteenth-century Spanish, "mestizo" often "referred to children born out of wedlock, thus uniting it with the term bastard."[14] The colonial-era relationship between racial mixing and sexual immorality in the formation of alternative families is epitomized in the history of Hernán Cortés and La Malinche, which is a national myth of origins in Mexico. La Malinche was Cortés's indigenous slave, mistress, and translator; she gave birth to his son Martín, one of the first mestizos. As such, La Malinche is a complicated figure in Mexican culture: traitor, victim, and mother to the nation. The story of Cortés, La Malinche, and Martín underpins the familial ties and moral judgments inhering in mestizo identity in the era of conquest.

In the early nineteenth century, Fray Servando Teresa de Mier (1765–1827), a Roman Catholic priest and politician who supported independence from Spain, claimed: "All we Creoles are mestizos . . . in our veins flow the pure blood of the lords of the country."[15] Despite this early celebration of the mestizo as Mexican symbol, D. A. Brading claims that Mier (like his fellow pro-independence revolutionaries) focused on elite patriotism, rather than imagining a truly *mestizaje* Mexico.[16] Accordingly, after Mexico's independence in 1810, creoles continued to be the dominant caste, in maintenance of the racial regime of the colonial era. When Porfirio Díaz rose to power in the late nineteenth century, the U.S. press frequently emphasized his Indian heritage as authentically Mexican, auguring the end of colonial-era race and class privilege and the beginning of "modern" (that is, Western-style) statehood.[17] However, Díaz's thirty-year reign more accurately relied upon neocolonial social and economic hierarchies that accelerated racial and class divisions, rather than mitigated them. The Porfiriato revised the family model, with Díaz depicting himself as "patriarchal" father to a nation of unruly children-citizens who were not yet prepared for the "duties" of democratic government.[18]

Díaz's economic policies were especially detrimental to Mexico for they industrialized the nation to the benefit of elites while further impoverishing its peasants. Such economic policies had an obvious racial component. According to Ben Fallaw: "The Porfiriato impeded cultural mestizaje by modernizing colonial ethnic prejudice. In the early nineteenth century, Latin American liberal states abolished colonial castes, but by the end of the century export-oriented commodity booms demanded cheap, disciplined labor, so elites re-created a socio-ethnic hierarchy. But they justified neocolonial castes with European and North American pseudoscientific racism and imported notions of progress."[19] Mena's *Century* stories depict the racism and classism of the neocolonial policies of the Porfiriato and U.S. imperialism, criticizing the cultural logic that justifies oppression in the guise of parental concern. Mena rejects the false familiality of Díaz and his U.S. cronies in favor of multiracial, cross-class, and egalitarian gender alliances under the banner of the Mexican Revolution. Her fiction imagines an alternative cultural order for North America in which cultural *mestizaje* is more than a slogan, and familiality is no longer a cover for despotism.

The Mexican Revolution revived interest in the Indian and the mestizo as two distinct, yet related alternatives to creole privilege, with both terms circulating widely as nationalist symbols for a modern Mexico. "Indian"-identified revolutionary politics were represented by Emiliano Zapata in the South, while the mestizo was popularly embodied by Pancho Villa in the North.[20] Yet beyond these particular revolutionary figures, the terms themselves had distinct resonances: "Indian" suggests a nostalgic return to precolonial social relations and racial categories, while "mestizo" emphasizes the history of interracial contact.[21] While both identities figured in the national imagination, the mestizo offered a postcolonial identity that spoke to (and for) an already racially mixed populace, particularly the more educated middle classes. Accordingly, Mena (like later writers such as José Vasconcelos) focused on the mestizo as the model for a multiracial future.[22]

By the twentieth century, the mestizo had become the dominant symbol for Mexican nationalism. According to John K. Chance, it was the Mexican Revolution's "ideology of 'power to the people' that brought the mestizo back again, and this time to center stage. The creole was transformed into a new kind of person. The revolution effectively did away with the white-Spanish-creole category and the mestizos—now officially sanctioned by the government and popular opinion—inherited the reins of power."[23] Writers like Andrés Molina Enríquez, Manuel Gamio, and José Vasconcelos gave public voice to the mestizo as symbol of a new nation. For example, in 1909, Enríquez professed the view that the mestizo was an example of Darwinian natural selection, and that *mestizaje* represented the nation's inexorable march toward progress.[24] According to the historian Ana María Alonso, Gamio's *Forjando patria* (*Forging the nation,* 1916) was significant for asserting the view that "the Porfirian elite was the enemy, the Indians were the shock troops, and the northern mestizo was the real protagonist of Mexico's 'second independence.'"[25] Most famously, José Vasconcelos's *La raza cósmica* (*The cosmic race,* 1925) described the mestizo as the "hyphen of the meeting point of . . . Spanish-Indian Tragedy" and "a bridge to the future."[26] Vasconcelos's image of the mestizo as a unifying symbol for Mexico permeated intellectual thought about Mexican identity throughout the twentieth century.[27] Such inclusive language by the intellectual leaders of the Mexican Revolution was often more rhetorical than practical, for Vasconcelos and others liked the idea of cultural mixing more than racial mixing with the overwhelmingly poor, rural, uneducated indigenous peoples.[28] Mena is significant not only because her stories predate the better-known works of these (male) authors, but also because her fiction features multicultural, multiracial, and cross-class alliances during the Mexican Revolution. Moreover, while similarly celebrating (and romanticizing) the mestizo as a model for revived national identity (including the occlusion of the indigenous), she nevertheless offers a more gender-inclusive, anti-elitist, and transnational perspective on *mestizaje* than these better-known male authors. Most importantly for my purposes, she did so for a distinctly U.S.–based audience, offering an unusual vantage point on the meaning of multiculturalism in the early twentieth century.

Mena's stories published in 1914 participate in these national conversations, offering fictionalized illustrations of the battle over cultural symbols for Mexican identity. Her fiction notably rejects nationalism or racial essentialism in favor of a more complicated relationship between "sister" nations and among ethno-social classes. No doubt influenced by her own experiences as an expatriate, Mena illustrates the transformed ties of mixed-race, familial identification in a transnational world. I argue that Mena shows Mexico's and the United States' futures to be inevitably linked—romantically, politically, economically, and culturally. Mena provides a vision of a Pan-American, multiracial, proletarian identity that is liberated from religious dogma, racial hierarchy, and Eurocentrism. The romance of race here speaks to continental concerns, expanding the reach of U.S. ideals throughout North America, while critiquing contemporary U.S. racial, economic, and gender hierarchies. Transforming the nation-as-family model in multiracial and hemispheric terms, Mena's modern Mexico redefines "E Pluribus Unum" for a new century. Mena's Mexico provides a model for a sexually and socially egalitarian hemispheric national family, combining many racial and cultural strands to imagine a revolutionary future freed of colonialisms past and present.

In her emphasis on the mestizo/a as a revolutionary model in and for North America, Mena is an important precursor to Gloria Anzaldúa, whose *Borderlands/La Frontera: The New Mestiza* (1987) imagines a multiracial, multicultural, egalitarian future to be created in the meeting place of European, Indian, and African cultures. Anzaldúa describes the "new mestiza" as a perpetual outsider: "The new *mestiza* copes by developing a tolerance for contradictions, a tolerance for ambiguity. She learns to be an Indian in Mexican culture, to be Mexican from an Anglo point of view. She learns to juggle cultures. She has a plural personality, she operates in a pluralistic mode—nothing is thrust out, the good the bad and the ugly, nothing rejected, nothing abandoned. Not only does she sustain contradictions, she turns the ambivalence into something else."[29] Like Anzaldúa more than seventy years later, Mena's mestizo/a identity is not a reiteration of facile multiculturalism, but is a historically minded and politically conscious identity balancing multiple influences and competing loyalties. In the early twentieth century, Mena participates in the popularization of the familial imagination—alongside other public figures in the United States such as Jane Addams, Pauline Hopkins, and Winnifred Eaton—while giving it her particular transnational Mexican American spin decades before the emergence of Chicano identity.

Like her contemporaries, Mena uses the national romance to speak to political concerns over racism, sexism, and class inequality. She illustrates her larger concerns through allegorical stories of interracial romance and generational conflict. In Mena's fiction, romance (familiarly representing futurity) has been distorted in Mexico by Spanish colonialism and U.S. neo-imperialism: in its history with Spain and contemporary relationship with the United States, Mexico has been a member of a pathological family, given the role of (recalcitrant) child to its colonial "parents." In "The Education of Popo," the United States and Mexico are inextricably linked through modern-day economic and cultural imperialism; Mena depicts Mexico as a "juvenile" in relationship to its more cosmopolitan "Sister Republic" to the north, a model of romance that precludes any genuine equality or intercultural exchange.[30] In "Doña Rita's Rivals," Spanish colonialism is represented by an aristocratic creole mother who attempts to control the romantic and political passions of her son, resulting in his enervation, hysteria, and arrested development.[31] Such hierarchical models of national identity and multicultural contact, modeled on U.S. economic intervention and Porfirio Díaz's government, are clearly unhealthy. Mena suggests an alternative through her depiction of the egalitarian possibilities of the Mexican Revolution.

In Mena's fiction, the Mexican Revolution offers a social order based in comradeship—nonsexual, quasi-sibling affection—that unites members of various classes in a familial-cum-political alliance. The ideal love is for patria, for the Mexican Revolution, which represents an inclusive, hybrid order merging various strands of identity: European and indigenous religion; European, Indian, and African races; upper, middle, and working classes; and men and women. As Doris Sommer has argued, Latin American historical romances were a nationalistic tool "to bind together heterodox constituencies: competing regions, economic interests, races, religions."[32] However, in contrast to Sommer's claim that historical romances reify hierarchical values, Mena effectively imagines a nonsexual racial romance, creating a platonic (rather than romantic) model of (trans)national diversity and identification.[33]

Neo-Imperial Romance

Published in March 1914 in *Century*, "The Education of Popo" highlights American economic and cultural imperialism in Mexico through an allegorical romance plot. Mena humorously depicts a failed romance between the twenty-six-year-old, bleached-blond American divorcée Alicia Cherry and her fifteen-year-old Mexican suitor, Próspero "Popo" Arriola, son of the regional governor. Alicia arrives in Mexico with her parents; her father is a businessman charged with "manipulating the extension of certain important concessions in the State of which Don Fernando [Arriola] was governor" (47). Like her father, who is in Mexico to complete "one of his schemes" with his "syndicate," Alicia Cherry treats Mexico as her personal playground, and its inhabitants as mere resources for her benefit (52). Appropriately, her attentions toward the governor's son Popo are described by her mother in the economic terms of "monopolizing" the town's sole English-speaker. Alicia's monopolization of Popo is akin to U.S. corporations' massive investments in Mexico under Díaz's regime, during which time U.S. industries and cultural products transformed its southern neighbor. Mena thus emphasizes, and satirizes, the inequalities between the two nations through the "romance" of Alicia and Popo.[34]

Mena plays with a number of familiar romantic conventions in her depiction of Alicia and Popo's relationship in order to highlight the United States' ascendancy as a neocolonial power. Reversing Henry James's familiar configuration of the United States as a young, naïve woman seduced by Old Europe, Mena depicts the American woman as the cynical and sexually experienced elder, while her Mexican suitor plays the ingénue. Inverting the racial and gender roles of transcultural contact, in which the white male seduces the brown female (as in Hernán Cortés and La Malinche in the conquest of Mexico), Alicia is the colonizer here; however, in contrast to the colonial ambitions of a Cortés, Alicia attempts to take advantage of her inexperienced Mexican paramour merely as a diversion, to flatter her ego and pique her ex-husband's jealousy. Finally, Mena replaces the physical domination that occurred under Spanish colonial conquest with the subtler domination of contemporary capitalism. Alicia represents the seductive quality of contemporary U.S. capital and popular culture: Popo is attracted to her modernity. However, while Alicia seems to possess all the power in this relationship, Popo ultimately rejects *her,* recognizing her shallowness and selfishness. This reversal marks a new era in Mexican history, as well as in U.S.–Mexican relations.

"The Education of Popo" is also a retelling of another familiar colonial script, that of Shakespeare's *The Tempest*.[35] Diana Taylor describes the "scenario of discovery" in the Americas—from Christopher Columbus to *The Tempest* to Manifest Destiny—as "explaining why 'we' have a right to be there."[36] In twentieth-century Latin American literature, the story of Prospero and his servants, Caliban and Ariel, has repeatedly been reinterpreted in order to comment on the discovery scenario.[37] The Uruguayan philosopher José Enrique Rodó's *Ariel* (1900) revised Shakespeare's association of Caliban, the cannibal, with the New World, declaring Latin America instead to be Ariel, the spirit of beauty, culture, and morality; the United States, by contrast, fulfilled the role of rough Caliban due to its obsession with vulgarity and materialism. In Mena's version, Próspero (Popo) is an unlikely hero, an immature boy eager but unprepared for romance and leadership. His father is Governor Fernando Arriola, a play on Duke Ferdinand, who displaced Prospero from his rightful place; Mena makes Popo the younger man, suggesting that while the Mexican Prospero is poised for power in his own right, he (like the mestizo as a national symbol) has yet to fully grow into his authority.

In "The Education of Popo," Mena portrays Mexico as underdeveloped economically, with even its leading citizens behaving like younger brothers or sisters attempting to impress their visiting northern siblings. Marking their childlike willingness to please, the Arriolas provide the Cherry family with a preponderance of American products: "canned soups," "ready-to-serve cereals, ready-to-drink cocktails, a great variety of pickles, and much other cheer of American manufacture" (47). As Edward Simmen explains, Mena here "explores the effects on Mexico and Mexicans of the cultural invasion from the United States in the form of technological advances."[38] Yet these "technological" innovations represent the nadir of progress, an array of generic comestibles devoid of cultural or regional specificity, let alone health benefits. Through this scene of Mexican hospitality, Mena implicitly contrasts the Spanish colonizers' violent acquisition of Mexican resources with the apparent generosity of modern Mexicans eager to *give to* the United States. In this way, Mena reveals the gravitational pull of U.S. capitalism, which paradoxically manages to appear as both the source of modern goods (U.S. corporations manufactured these products) and the recipient (the Cherry family is served these goods by their hosts). Mexicans themselves become mere conduits to and markets for U.S. capital.

With their overwhelming (and naïve) hospitality, the Mexicans unwittingly set in motion the transformation of their home (and by extension, nation) through contact with U.S. products and people. Popo transforms himself linguistically and sartorially for his American guests in order to merit their regard. "[H]e bought some very high collars, burned much midnight oil over his English [language] 'method,' and became suddenly censorious of his stockinged legs" (48). In Mena's version of *The Tempest*, the Caliban figure learns the master's language all by himself; he does not need a foreign magician to teach him. Popo dons manly trousers for the first time in his life in preparation for the Americans' arrival, allowing him to appear more mature, more masculine, and of a higher class. These changes reflect the impact of American economic authority across North America, but they also allegorize Mexico's changing relationship to the United States. Popo represents a modernizing Mexico not yet prepared for the realities of industrial progress and "development." Popo thinks of his new clothes as evidence of his maturity, but readers know that he is just a boy playing dress-up. Real independence will take quite different form.

The Americans, needless to say, do not similarly adapt themselves to their host nation. Rather, they are worldly, cosmopolitan neo-imperialists more interested in the "picturesque" aspects of Mexico and its inhabitants than in genuine exchange. Popo is patronizingly appreciated as a charming specimen of exoticism and backwardness: in short, as a Caliban. To Alicia, Próspero is "an amazingly cute little cavalier" and "a perfect darling" (51). While Popo reads her attention as a sign of love and equality, Alicia sees herself as Popo's teacher, initiating him into the clichéd world of dime-store romances that she expects he will encounter when he attends university in the United States in a few years' time. She tells her ex-husband, Ned Winterbottom, "I told [Popo] that he could thank his stars for the education I had given him . . . and I gave him a few first-rate pointers on the college widow breed" (62). Such a model of interracial romance is nothing more than neo-imperialism, offering little of value to Mexico or Mexicans at the present time. While Alicia Cherry may see herself as a female Prospero, teaching her ignorant Mexican Caliban about the ways of the world, Mena suggests that she is, in fact, a crude, capitalist Caliban à la Rodó.

Accordingly, in Mena's story, U.S. cultural influence is most powerfully symbolized by cheap popular theatricals. Mena describes Alicia Cherry as "a confirmed matinée girl" of twenty-six, who looks like a blond bombshell from the stage or the emerging technology of screen (56). Her ex-husband is every inch the U.S. theatrical ideal: "Extremely good-looking, with long legs, a magnificent chin, and an expression of concentrated manhood" (58). Ned fits the "national ideal" of "foot-ball hero, triumphant engineer, 'well-known clubman,' and pleased patron of the latest collar, cigarette, sauce, or mineral water" (58). Straight out of central casting, Ned is "one of those fortunate persons who seem to prefigure the ideal toward which their race is striving" (58).[39] With characteristic irony, Mena shows that the U.S. "racial ideal" is attractive but shallow, an invention of advertising rather than a genuine expression of cultural progress—rather like the canned soup imported from the United States. In contrast, Popo is "a thorough juvenile," who charmingly plays at being her "leading man" but is fundamentally unequal to the task (56).[40] This U.S. model of romance precludes any genuine intercultural exchange, relegating the Mexican youth to the role of proxy for Ned and Alicia's romantic comedy reunion. The entire exchange between Mexico and the United States turns out to be a put-on, a parody of equality rather than an expression of it. Popo's feelings are irrelevant to the scripted proceedings, just as Mexican development is unimportant to U.S. economic policy. This is a scenario of U.S. dominance, an updating of colonial conquest for the twentieth century.

Mena hints at other troubling consequences of U.S. cultural imperialism. The air of entitlement possessed by the northern visitors produces self-loathing and internalized racism in the Mexican youth. Popo marvels at Alicia's foreign beauty, quickly learning to prefer the Aryan ideal to his own darker complexion: "Never before had he seen a living woman with hair like daffodils, eyes like violets, and a complexion of coral and porcelain. It seemed to him that some precious image of the Virgin had been changed into a creature of sweet flesh and capricious impulses, animate with a fearless urbanity far beyond the dreams of the dark-eyed, demure, and now despised damsels of his own race" (49). The Mexican imagination shifts, overlaying Catholic ideals with a U.S. popular-culture patina. Despite Popo's rosy-eyed view, Alicia is as unlike the Virgin Mary as a woman can be. Her beauty comes from bottles, not from God's favor. Mena's irony is heightened by her use of names, for Alicia Cherry is neither "noble" nor virginal. In turn, Popo's "prosperity" is not inherent in his name, but rather lies in the future, when he learns his own worth and power; only after he refuses to see himself as Caliban can he truly become *Próspero*. Mena thus suggests that contemporary U.S.–Mexican relations benefit the former to the detriment of the latter. However, the story suggests that Popo has in fact learned a lesson that he will not forget: he has the power to spurn current inequalities and demand something better. Whereas his parents remain in thrall to the United States, Popo's disillusionment will serve him well.

As with all forms of colonization and imperialism, it is the colonizer who stands to gain the most from the intercultural encounter. Alicia's flirtation with Popo serves as a form of "discipline [that] would go far toward regenerating him [Ned] as a man and as a husband" (60). For the U.S. Americans, Mexico is a site of sexual regeneration, akin to Theodore Roosevelt's foray with the Rough Riders during the Spanish-American War. Mena thus aligns interracial romance with masculinization for both Popo and Ned, although with differing results. Romance at the borderlands provides the Mexican youth with experience in cosmopolitan courtship, while the man from the United States gets a lesson in chivalric masculinity. Nevertheless, it is not an equal exchange. Mena shows Alicia in the role traditionally held by privileged white men—such as Winnifred Eaton's Norman Hilton. The U.S. woman is as guilty of neo-imperialism as her male counterparts—there are no separate spheres here!

The colonizing impulse is further evident in the language of Alicia and her family, who conflate the nation-state and its imagined community. For example, Alicia wishes to show the Mexicans "how such things were managed in America—beg pardon, the United States" (50).

Neo-imperialism is implied in the slippage between the geographic nation-state (United States) and the imagined community (America), threatening to annex all of North America, and perhaps even South America, as United States territory.[41] (This linguistic problem is one that continues to bedevil American studies work, including this book.)

"The Education of Popo" ends with a rejection of colonial and neo-imperial relationships between Mexico and the United States. Upon learning that Popo did not take advantage of Alicia's patronizing offer for him to "help himself" to "a few kisses," Ned (equally patronizingly, but with irony) declares that Popo "is worthy of being an American" (62). The irony, of course, is that Popo's admirable behavior is not owed to "American" ideals of self-restraint, which neither Ned nor Alicia possesses. For her part, Alicia reads Popo's rejection of her as Caliban cursing his master; she retorts to Ned that Popo's apparent chivalry was a sign of his indigenous blood: "Why, that was his Indian revenge, the little monkey! But he was tempted, Ned" (62). Adding another layer of allusion, Mena casts Alicia here as a seductive Satan figure, "tempting" the innocent Popo with sexual and colonial knowledge; her last name, Cherry, adds an ironic valence on the threat she represents to Popo's virginity and innocence. While Ned projects the U.S. national value of self-restraint onto Popo's dignified rebuff, Alicia sees the Indian's mocking rejection. Both of their responses elide the thoughts and feelings of Popo himself.

Popo's refusal to play his part in the colonial script suggests the possibility of an alternative Mexican American identity—one that is truly multicultural or *mestizaje*. Popo's rejection of the experienced American divorcée might be understood as a result of his aristocratic Mexican upbringing, which presumably has been shaped by Catholic morality, class propriety, and perhaps indigenous custom. In this case, he maintains the traces of Spanish colonialism in his culture, rather than accede to the "modern" morality that the Cherry family represents. In terms of *The Tempest,* Mena implies that Popo represents a merging of Prospero, Ariel, and Caliban into a new model of culture, sensibility, and learning. He promises a fusion of New World characteristics: multilingual, educated, morally upright, transnational, yet firmly anti-imperial. As a representative of the mestizo in the Mexican American imaginary, Popo bears the traces of several cultures colliding: of the Spanish conquest of indigenous peoples in centuries past and of U.S. expansion in the present. Mena does not give us Popo's interpretation of these events for this entire encounter is presented from the biased point of view of the foreign visitors. The mestizo is a figure of futurity, and Popo's actions will be read in contradictory ways—until he speaks, not only for himself (such as by refusing Alicia's advances), but for his nation and culture (perhaps by becoming a governor himself).

Given this story's attention to the perceptions that U.S. citizens have of Mexico, "The Education of Popo" ends with Alicia appropriating the discourse of hybridity to explain her own bad behavior. Having been labeled both a saint and a sinner by Popo, she declares, "I suppose we're all mixtures of one kind and another" (62). Moving from racial mixture to moral ambiguity, Mena here mocks the U.S. citizen's idea of hybridity as merely a cover for neo-imperialism, an ideological justification for selfishness. Alicia certainly represents the combination of self-interest and carelessness that mark the United States' economic relationship with Mexico; this kind of moral "hybridity" marks the limits of twentieth-century U.S.–Mexican relations. However, Popo offers a different model of a multicultural future. He is the future citizen of Mexico's intercultural encounters—the revolutionary mestizo. Newly aware of the power inequalities between nations and races, he will become powerful and useful after he has grown up and completed his "education" at a university in the United States. Then Próspero "Popo" Arriola and his homeland will indeed prosper from his hard-won knowledge of the modern world.

In conclusion, "The Education of Popo" allegorizes the relationship between the United States and Mexico as an asymmetrical, and ultimately failed, romance. Popo, a model for future Pan-American sovereign identity, rejects the false egalitarianism and "moral mixture" of Alicia Cherry in favor of a future in which genuine cultural exchange is possible between "sister republics." As such, Mena imagines a future outside the colonial script, where North American nations encounter each other as equals, and value each others' racial and cultural differences.

Further underscoring the corrosive influence on colonialism on contemporary familial/political relationships in Mexico, Mena's story "Doña Rita's Rivals" reveals the pathology of the Spanish colonial order and its Porfirian-era reincarnation through the generational struggle between creole mother and son. This story stresses the need for the younger generation to create a healthier future, where exogamy trumps endogamy, sibling comradeship replaces mother-son incest, the Mexican Revolution eclipses Porfirian politics, and multiculturalism displaces racial hierarchy. Love, loyalty, and politics converge in this allegory of contemporary Mexican identity.

Colonial and Revolutionary Romances

Published in the September 1914 issue of *Century* magazine, "Doña Rita's Rivals" tells the story of Doña Rita Azpe de Ixtlan, a powerful, aristocratic Mexican Catholic mother whose obsessive love for her son Jesús María very nearly kills him. The "rivals" of the title are the two competitors for her son's affection and attention: (1) a beautiful young mestiza who has captured his heart, and (2) the Mexican Revolution, which has inflamed Jesús María's passion for patria (77). Doña Rita represents the old Spanish colonial hierarchy revived under Porfirio Díaz, which denigrates indigenous culture and privileges the elitist, racist order of Spanish rule and neocolonial industrialization. In contrast, Jesús María's love for Alegría Peralta, a middle-class girl, is harmoniously conjoined with his love of country. According to the political and social order of Doña Rita's household—and of the power structure in Mexico historically and during Porfirio Díaz's regime—both of Jesús María's loves are taboo, as they are incompatible with the old, aristocratic order. His romances with Alegría and the revolution represent a new romantic/political system for Mexico, one that is multiracial, cross-class, and comparatively egalitarian.

Doña Rita plays the role of Machiavellian director in this Mexican production of *Romeo and Juliet,* conspiring to end her son's two passions by telling Alegría that Jesús María has broken off their romance in deference to class divisions; as a result, the girl commits suicide. Despondent over Alegría's death, Jesús María goes mad himself, returning to a childlike, dependent, hysterical state that thrills his mother until it threatens to kill him. While out to find a priest to give her son last rites, she discovers a doppelganger for the dead Alegría. This double is Piedad, a prostitute working under the name La Palma, and sister to the dead girl. Convinced that the only way to return her son to consciousness is to resurrect his beloved, Doña Rita brings Piedad home to impersonate Alegría. Jesús María does indeed respond to Piedad's ministrations, and with sisterly affection she nurses him back to health and encourages his revolutionary idealism; in fact, Piedad pushes her patient to greater radicalism than did her more respectable sister. Unable to cope with these breaches of class boundaries, religious propriety, and filial devotion, Doña Rita goes mad herself and dies a dinosaur of the *ancien régime,* unable or unwilling to adjust to the changes in her son and in her country. She is found seated in her carriage, "her head against the faded upholstery, her face serene in the inviolable aristocracy of death" (86). Her death functions as a kind of expiation of Mexico's colonial past and its neocolonial present, in that it frees her son to participate in the Mexican Revolution, becoming both a man and a representative of modern Mexican nationhood.

Doña Rita is a castrating mother whose love for her son is politically conservative, incestuous, and pathological. More than anything, she represents the class hierarchy of Spanish colonialism and its maintenance under Porfirian neocolonialism. As the narrator explains, at the top of this hierarchy are those women of the hat class (*de sombrero*), of which Doña Rita is a proud member. Lower down the ladder is the shawl class (*de tápalo*), consisting of the middle classes. Last, and beneath Doña Rita's contempt, are the *rebozo* class, those "women of petty tradespeople, servants, artisans" (70). Doña Rita's insistence on class status as marked in women's clothing shows how upper-class women benefit from the status quo, while obscuring the racialization of these class distinctions (after all, the *rebozo* is the clothing of the indigenous). The narrator gives voice to Doña Rita's privileged perspective, reaffirming class differences through the language of religion (rather than race): women of the shawl class "do not aspire to decorate their heads with millinery, for the excellent reason that God has not assigned them to the caste *de sombrero*" (70). Mena here highlights the role religion plays in Mexican class politics, and how upper-class women work to maintain class distinctions.

Doña Rita echoes Díaz's regime by emphasizing class difference according to one's role in economic production—such that the implicitly indigenous "women of petty tradespeople, servants, artisans" are necessarily inferior to middle-class middlemen or aristocratic women of leisure. However, Mena also calls the reader's attention to the implied racialization of class distinctions within Mexico. Those *de sombrero* like Doña Rita clearly identify with their Spanish heritage; middle-class women of the shawl class fit with the racial typology of the mestizo; and the working-class women *de rebozo* are aligned with *indígenas*, the peasants for whom revolutionaries like Emiliano Zapatista fought during the Mexican Revolution. While Doña Rita's hierarchy based on (Western) clothing is clearly a legacy of Spanish colonialism, her emphasis on a caste system defined by one's position within the economic system reveals the transformations wrought under the Porfiriato.[42] Díaz's regime effectively dressed up colonial class and racial divisions in the guise of progressive economic policy. Doña Rita's language of caste, predestination, and Spencerian evolutionary order echoes the discourse of the Porfiriato.

Doña Rita's rival for her son's affections, Alegría Peralta—"the bandmaster's daughter"—is a woman of the (middle) shawl class whose physical appearance highlights the multiracial character of the mestiza (70).[43] Her cheeks, when pale, were "the color of burned milk," highlighting, paradoxically, the "impurity" or imperfection of her whiteness (71). In addition, we learn that Alegría "was a tall girl, slim and square-shouldered, not considered handsome. Her eyebrows were too thick, her mouth was too large, and her temples and jaws were veiled with a fine, bluish down, shading into the line of her hair. However, her nose was delicately aquiline, and her eyes were of the type most admired in Mexico—very long and oblique, shadowed with heavy lashes; the irises were the color of cognac" (71). As Mena's description makes clear, Alegría combines Spanish and Indian phenotypes, bearing the traces Mexico's history of conquest on her face and body. Her tall, thin frame fits the European ideal, as does her aristocratic nose. Yet her hirsuteness and sensual lips indicate a more diverse genealogy. More than any single feature, her beautiful, languid eyes represent Mexico's mixed heritage: neither blue nor black, European nor Indian. Alegría Peralta is a mestiza, bridging the divide between the aristocracy and the *peones,* symbolizing the nation as it is positioned to transform from feudalism to a form of democratic socialism.

Despite Doña Rita's emphasis on her family's aristocratic heritage, she selectively claims Mexican indigenous lineage when it corresponds with her ideas of class privilege. Thus, she describes Jesús María as the "son of a general immortalized equestrianly in bronze, student at the military college, [and] sole surviving hope of a line the perspective of which vanished among the lords and priests of an extinct civilization" (72). Doña Rita is willing and eager to claim her son's link to extinct Aztec royalty, but not to contemporary indígenas. Similarly, her own full name—Doña Rita Azpe de Ixtlan—reveals a history of racial mixing between Spaniards and indigenous cultures that she disavows by her horror over her son's love for the mestiza Alegría.[44] Doña Rita's selective memory of her family's racial hybridity must give way to more complex representations of the nation's past, present, and future. Thus, in "Doña Rita's Rivals," Mena presents Jesús María's health—and, by implication, the health of the entire leadership class—as dependent upon shedding such hierarchical, racialized, pseudoscientific, and religiously justified systems of class privilege. Jesús María allegorizes a diseased body politic in need of healing through democratic politics, while Doña Rita is the enemy of progress, representing the combined authority of caste, Catholicism, and the castration complex.

The Azpe de Ixtlans are thoroughly aligned with Mexico's elite, representing the power, privilege, and racism of Spanish colonialism and

the neo-imperialism of the Porfiriato. The family is from the conservative center Puebla, a city founded by Spanish conquistadores in 1531.
Doña Rita's dead husband was a general, presumably against the French
in the 1862 Battle of Puebla (which continues to be celebrated as Cinco
de Mayo), during which Porfirio Díaz became a war hero.[45] Doña Rita
represents the rear-guard politics of the Porfirian elite, looking affectionately back to Spanish colonialism, and viewing Mexico's indígenas
as pathetic wards. She attempts to gain her son's sympathy by "pointing
out the indolent and pious resignation of the dear Inditos, and wonder-
ing naïvely whether education, property rights, and an audible voice in
government might not spoil their Arcadian virtues and dispel their truly
delightful picturesqueness" (79). Her condescending description of Mexican peasants is obviously out of step with her son's awakening politics, as
well as with the mood of the nation. Illustrating the end of the colonial,
military era of Mexican history, Mena reveals that the aristocratic classes
could no longer expect special treatment: "In due time Jesús María was
expelled from the military college. His father's name had less potency in
the capital than in Puebla" (78). Mena's stories show that the old military
regime symbolized by Díaz is waning in power. Doña Rita's politics are
nostalgic and out of touch. A new political system is emerging.

Like her racial and class politics, Doña Rita's ideas about gender are
outdated. Despite her own formidable authority, she repeatedly denigrates women's capacities. Mena's narrator explains, "Her religion, it was
true, countenanced the doctrine that women had souls; but her intelligence forbade her to attach the slightest value to a man's judgment
of such recondite accessories in the case of her sex" (84). While Mena
distinguishes between Rita's religious education and her personal attitudes, Doña Rita is portrayed as a product of her time and upbringing,
and therefore subject to evolutionary extinction. As such, her certainty
that women are the "weaker sex"—notwithstanding her own iron will—
should be understood to be the result of her indoctrination in Spanish
colonial elitism, with its racial, class, and religious hierarchy. She is
unable to adapt to the changing attitudes of the younger generation.

As a result of her inflexibility, Doña Rita chooses insularity over
cosmopolitanism, the familiar over the new, endogamy over exogamy.
In "Doña Rita's Rivals," Mena reverses the Oedipal conflict so that the
mother desires her son's exclusive, unwholesome attention. This desire
is both personal and political, as it is an expression of Doña Rita's class
identity. Accordingly, Jesús María's transgressive love for a middle-class
woman is inseparable from his enthusiasm for the Mexican Revolution.

This is made evident when Doña Rita reads her son's love letters to Alegría: "All her maternity, all the sex in her, vibrated to the passion of his phrases. . . . She wept. Why, why had she never divined and absorbed her son's heart, she who had adored him? She read on through later letters, born of ripened sympathies of heart and mind, and then through letters which told her that Jesús María was infected with that most dangerous of distempers, patriotism" (72).[46] Jesús María's personal love for Alegría is fused with his political passion for democratic politics. Mena hereby emphasizes the allegorical nature of the story, with cross-class romance embodying the principles of the Mexican Revolution.

Appropriate to her class sensibilities, Doña Rita is shocked by her son's interest in revolutionary politics. She is amazed that he would risk "his future by concerning himself about the base fortunes of *los enredados!*" (73). *Los enredados* are, in Mena's text, members of the lowest class (those of *rebozo*), who are rural people working for revolution.[47] Mena feminizes these revolutionaries by associating them with the shawl of the indigenous (recall the women of the *rebozo* class described earlier), even as the noun is masculine in Spanish. In this way, Mena suggests a hybrid identity, where regime change might be simultaneously masculine and feminine, as well as forged by a cross-class alliance. As I discuss in chapter 5, in Jane Addams's labor museum, women's hand-made textiles are political symbols, linking class and gender solidarity. Doña Rita's dismissal of the *rebozo* marks her as a traitor to her gender, as well as the future of her nation.

Importantly, despite the *enredados'* association with indigeneity, rurality, and the lower classes, Mena describes them in terms nearly identical to their mixed-race cousins, the half-caste, the mulatto, and the mestizo: "They are pleasing to the artist eye, and are full of sorrows. Strong, supple, ingratiating, skillful at fashioning curious and exquisite treasures out of nothing, they are natural minstrels and persifleurs, prone to humor, irony, hypocrisy and the melancholy that complains as a requiem in their very dances. Easily moved to tears, sensitive in love, swift and treacherous in quarrel, with plastic gestures, and eyes as lovely as those of Jersey cattle, they are ignorant of all save the saints, who do not help them" (73). In the Mexican context, the same melancholic features that define the mixed-race subject in the United States (physical attractiveness, emotional instability, moral laxity) are attributed to the "enredados." These working classes are, quite literally, of mixed-race, given the long history of mixed marriages under Spanish colonialism. Yet their seemingly biological traits have social causes. If they are quick to anger, this is likely because they suffer at the hands of the upper classes (see Doña Rita's treatment of Alegría). If they have eyes like "Jersey cattle," it is because they are seen and treated merely as domesticated animals, necessary to developing the land, but not equal to their masters. And they are manipulated rather than helped by religion, kept in their lower status by a Spanish Catholic doctrine that tells them their reward will come in heaven rather than on earth. Jesús María's allegiance with their cause marks a new era in cross-class politics, one that is relevant to Mexico's northern neighbor.

The *enredados* are the base (in both senses) of Mexican society. As Mena's narration explains, "Sometimes they are slaves in all but name, and sometimes they are bandits—one chooses one's trade—but for the most part they live in peaceable squalor" (73). This description specifically refers to Pancho Villa, whose revolutionary forces were delegitimized as "bandits."[48] In any case, they are the class on which the entire nation depends: "The social superstructure, with its mines, plantations, and railroads, its treasure-house cathedrals, and its admired palace of government, rests on their backs—for they are the people, prolific of labor and taxes—but otherwise they do not count, unless it be with God" (73). Economic development, the church, and government are all built on the backs of the *enredados*, yet the poor get no respect, recognition, or recompense.[49] As in the United States in an era of sweatshops, sharecropping, and "coolie" labor, the working classes of the Porfiriato are beasts of burden, doing all of the work without receiving their fair share of the benefits of their labor. By contrast, Doña Rita and her dead husband are parasites on the state's resources: "The estate left by the general had consisted chiefly of debts, law-suits, and magnificent, but dubious, claims against the Government. Mother and son had come to the capital with the retainers, the peacocks, and the cumbersome carriage, tokens of the Ixtlan quality . . . partly to enable his [Jesús María's] mama to smile the powers of the national treasury into paying the general's claims" (78–79). The Ixtlans are an unholy, unhealthy combination of Spanish feudalism and American robber-baron greed. Mena's lesson is clear: such an unjust system ought not to continue, on either side of the Rio Grande.

Highlighting the perverse relationship between the personal and the political, in her efforts to keep her son out of nationalist politics, Doña Rita's behavior is nothing short of incestuous. Desperate to break up her son's love affair with Alegría, she "searched her brain for a policy that might attach to herself the wandering heart of her son" (73). Her solution is to attempt to seduce her son. After dressing "with the care of a coquette, [she] asked him to play [violin] to her" (73). Mena continues, "She took his violin from its case, placed it graciously in his hands, and fluttered into a chair in a bewitching attitude of attention, with her profile toward him (her profile had always been admired). Unconsciously, she was employing with him the arts by which she had striven, alas! without success, to keep his father, the general, at her side. She felt a great necessity of preventing him from seeing that girl tonight. Her rival!" (74). Doña Rita's jealousy and feminine wiles expose the sexual tinge of her parental concern. She continues to cajole and manipulate her son with guilt and bribery: "Pale beneath her powder, she begged him not to leave her. She urged a hundred reasons of loneliness and affection, employed a hundred graces of appeal and persuasion. She grew magically younger. Tonight she would be his sister, and they should have a fiesta, just they two. More music, and games of the ping-pong, yes, and even a waltz to the music of that barbarous *fonógrafo* from the United States. A late supper, too, and a bottle of champagne" (74). The overt incestuous eroticism here is fascinating. Doña Rita seems intent on seducing her son, and she uses all of her tools to achieve it: makeup, flirtation, food, music, alcohol.[50] In promising to be Jesús María's sibling instead of his mother, Doña Rita speaks the language of the revolution and attempts to substitute for Alegría in her son's affections. Doña Rita's jealousy over Alegría is both personal and political, and she is pathological on both counts.

Moreover, in her promise of ping-pong, the phonograph, and champagne Doña Rita tries to tempt her son with expensive foreign goods available only to Mexico's wealthiest and most cosmopolitan citizens. The phonograph from the United States in particular echoes the seductive power of goods and popular culture across the border, which I discussed in the story "The Education of Popo." Doña Rita, however, offhandedly dismisses U.S. technology as "barbarous," indicating her continued allegiance to European culture as a residue of Spanish colonialism. The failure of Doña Rita's attempts at seduction indicates the righteousness of her son's passion and the perversity of her obsession.

Just as Jesús María represents the solidarity between the upper classes and the working classes in the revolution's reform of Mexican politics, his name emphasizes a new egalitarianism emerging. In contrast to his mother's chauvinism, Jesús María embodies the collaboration between men and women in the revolutionary future. His name honors both Jesus and the Virgin Mary, indicating the revitalization of religion (not its abandonment) during the Mexican Revolution. Jesus and Mary were a son and mother operating outside of Oedipal fantasies, promising equality, rather than hierarchy or jealousy, as the theological/psychological basis of the new regime. His name and political affiliation also echo the egalitarian promise of the revolutionary troops, who included women "soldaderas" as supporters, soldiers, and officers. Jesús María, in short, signals both a return to and a reinvigoration of the revolutionary message of the New Testament.

In a similar fashion, the names of the women Jesús María loves signify his evolution from selfish desire for happiness (Alegría) to piety (Piedad). Mena emphasizes devotion to noble cause over religious devotion or personal happiness, thereby urging Mexico to look forward to a new political future. Importantly, in Mena's vision, the revolution depends on the sacrifices of the upper classes as much as on the proletariat, on women as well as men. Her Mexican Revolution can only be achieved by the effort of all groups working together for change. In this way, Mena departs from the actual history of the Mexican Revolution—which was not much shaped by cross-class solidarity[51]—in order to resonate with her U.S. readers, who were living in a time of profound class inequality. For example, in East Coast urban areas, such as Mena's adopted home of New York City, the most affluent 10 percent of the population possessed an estimated 90 percent of the wealth.[52] In this way, Mena's depiction of Mexico and the Mexican Revolution subtly critiques the cushy lives of her audience of *Century* magazine readers, prodding them to similar cross-class and interracial sympathies.

Doña Rita's perverse attentions toward her child are a feminine variation on the male acquisitiveness evident in Winnifred Eaton's stories of white male colonial appetite, and Jesús María accordingly fulfills the familiar role of hysterical mixed-race subject. His state of enervated dependency following his lover's suicide suits his mother just fine: "Jesús María was to be the invalid now. He had returned home drunk, not drunk in the competent Northern fashion, but *borracho* in the poignant, morbific mode of Indian blood newly inoculated with alcohol in its ungentler tropical disguises" (76). According to Doña Rita's upper-class taxonomy, melancholia is evidence of the "Indian" temperament; yet the fact that Jesús María is in this position, and this condition was the result of his mother's unwholesome attentions, points out her specious racial logic. The causes of melancholia are social, not biological. It is not his personal psychology that needs to change, but the nation's (his family's) politics. In his justified discontent, Jesús María is the revolutionary-era mestizo, a mixed-race, multicultural subject.

Doña Rita, in turn, represents the unhealthy status quo of Mexican neocolonialism. The result is a pathological cycle: her obsessive interest makes her son sick, which allows her further access and control, which makes him even more ill: "For the first time since his babyhood Doña Rita had her son all to herself. He was very ill for many weeks, during which time she joyously wore out her strength in loving and jealous service, dethroning the indignant *nana*, and sleeping fitfully, when she slept at all, on a stretcher beside his bed. Even in his babyhood she had never possessed him so richly. He was helplessly dependent on herself alone, thus appeasing for a time the supreme soul-and-life hunger of the implicit mother toward the man-child, and drenching her being in a wild sweetness such as she had never known. His convalescence arrived as a dear autumn to crown that dearest of summer-times. Laughably weak, he adored her first from his pillow and then from his chair" (76–77). Mena here reveals the pathology of the Porfirian-era elite, where class anxiety has created a hothouse atmosphere that threatens the health of the younger generation of Mexicans. Alegría is dead and Jesús María in a second infancy because of Doña Rita's meddling.[53] Her refusal to acknowledge the multiclass, multiracial constitution of modern Mexico—symbolized by the forbidden love affair—results in Alegría's death and her son's hysteria. The upper-class denial of modern *mestizaje* thus threatens the health of the nation. During this relapse, Jesús María is expelled from the Young Scientifics, symbolically hastening his own break with Porfirian politics, eventually resulting in his strengthened allegiance with the revolution, in particular through Piedad/La Palma.[54]

In contrast with Doña Rita's claustrophobic love, Piedad/La Palma augurs a more egalitarian, healthy future. Whereas Doña Rita's obsessive love causes her (quite unnaturally and incestuously) to attempt to become her son's sister/lover, Piedad/La Palma is a literal twin of Alegría and a figurative sister for Jesús María; Piedad is a vital, living substitute for the woman whose death sent Jesús María into a melancholic fugue. Piedad's entrance is both the return of and an outlet for Jesús María's love for Alegría. Echoing Mena's earlier description of Alegría as a mestiza, Piedad's "cheeks, where the paint ceased, were the color of burned milk" (80). The only difference between the two sisters is that Piedad wears makeup, presumably lightening her skin and reddening her cheeks to increase her desirability; the artificiality of makeup signifies her moral fall from grace into prostitution. The new love affair between Jesús María and Piedad completes a circuit: his love provides Piedad a chance for spiritual redemption, while her ministrations facilitate his physical regeneration. Doña Rita is forced to acknowledge the salutary effect Piedad has on him: "What anguish of spirit it cost Doña Rita to breathe the same air with this creature, sometimes of necessity even to touch her, and, worse than all, to see her caressed as a bride by Jesús María, cannot be described. However, it was impossible to shut the eyes to the truth that the girl was his medicine" (82).

Despite the description of Piedad being "caressed as a bride" by Jesús María, she does not become a replacement love object for her dead sister; rather, she rechannels Jesús María's passion toward political ends. Piedad might be understood to represent the Catholic idea of *caritas,* universal love; it is this nonromantic, nonsexual passion that facilitates Jesús María's recovery. Piedad represents a renewed religious faith that truly offers redemption. A prostitute substituting for her respectable sister, Piedad is reborn into social acceptance, just as Jesús María was brought back from the dead. Jesús María welcomes her as an adopted sister, telling her that Doña Rita "is now thy mother, too. Consider how she found thee, as Pharaoh's daughter found the Jewish babe" (83). Piedad becomes not only a sibling, but a second Moses, a revolutionary leader. The romance with revolution thus promises to transform personal passions into political acts, and turn social outcasts into moral leaders.

Moreover, in the typological indexing of Old Testament story (Moses and Pharaoh) with modern political events (the Mexican Revolution), Mena offers a syncretic model for understanding Mexico's history and its future. Under the banner of the Mexican Revolution, Old Testament and New Testament, Aztec religion and Indigenous history, Spanish colonial history and U.S. imperialism all correspond and combine. The Mexican Revolution thus offers an alternative sense of temporality, a densely networked cycle, rather than a linear, progressive sequence. Néstor García Canclini describes this phenomenon as the "multitemporal heterogeneity" of Latin American nations "in which coexist multiple logics of development."[55] Mena's vision offers a way out of the hierarchies of the past, choosing a multiracial, multicultural, transnational, transhistorical model of identity.

In this way, Piedad is the ultimate figure for the Mexican Revolution, transforming class and religious hierarchy. She is a "girl both of shawl and of sin, [Doña Rita's] latest and greatest rival" (84). Accordingly, as Jesús María recovers, his love of country returns: He plays on his violin "the Indian airs that he loved best" followed by "a *danza* of his own composing, dreamy and pensive, as a *danza* must be, but wedded to verses of his own which throbbed with love of the mother-soil and a latent wistfulness for liberty over all its length and breadth . . . Jesús María wept as he told her [Piedad] how he had once dreamed of working for the regeneration of Mexico, but how he had failed in the test of manhood, and was now a broken creature whose dreams lay all behind him. But Piedad refused gaily to listen to that and they began to discuss plans; and presently he was all on fire with a new scheme of patriotic service" (85). With Piedad's encouragement, Jesús María merges his political sympathies with his artistic impulses to create new, hybrid musical forms that will serve the revolution.[56] Whereas when ill he had "caressed [Piedad] as a bride," now it is folk music that becomes "wedded" to his own revolution-inspired lyrics. Jesús María decides to "fertilize the soil of freedom with his songs," working to challenge "the jealous forces of feudalism and foreign capital" (85). In this way, he can become a modern mestizo himself, transforming Mexico into something new that does not re-create Spanish colonialism or Porfirian-era neocolonial economics. The revolution becomes his one true love. Indeed, even Jesús María's mother's incestuous love for him is redirected, becoming *his* "love of the mother-soil." The threat of literal incest from an outdated racial/class hierarchy is transformed into patriotic fervor and platonic equality.

While her son grows stronger with dreams of a transformed Mexican future, Doña Rita weakens and goes mad; "Tortured by the present, appalled at the future, her mind took refuge in the past" (86). Unwilling and unable to accept the changing historical and political climate in her country, Doña Rita dies. The older generation must expire in order to expiate Mexico's colonial history and allow for an alternative social order to emerge. Her death marks the end of aristocracy, feudalism, traditional gender roles, and manipulative religious dogma. Mena suggests that Mexico's future will look very different from its past, marked instead by democratic engagement, class solidarity, and equality.[57]

Mena romanticizes the Mexican Revolution as a quasi-family of comrades united by a noble cause, where all might be equal, regardless of race, class, gender, or prior moral lapses. This sibling relationship differs markedly from the political language of "Sister Nations," which occluded the power imbalances between two North American nations under the rhetoric of kinship, as well as from the power inequality between Caliban and Prospero. In "The Education of Popo" and "Doña Rita's Rivals," Mena creates a narrative of development in which the mestizo/a grows up, gains authority, and fights for the nation's future. Her vision of a more egalitarian future for Mexico also offers a potential model for U.S. Americans. The Mexican Revolution, embodied by the quasi-sibling, cross-class, multiracial alliance between Jesús María and Piedad, offers a truly non-Oedipal dynamic, an intentional family joined together for the betterment of their country and the continent. I explore another version of the intentional family in the following chapter, in which I discuss the alliance of Native American "half-breeds" and immigrant homesteaders in the western United States.

María Cristina Mena's vision of Mexico's future presages the politics of Gloria Anzaldúa's *Borderlands/La Frontera* far more than the facile multiculturalism of twentieth- and twenty-first-century advertisements featuring smiling crowds of rainbow-hued children. As Raphael Pérez-Torres explains: "The rhetoric of multiculturalism has been used to replicate the ideology of the melting pot, suggesting that all racial/ ethnic groups in the United States stand in equal positions of power. This neotraditional vision of the multicultural erases the unequal distribution of power among diverse constituencies. What is called for is a resistant understanding of multiculturalism."[58] Mena fulfils the criteria for Anzaldúa's mestiza consciousness and Pérez-Torres's "resistant" *mestizaje*, while also highlighting the range of turn-of-the-twentieth-century discourse of the multicultural family and the racial romance.

Mena's *Century* magazine fiction offers a radical, politicized version of multiculturalism, class solidarity, and gender equality in the image of a healthy, intentional family of comrades. Rejecting the colonial, neoliberal, and imperial inequalities that defined Mexican identity in the previous three centuries, she presents the Mexican Revolution as a healthy alternative. In Mena's fiction, Western linear narratives give way to a cyclical, indexical, heterotopic model of time and space. Refusing the binary between religion and rationality, Mena's Mexico finds room for Catholicism, Aztec religion, and mysticism, alongside democratic politics and contemporary geopolitics. Finally, she articulates a Mexican future that is inseparable from its neighbor to the north, a hemispheric model for interdependence without dependency. In Carlos Fuentes's explanation, "only independent nations can become interdependent partners. If not, they become protectorates, neocolonies, subject states."[59] Applying the racial romance to North America and Latin America, Mena extends the symbolic reach of multiculturalism and sets the stage for Chicano identity more than a half century later.

4 / Half-Breeds and Homesteaders: Native/American Alliances in the West

I have now illustrated several variations of the racial romance as used by women authors to urge their U.S. readers to recognize nonwhite minorities as members of the national family. Fictions featuring mulattos, half-castes, and mestizos made visceral the nation's history of exploitation, while also modeling more egalitarian social relations. Mourning Dove's novel *Cogewea: The Half Blood, A Depiction of the Great Montana Cattle Range* features the mixed-race offspring of Native American and white parentage. This novel's version of the racial romance emerges in response to the particular historical inequalities facing Native Americans in the United States in the age of allotment, and offers distinct identification strategies. Mourning Dove repeatedly rejects the biological essentialism of turn-of-the-twentieth-century racial discourse. She refuses to accept blood as the only measure of identity, opposing the prominent discourse of "blood quantum" in U.S.–Native American policy. Her novel defines Native American identity *as* American identity, shaped equally by biology and culture, nature and nurture, blood kinship and adoption, endogamy and exogamy. Refusing the trope of Native Americans as tragic and vanishing Noble Savages, Mourning Dove depicts contemporary Native Americans as survivors who maintain tribal culture and traditions by creating hybrid identities. Mourning Dove aligns the early twentieth-century Native American with the European immigrant settler, imagining new (and future-oriented) forms of kinship and national belonging. *Cogewea* imagines a new model of familiality in the West, made up of half-breeds, immigrant cowboys and homesteaders, and other outsiders.

I read Mourning Dove as expanding both Native American and U.S. identities for the twentieth century through her vision of a half-breed ranch in the American West. She expands Native American identity by insisting that the half-breed is a legitimate heir who honors tribal traditions while participating in mainstream (white-identified) U.S. culture. And her vision of a multicultural, adoptive family in the West is an alternative to assimilationist and Nativist policies toward American Indians. Rejecting any notion of racial or ethnic "purity," *Cogewea* suggests that all modern Americans would do well to forge new identities out of many cultural influences. Accordingly, the novel defines kinship through shared endeavor, not shared blood, in order to plot a multicultural future in the American West.

Mourning Dove (Hum-ishu-ma) is the Salish name of Christine Quintasket, a Native American woman of mixed Okanogan and Colville descent.[1] Throughout her life, she self-identified as a "mixed blood," though there is disagreement as to whether she had a white biological father, grandfather, or stepfather.[2] Regardless, Mourning Dove identified with both Native American and "white" cultures, asking her readers, as Martha L. Viehmann puts it, to "rethink the divisions between the two cultures and between 'pure' and 'amalgamated' individuals."[3] Mourning Dove was an activist in Native women's organizations, as well as on behalf of Native American rights. Intimately familiar with the challenges of living "between two worlds," she was also a dispute mediator. Like the other writer-reformers I have discussed, Mourning Dove merged political activism with mainstream publishing in order to draw attention to minority rights in an age of rampant U.S. expansion. By the early twentieth century, Native Americans had been thoroughly marginalized and oppressed by the U.S. government, with the ideology of Manifest Destiny justifying white settlement and Native American displacement from coast to coast.

Well aware of literature's capacity to influence public sentiment— a connection made vividly by the publication of Helen Hunt Jackson's *Ramona* (1884), which sought to be a Native American version of *Uncle Tom's Cabin* (1852) through its illustration of the plight of displaced tribes in California—Mourning Dove used popular fiction to gain sympathy for and draw attention to Native American rights. In *Cogewea*, Mourning Dove shows the marginal position of Native Americans, particularly those of mixed blood, in the early twentieth century. Her novel combines the stock plots of a dime novel with Okanogan oral traditions, both evoking and criticizing the myth of the Vanishing Indian. Mourning Dove first drafted her novel in 1912, though failed to find a publisher. She revised the novel in 1916 with the assistance/collaboration of Lucullus Virgil McWhorter, a folklorist committed to documenting Native American history and culture. McWhorter dramatically altered aspects of Mourning Dove's text, adding extensive ethnographic footnotes, lengthy historical asides, epigraphs from the poems of western writer Badger Clark and Henry Wadsworth Longfellow's "Hiawatha," and taking other editorial liberties.[4] The book's publication was delayed for more than decade due to paper shortages during the First World War and then to publisher skepticism about the profitability of a Native American novel. *Cogewea* was finally published in 1927 by the small, inauspicious Four Seas Press, after Mourning Dove and McWhorter agreed to supply part of the financing themselves. The final product—at the time of its appearance, it was one of the first novels by a Native American woman in the United States—is, as Dexter Fisher diplomatically describes, an "intriguing blend of oral and written forms."[5] *Cogewea* merges the western romance with Native American folklore in a thoroughly original way. However, most critics argue that the inconsistent voice of the novel is a sign of its historical conditions and compromised integrity; for example, Alanna Kathleen Brown mourns that "in English and on the printed page it [Mourning Dove's 'family story'] is removed from the expressiveness of its own language and the power of immediate performance."[6] As I have argued with regard to Winnifred Eaton, debating whether a novel (or its author) is inauthentic or politically rear-garde is counterproductive, distracting readers from understanding the novel's message and its means of expression. By writing in English for a popular audience, Mourning Dove necessarily responded to the particular expectations of white readers. Since much of the novel's production history simply cannot be known, I think we must analyze the novel on its own terms. Without evidence to the contrary, I choose to take seriously Mourning Dove's voice in the final product, particularly the novel's strategic use and revision of familiar tropes like the Noble Savage and the Vanishing Indian that were used in mainstream popular culture and politics to situate contemporary Native Americans and Native American cultures as historical relics. I read Mourning Dove's authorial agency, in both the conservative and radical elements of the novel, as evidence of the creative and political options available to a mixed-race Native American woman writing in English for largely white audiences in the first decades of the twentieth century.

In any event, while the novel bears the traces of McWhorter's influence (such as in didactic footnotes explaining Native American traditions and

U.S. policy), the plot may well have been Mourning Dove's, particularly its adaptation of the conventions of the western romance to tell the story of "half-bloods" or "half-breeds" in Montana territory. The eponymous heroine of *Cogewea* is a "breed" on the Flathead Reservation.[7] Her Okanogan mother died long ago, and her white father abandoned the family for the lure of the Alaskan gold rush, leaving her to be raised by "the Stemteemä," her "old Indian grandmother," along with her two sisters, Julia and Mary. After being educated at a local convent school and then sent away to the Carlisle boarding school in Pennsylvania, Cogewea returned west to live on, and help manage, the Horseshoe Bend Ranch with Julia and Julia's husband, John Carter, a good white man of "Scotch descent" (19). A feisty tomboy, Cogewea is beloved by Jim LaGrinder (the "Westerner"), the ranch foreman and another "breed," but she views him only as a big brother. Soon Cogewea meets a smooth-talking "Easterner" named Alfred Densmore who finds her irresistible, especially when he believes her to be the ranch owner.[8] After months of seduction, she finally elopes with Densmore, but when he discovers that she is not the possessor of a great fortune, he beats her, ties her to a tree, and robs her of her modest savings—behavior befitting a villain out of a dime novel or silent movie.

Meanwhile, sensing danger, Jim rescues Cogewea, precipitating her recognition that she does, in fact, love him as more than a sibling.[9] Further underscoring the happy ending, Cogewea and her sisters gain unexpected wealth after their long-lost father's death. Due to a legal technicality, their father's will—in which he left his multimillion-dollar mining fortune to his new white wife, while bequeathing a mere twenty dollars to each daughter—is thrown out; instead, each of his "breed" daughters inherits $250,000. For once, the law works in the Native Americans' favor. The romance is complete when Cogewea marries Jim (whom John Carter plans to make a partner in the ranch), and her younger sister Mary (the "shy girl") marries "Frenchy" LaFleur, a comical but kindly Frenchman-turned-cowboy. The novel thus ends happily for all three half-breed sisters, as each marries a good man and receives her rightful inheritance. Meanwhile, Densmore reads of Cogewea's windfall and is sorely disappointed at his missed opportunity.

Cogewea effectively revises the Sacagawea story for a new generation. In the eighteenth-century narrative, the Native American girl-woman serves as child-bride, translator, and guide to white men, unwittingly ensuring the loss of Native American lands and her own early death. As Beth Piatote argues, in mainstream popular literature, "Indian women emblematized a sacrificial love that would resolve the settler-native conflict," usually in terms favorable to whites.[10] (The tragic love story shares many features with the myth of La Malinche, Hernán Cortés's slave, mistress, and translator in the founding of Mexico, which I discussed in the previous chapter.) Mourning Dove's twentieth-century version stars a grown-up, mixed-race heroine who is the product of a previous interracial encounter that ended badly, with her mother's death and her father's abandonment. Mourning Dove's racial romance features a biracial heroine who lacks a social place, with the added sensationalism of a dramatic love triangle, a dastardly villain, and an unexpected inheritance. Most important, Mourning Dove applies the racial romance to the half-breed and expands kinship beyond the boundaries of blood. Like Winnifred Eaton's extension of half-caste status to an adopted sibling in *The Heart of Hyacinth* (see chapter 2), Mourning Dove's novel extends kinship to those culturally identified with Native American tradition and the western cattle ranch. Importantly, though, Mourning Dove insists that Native Americans are the stars of this story. The West is the geographic home, and Native American half-breeds are the head, of this multicultural family. This message is almost certainly Mourning Dove's alone, for she was responsible for the novel's happy ending; McWhorter suggested that the tale end tragically, in keeping with the literary tradition of the Vanishing Indian (as in Jackson's *Ramona*).[11]

Yet critics have distrusted the novel's optimistic ending, seeking uncertainty even when there is little evidence for it. For example, Louis Owens describes Cogewea's marriage to Jim as "a note of stasis, with nothing resolved, none of the many questions answered."[12] Susan M. Cannata declares that "Mourning Dove uses conventional elements of a happy ending, but she does not revise them to accommodate her mixed-blood heroes. Because the protagonists are not white, a conventional happy ending cannot occur."[13] Arnold Krupat inserts a note of skepticism, warning in a footnote that "the novel does not offer hints as to how M. and Mme. LaFleur will live—whether they will reside in the American West, in Europe, or elsewhere. Is it not perhaps relevant to think here of the fate of Hester Prynne's daughter Pearl in *The Scarlet Letter*"?[14] The comparison of *Cogewea* to *The Scarlet Letter* is revealing, suggesting that Krupat associates mixed-blood marriage with community shame, though Mourning Dove most certainly does not. All of these critics find a happy ending incompatible with half-blood identity. The most frequently cited line used to justify critical skepticism appears a paragraph before the end of the novel, when the narrator describes how the "moon, sailing over the embattled Rockies, appeared to smile down on the dusky lovers, despite the ugly Swah-lah-kin [rain cloud] clinging to his face" (284). While the presence of a rain cloud might suggest a shadow looming over the couple's happiness, the novel's final lines are fully triumphant: from a cheap boardinghouse out East, Densmore reads of the marriages of Mary and Cogewea, and of the girls' inheritances. Given the novel's commitment to the heroines' happy ending (and the villain's punishment), I find the skeptical readings of critics such as those I quoted above to be overly insistent, revealing more about contemporary politics than historical conditions. Ingrained patterns of suspicious reading blind us to other narrative and political possibilities, particularly the idea that Mourning Dove might truly mean to celebrate all three sisters' marriages as happy endings. By reading *Cogewea* credibly, I aim to show how Mourning Dove's novel imagines an alliance of Native Americans and European immigrants. *Cogewea* effectively transforms European immigrants into members of an extended multicultural family in the American West. The novel's series of mixed-blood marriages might thus be understood as a kind of canny survival strategy, providing an alternative to the myth of the Vanishing Indian. The novel depicts a new model for Native American kinship in the United States, an intentional family defined by shared culture and commitment, rather than blood alone.

In her formulation of the racial romance, Mourning Dove offers a distinct counterpoint to popular practices of white co-optation of Native American culture. For centuries, but especially in the turn-of-the-twentieth-century period, whites relished practices of "playing Indian" or "going native" as the means to counteract the enervating effects of modern life and labor.[15] However, whereas those cultural acts of identification served to control and displace real Native people, *Cogewea* is committed to Native American agency and Indian landholding. Her model of multicultural familiality begins with Native American subjects on Indian lands, and extends kinship only to those European immigrants who share the half-breed's values. Multiculturalism here works *for* Native American half-breeds, not against them in the form of coercive assimilation policies. Indeed, the half-breed redefines assimilation, such that good European immigrants are those who adapt to the half-breed's values.[16] In a time when Native American autonomy was under threat, Mourning Dove's strategic usage and redefinition of the racial romance was truly radical.

The "Half-Breed" Caught between Two Worlds

Underscoring her use of the racial romance, Mourning Dove's descriptions of the half-breed echo the melancholic (and frequently orientalized) attributes of the mulatto and the half-caste. Cogewea has "hypnotic" and "mesmeric" eyes as "inscrutable as the Sphinx" (16, 81, 192). Her temperament tends toward "dreaming," "brooding," and "an undefinable [sic] restlessness" (16, 18, 22). Jim, her half-breed paramour, is similarly described, but in masculine terms: "His black eye was keen and restless. A scanty mustache adorned his sensitive lip, which he was wont to pull and twist when in deep thought or anger. . . . Quick-tempered and a dead shot, with his suspicious Indian nature, he was not regarded as a safe man to cross" (18).[17] Like Cogewea, Jim is "restless" and mercurial, but his melancholia is expressed through a hot temper. Mourning Dove's depictions of Jim and Cogewea echo the mulatto's "passionate, nervous temperament"[18] and the half-caste's "erratic and moody" nature.[19] Mourning Dove clearly relies upon the discourse of mixed-race psychology familiar to her readers.

Cogewea likewise relies upon the literary convention of the mixed-race subject in social limbo, trapped between two worlds. The "half-breed," the narrator sighs, is "regarded with suspicion by the Indian; shunned by the Caucasian; where was there any place for the despised breed!" (17). As Cogewea explains to the reticent cowboy Silent Bob, the half-breed lives a fraught existence: "Yes, we are between two fires, the Red and the White. Our Caucasian brothers criticize us as a shiftless class, while the Indians disown us as abandoning our own race. We are maligned and traduced as no one but we of the despised 'breeds' can know. If permitted, I would prefer living the white man's way to that of the reservation Indian, but he hampers me. I appreciate my meager education, but I will *never* disown my mother's blood" (41). Cogewea expresses a preference for the privileges of "the white man's way" of life, though she stresses that she does not wish to forsake her Native American identity. To the contrary, she is bound to two bloodlines (the red and the white) and two families ("Caucasian brothers" and an Indian "mother"). In this articulation, the family tree is gendered and racialized along generational lines. The novel hereby acknowledges the common (and frequently tragic) trend of Native American women who married white men—such as Pocahontas and John Rolfe, Sacagawea and Toussaint Charbonneau. Following this historical pattern, Cogewea identifies Native American tradition with her "mother's blood." Importantly, however, Cogewea emphasizes the half-breed's "Caucasian brothers" rather than exploitative white fathers. Mourning Dove effectively looks away from past models of interracial contact in order to suggest the half-breed's contemporary ties to U.S. culture. In some ways, Cogewea has more in common with her white brothers—members of her own generational cohort—than her Native American mother, although she steadfastly refuses to choose one racial identity (or familial relationship) over the other. As Mourning Dove makes clear, the modern-day mixed-race subject is bound to both of her inheritances and must find a middle path; Cogewea notably features half-breeds who use their outsider status to build a new, alternative community. By implication, the nation likewise must reconcile its past with its future, acknowledging its diverse citizenry in an inclusive national identity. For Native American subjects, the result is the long-denied recognition of their central role in the United States' future; for U.S. citizens generally, Cogewea's intentional community models productivity, peace, and prosperity in the Wild West.

As I have shown in the previous chapters, violent histories must be acknowledged in order to imagine alternative futures. Accordingly, the tragic history of Native American women exploited by white men shadows Cogewea's choices. As the novel repeatedly shows, unscrupulous whites have long used the tradition of the "Indian marriage ceremony" as the means to a temporary relationship that can easily be broken, without legal consequence (this echoes the practice of white men entering into short-term "Japanese marriages" addressed by Winnifred Eaton). As Cogewea explains to Densmore, the essence of this ritual is a verbal declaration that the groom will support his wife. Stemteemä tells the story of Green-blanket Feet, whose white husband married her in this way, separated her from her family and tribe, and then abandoned her and kidnapped their children. Densmore similarly hopes to take advantage of the marriage custom in order to marry Cogewea, take her money, and move on quickly, without consequence. He attempts to convince her to marry him in an Indian ceremony, using the seductive rhetoric of the Declaration of Independence; he asks her, "is it not the inalienable right, as recognized in all reason, for every one to choose their own path in life? . . . What do you say? Let's elope!" (252).[20] Densmore's allusion to the "inalienable rights" of "life, liberty, and the pursuit of happiness" threatens to come at Cogewea's expense, for he privately imagines "a light marriage ceremony—acquirement of property title—accidental drowning while pleasure boating—fatal shooting accident while hunting—sudden heart failure—or safer still—the divorce court. In mad ecstacy [sic] he again unsuccessfully attempted to kiss" her (254).[21] Densmore's true villainy is revealed in his thoughts, which echo Aubrey Livingstone's treachery in *Of One Blood* (see chapter 1). Given the chance, Densmore will repeat the history of white men exploiting racialized women. Yet Mourning Dove refuses to implicate all white men in Densmore's wickedness, for she provides evidence of honest, faithful white men in the novel as well: John Carter, Frenchy, and Silent Bob. Mourning Dove underscores the moral responsibility of individuals, which provides the foundation for the intentional community that develops organically on the H-B Ranch. Such emphasis on the individual's moral agency offers a way out of the logic of racial destiny, embodied by the U.S. government's demand for Native American assimilation and extermination. By refusing to characterize people solely on the basis of racial essentialism (as Densmore does), Mourning Dove rejects the colonial script for U.S.–Indian relations and makes it possible to imagine a new social order populated by a multicultural family of mixed-bloods and immigrants. This vision of harmonious community ensures Native American survival and voice in the context of U.S. expansion.

The possibility of an alternative, hybrid identity recurs throughout the novel. Accordingly, while Cogewea describes her racial inheritances as both "red" and "white," she just as frequently posits her doubleness in anthropological terms, as "Caucasian" and "American" (70, 91, 95). In so doing, she proclaims Native Americans to be the rightful possessors of the land, stressing that the fundamental difference between the two groups is geographic, not racial: "Caucasians" originally came from Europe (the Caucasus Mountains), while "Americans" are from America. Using anthropological language, Mourning Dove highlights how whites came from somewhere else, that they are immigrants to the North American continent, not native inhabitants. Consequently, the half-breed's doubleness (and resulting alienation) is a cultural and historical phenomenon, which makes room for a potential alignment of interests between immigrants and Native Americans in the present generation. Mourning Dove thereby opens the door for an alternative family-community model defined by inclusivity rather than exclusivity, shared values rather than shared bloodlines, in a common geography. Rita Keresztesi Treat describes this formula as Mourning Dove's celebration of "hybridity over white cultural domination or fullblood cultural and racial resentment."[22] Rejecting a purely quantitative notion of racial identity, Mourning Dove's half-breed is neither "white" nor "Indian," but a cultural (and not merely genetic) combination of the two. As such,

Cogewea represents a rejection of the U.S. policy of blood quantum, which, as I will discuss later in the chapter, calculates Native American blood in order to dilute it in the national bloodline, and uses the logic of racial difference to justify a land-grab.

To underscore her redefinition of the Native American as authentically, native "American," Cogewea insists on her "proud descent from the only true American—the Indian" (15).[23] In demanding recognition that the "Indian" is the "only true American" our heroine asserts the primacy of geography and culture, and of familial ties, in defining national identity. While she is clearly reclaiming the term "American" for the continent's original residents, Mourning Dove might be after something even more politically powerful: by eroding the distinction between "American" and "Indian," the former term either becomes exclusive (simply reversing the racial hierarchy) or it is truly transformed, becoming capacious enough to contain both white and minority identities in the United States. That is to say, in taking back the term "American," which has been used as shorthand for whiteness, Mourning Dove redefines and expands U.S. citizenship to those who have been left out of "American" culture and politics. "American" becomes an adjective describing a geographic and cultural identity, not a racial identity.

The importance of both white-identified U.S. culture and Native American culture is made clear in Mourning Dove's description of Cogewea as both a typical Native American girl and an immigrant striver. Mourning Dove describes her heroine as a voracious reader: "Fond of books, the best authors claimed her attention when she was not riding or helping with the routine work of the house" (17). Like the heroines of countless immigrant bildungsromans—Mary Antin in *The Promised Land* (1912), Sara Smolinksy in Anzia Yezierska's *Bread Givers* (1925)—Cogewea is marked as a worthy citizen in part through her love of learning. Importantly, however, Mourning Dove insists that Cogewea is equally defined by her Native American heritage. Cogewea listens intently to Stemteemä's stories of "Green-blanket Feet" and Stemteemä's aunt Wan-na-ke, Native American women who were betrayed by their white ("Shoyahpee") husbands. These bad white men severed their wives' ties to Native American culture and kinship. As a modern mixed-race girl, Cogewea's journey is to find an appropriate husband who will respect her two heritages as part of a unified whole.

Mourning Dove's notion of hybridity emphasizes the role of culture (kinship) more than race (blood) in defining one's identity. Nevertheless, Mourning Dove relies upon entrenched stereotypes of Native Americans as "Noble Savages," if only to debunk them by emphasizing the effect of experience (that is, of culture) on personal psychology. For example, while Jim and Cogewea are both half-breeds, that fact alone does not guarantee their suitability as lovers since Cogewea is an educated woman, while Jim's "schooling was limited to indifferent reading and writing. Twenty-seven years of age, with a life on the range, he was a typical Westerner—a rough nugget—but with an unconscious dignity peculiar to the Indian" (19). Mourning Dove's description of the "unconscious dignity peculiar to the Indian" echoes the myth of the Noble Savage, implying that Jim's "type" is doomed to extinction (like Alessandro Alessi, the Luiseño hero of *Ramona*). Clearly, Mourning Dove relies here on readers' familiarity with the trope of the Vanishing Indian, though she does not simply reiterate the stereotype.[24] In fact, Mourning Dove is careful to stress how Jim's life experiences—defined by hard work, limited opportunity, and social ostracism—have shaped him into the "rough nugget" he is. In her emphasis on nurture over nature, and culture over race, Mourning Dove offers a more complex vision of early twentieth-century Native American life. By describing Jim as "a typical Westerner," Mourning Dove further suggests that this half-breed is, in fact, a modern paradigm of western masculinity. Such details accumulate in *Cogewea* to redefine "American" as a modern, multicultural identity, shaped by culture more than race, nurture more than nature, consent more than descent.[25]

By differentiating U.S. national identity from the nation's history of exploitation, Mourning Dove makes possible new forms of kinship in the American West. The H-B Ranch becomes an intentional family of half-breeds, immigrant settlers, and other outsiders. Mourning Dove's expansive notion of kinship offers a stark contrast to the racial regulations governing the U.S. government's Native American policy in the late nineteenth and early twentieth centuries. Mourning Dove's rejection of a purely blood-based formula for identity is a repudiation of U.S. law in the era of the Dawes Act.

In this period, assimilation (including miscegenation) was an official policy designed to ensure tribal extermination, making the racial romance an especially fraught literary genre. For Mourning Dove, a mixed-race Native American author who did not desire the extermination of Native Americans or Native American cultures, the challenge was to figure out how to urge readers to imagine Native Americans as part of the national family without reaffirming an assimilationist agenda. Another question was how to reject coercive U.S. policy without resorting to a kind of Native American essentialism that requires "pure blood" in order to be recognized as "Indian"? Mourning Dove answers these questions by creating a romance about half-breed heroines and heroes who provide a model for intentional community formation in the early twentieth century. Mourning Dove's novel rejects both the vanishing of Native Americans (and their cultural traditions) and the institution of a wholly blood-based definition of cultural authenticity. Instead, she depicts tradition as an inheritance to be passed on to, and down through, adopted members of the family.

Native American Policy and Blood Quantum in the Progressive Era

Much as African American lineage popularly was deemed "tainted" according to the one-drop rule of hypodescent, Native American ancestry frequently had been treated in U.S. law as a kind of stain in the bloodline that should be tracked and managed.[26] At the same time, Native American blood was assumed to have a shorter half-life than black blood, and thus was capable of dilution through marriage with whites.[27] By the turn of the twentieth century, miscegenation between Native Americans and whites was widely encouraged by white politicians and social scientists as a desirable, even inevitable, step in the assimilation of Native Americans. Such anthropological policies were predicated on the belief that Native Americanness could be erased through selective breeding. As Dr. Aleš Hrdlička, the Czech anthropologist who served as the first curator of physical anthropology at the U.S. National Museum (now the Smithsonian Institution National Museum of Natural History), explained in 1898, "The future of the North American Indian would be extinction as a separate race" through marriage with whites.[28] In other words, as it applied to Native Americans, extermination and miscegenation were identical strategies; both promised to eradicate Native American culture. Such faith in the virtue of assimilation continued to shape the U.S. government's policies toward Native American tribes well into the twentieth century.

Whereas Nativists and white supremacists continued for decades to believe that interracial marriage with African Americans, Asian Americans, as well as some European immigrant groups (such as eastern European Jews) threatened (white Anglo-Saxon Protestant) American culture, miscegenation with Native Americans was widely advocated as a social good. Whites who supported miscegenation for Native Americans did so knowing that the minority populations were small and dispersed enough not to challenge the white majority or overwhelm the national bloodline. Indeed, thorough assimilation, such advocates believed, might actually strengthen white hegemony against other minority populations. For Native American tribes, then, miscegenation was commonly represented as a path toward race suicide. In such a climate, half-breeds might be perceived as insidious threats to the future of Native American culture.

Mourning Dove rejects the conflation of miscegenation and extermination. In *Cogewea*, Mourning Dove instead shows how the future of Native American culture might lie with embracing marginality, with accepting half-breeds and immigrant settlers as members of a kind of mongrel American family. In this view, miscegenation might be a necessary strategy to extend and expand the Native American population. Through identification with immigrants, Native American culture lives on. Rejecting the static, tragic figure of the Vanishing Indian, Mourning Dove's half-breed is an ever-evolving representative of American (in both senses) culture: of its indigenous past and its multicultural future. In this, she went against the grain of U.S. policy toward Native Americans.

As early as the 1880s, the U.S. government had begun to emphasize assimilation in its Native American policy. This shift in focus was both an extension and a rejection of the prior era of extermination through war and dislocation. For more than a hundred years, Native Americans had been denied the rights of either independent nations or U.S. citizens, decimated by wars and European diseases, forcibly moved off of their lands and relegated to reservations. With the recognition that nineteenth-century policies had failed to permanently "solve" the "Indian problem," the U.S. government instead began to focus on breaking tribal ties by ending collective landowning. Turning away from the direct violence of the previous era, the 1887 Dawes Act (or General Allotment Act) was a coercive policy designed to incorporate Native American tribes by forcing them to accept the Euro-American dogma of private property ownership; a secondary goal of the act was to encourage Native Americans to sell their allotment lands to white homesteaders.[29] The Dawes Act was remarkably effective in terms of the redistribution of property; two-thirds of all tribal lands—more than 90 million acres—were transferred out of Native American control.[30] However, Native American identity proved to be a more complicated equation. The Dawes Act also urged assimilation by granting greater tribal authority to Native Americans with white ancestry. Correlating miscegenation with assimilation, the Dawes Act was predicated on the belief that Native Americans with white ancestry were more "competent" than full-bloods to exert the rights of voting and land ownership.[31] Accordingly, the Office of Indian Affairs invested in mixed-blood Native Americans in the hope that they would guide their tribes toward assimilation.[32] In addition to blood quantum, the Dawes Act required that Native Americans "voluntarily" live "separate and apart from any tribe of Indians" and "adopt the habits of civilized life" in order to gain full land, legal, and civil rights. The allotment process featured many qualifications and was applied extremely inconsistently.[33] Nevertheless, the Dawes Act clearly sought to link land ownership and citizenship to assimilation and miscegenation.

The coercive strategies of the Dawes Act were also applied in class-rooms across the nation, as Native American children were aggressively recruited to attend boarding schools designed to transform them into model (white) U.S. citizens. These boarding schools stripped Native American children of their tribal identities by cutting their hair, dress-ing them in Euro-American clothing, converting them to Christian-ity, and demanding they speak only English. The goal was to provide training in manual, industrial, and domestic trades, creating a servant class who, presumably, would continue to assimilate within their new workplaces.[34] By the turn of the twentieth century, there were nearly 150 such schools nationwide, the best known of which was the U.S. Train-ing and Industrial School in Carlisle, Pennsylvania, which was founded by Captain Richard Henry Pratt in 1879. Pratt, a former U.S. cavalry officer, infamously declared it his intention to "kill the Indian, and save the man." Conjoining missionary zeal with military precision, Carlisle endeavored to convert its charges to the credo of private property own-ership, individualism, and Christianity, all on the campus of a former military barracks.[35] The mainstream public supported these efforts to "civilize" Native American "savages," as is evident in an 1887 *New York Times* article lauding the "wonderful progress of the Chippeways" as a result of boarding schools; the author celebrates "their transformation from worthless savage brutes into self-respecting farmers."[36] Meanwhile, Native American students resisted such assimilation in a variety of ways, such as by emphasizing "an intertribal, 'Indian' identity."[37]

Given this backdrop, Mourning Dove's characterization of Cogewea as a graduate of the Carlisle school illustrates the failure of government assimilation efforts. Instead of eradicating Native American culture, such programs produced culturally hybrid subjects—"half-breeds" who were simultaneously Native American and U.S. American, "red" and "white," and who were capable of defending their rights in a white-dominated world. Mourning Dove's novel thus challenges those national efforts to assimilate Native Americans and thereby destroy Native American culture. In contrast to the blood-based logic of the Dawes Act and Indian boarding schools, Mourning Dove's novel offers a more expansive and hybrid model of identity, in which recognition and adaptation work in two directions. That is to say, rather than seeking the wholesale transformation of Native Americans into normative U.S. citizens, Mourning Dove's half-breeds point the way for all Native Americans to learn white ways to better defend their interests. Meanwhile, U.S. citizens—particularly European immigrants with dreams of freedom, adventure, and prosperity—are shown that "true Americanism" echoes the values associated with Native American half-breeds: flexibility, adaptability, and inclusivity. Together, half-breeds and immigrants on the H-B Ranch offer a model of hybrid identity and cooperation vital for the nation's future.

Mourning Dove is particularly critical of the U.S. government's obsession with quantifying, managing, and attempting to dilute Native American blood. She describes the federal Indian Bureau as a "vampire! whose wing cools with the breeze of never-to-be-filled promises, the wound of its deadly beak, while it drains the heart's blood of its hapless 'ward'" (140).[38] Mourning Dove vividly illustrates the Indian Bureau as a sweet-talking monster intent on sucking the blood—the stuff of life, race, and tradition—from those it claims to help. The government is an undead creature, a perversion of the natural order. Just as significant as Mourning Dove's reference to blood is her invocation of the phrase "hapless 'ward'" to describe Native American tribes. This is a deliberate echo of the history of U.S.–Native American relations, and a criticism of the government's treatment of its internal minorities. In 1831, the U.S. Supreme Court declared that Native American tribes were "domestic dependent nations" whose "relation to the United States resembles that of a ward to his guardian."[39] That court case defied the long-standing federal policy of recognizing Native American tribes as independent nations with treaty-making power (though these rights were just as frequently trampled upon), ensuring that the U.S. government would henceforth claim tribal lands by portraying Native Americans as childish incompetents. Not unlike the rhetoric of slavery as a benevolent institution—according to which whites were racially superior "parents" responsible for their African American "children"—nineteenth-century U.S. policy portrayed Native American tribes as adopted or orphaned children in need of paternalistic protection.

By describing the federal Indian Bureau as a vampire draining the blood of its ward, Mourning Dove emphasizes how the United States' policy toward Native Americans was an unnatural perversion of familial relations. Far from being a benevolent guardian, the vampire offers its victims nothing but pain and loss. This U.S. government's history of racial exploitation is reenacted in the present in the figure of Densmore, who is another white vampire intent on bleeding the Native American half-breed of her (meager) inheritance; in contrast, good white men like John Carter and Frenchy honor their Native American wives by not treating them as wards (and, as I will discuss in the final section of the chapter, by bringing their own capital to their marriages).[40] Mourning Dove's use of the judicial language of "wards" reminds her readers of the filial inheritance that Native Americans are owed. In *Cogewea*, Mourning Dove implicitly demands that her "Caucasian brothers" acknowledge the Native American and the half-breed as legitimate siblings and heirs. Indeed, the novel ends with Cogewea, Julia, and Mary receiving sizable fortunes from their father's estate, suggesting that the United States' half-breed children will finally receive what is due them.

During the era of allotment, the U.S. government's legislative and educational policies seem to emphasize cultural traits, but they fundamentally insist on blood as the primary measure of civilization. Thus, while U.S. policy was predicated on the idea that Native Americans could be transformed into "proper" citizens, it reified blood as a totemic substance needing to be managed through selective breeding and careful domestication. Accordingly, while the Dawes Act did not explicitly require a particular percentage of Native American ancestry in order to claim allotments, it did mandate the creation and maintenance of tribal rolls. Thereafter, the U.S. government required individuals to provide evidence of one-quarter Native American blood in order to receive federal benefits. The government thus pursued a multipronged strategy: (1) to establish blood quotas such that only "blood Indians" would qualify for federal "benefits"; and (2) to encourage intermarriage so as (eventually) to decrease the number of eligible tribal members, while giving greater power to those of mixed descent. The Dawes Rolls ensured that "proof" of Native American tribal membership henceforth would be understood in terms of "degree of blood" or "blood quantum."[41] Yet while federal policy required proof of Native American blood, it sought to minimize the "Indianness" of Native Americans. Accordingly, though blood quantum was necessary to qualify for individual land parcels and other federal benefits, those benefits nonetheless could be withheld on the basis of cultural habits (rejecting white, middle-class domestic habits was commonly referred to as "returning to the blanket"). In essence, the government understood Native American blood as always threatening to "out" itself, requiring careful monitoring to prevent backsliding. Culture might mitigate the "taint" of blood, but blood remained constitutive of Native American identity.

The blood quantum system's emphasis on calculations and legal definitions reflects white cultural assumptions of identity rather than Native American beliefs. For centuries, Native American tribes had determined membership through a variety of kinship systems that were more flexible than the quantitative method favored by the Office of Indian Affairs, such as by accommodating individuals or whole tribes who had been "adopted" into another tribe. For example, the Washoe of Nevada and California had a "complex and situational" definition of tribal identity that was shaped by "kinship networks, residence patterns, linguistic practices, social roles, intratribal politics, appearance, and the like."[42] After the institution of blood quantum rules, many Native American tribes adapted federal rules to fit their own traditions of membership. Thus, in 1906–7, the Chippewa of the Minnesota White Earth Reservation redefined "blood" in cultural terms: those who lived with the tribe were "full bloods," while those living among whites were "mixed bloods," regardless of ancestry.[43] While some tribes put the law in the service of their own kinship systems, many more acquiesced to the U.S. government's blood quantum system. As a result, today approximately two-thirds of federally recognized Native American tribes rely on blood quantum as the sole measure of membership, despite the fact that such rules inevitably exclude some Native Americans who are deeply integrated into tribal life, while including others who are unknown to reservation residents.[44]

Even now, such narrow and bureaucratic understandings of identity threaten to permanently alter what it means to be a Native American. As Tiffany Waters explains, "By choosing to forsake traditional modes of community membership in exchange for blood quantum, Native nations are committing the ultimate act of self-colonization in that not only are they excluding a growing number of their 'mixed-blood' brethren, American Indian people are, in a self-colonizing act, breeding themselves out of an 'authentic' Indian identity."[45] The long-standing battle between self-preservation and tribal tradition plays out in Mourning Dove's *Cogewea,* which addresses the debate by insisting on more expansive notions of kinship. Mourning Dove rejects the logic of the Dawes Rolls, asserting the authenticity of the half-breed, and allying mixed-bloods with immigrants. By emphasizing adoption (such that

immigrants become kin to the half-breed through marriage or friendship), she avoids the threat of extinction; the various outsiders associated
with the Horseshoe Bend Ranch are, in effect, a "family" (42). Mourning Dove's method of extending kinship through processes of adoption
echoes certain tribes' traditional notions of membership far more than
the Dawes Act's prescriptive blood essentialism. Mourning Dove once
more rejects the all-or-nothing logic of U.S. racialism, which demands
that its subjects assimilate to normative whiteness or be left out of the
operations of power. Instead, flexibility and hybridity (virtues Mourning Dove associates with half-breeds) become the rules of community
formation.

Cogewea is a window onto to the evolving legal strategies of the U.S.
government in the twentieth century. In 1924, the U.S. government
granted Native Americans U.S. citizenship. While this may be read as the
act of incorporation that foreclosed tribal independence, many Native
American activists advocated for citizenship, as opposed to "wardship,"
as a way to ensure legal rights. For them, the act was a resounding victory. The same year, Congress passed the Johnson-Reed Act, which dramatically curtailed immigration based on national origins in an attempt
to reverse the ethnic diversity created by the previous century's open-
door policy for European immigration (Asian immigration had already
been restricted). It appears that the nation's politicians simultaneously
made "Indians" into "Americans," while declaring immigrants to be
Others incapable of assimilation. However, according to Walter Benn
Michaels, both the Johnson-Reed Act and the Indian Citizenship Act
"participated in a recasting of American citizenship, changing it from a
status that could be achieved through one's own actions (immigrating,
becoming 'civilized,' getting 'naturalized') to a status that could be better
understood as inherited."[46] Michaels's point is that the 1920s were suf-
fused with racism and nativism directed against all nonwhites through
blood-based notions of difference.

In contrast to the government's emphasis on blood-based citizenship,
Mourning Dove imagines an alliance of immigrants and half-breeds to
form a multicultural family, all of whom are true "Americans." Importantly, Mourning Dove emphasizes the context of the western frontier
as the site of this inclusive intentional community. As Kris Fresonke
and Mark Spence explain, the frontier "is not the boundary between
civilization and wilderness, nor between white and red. Rather, it is
a simultaneously wild and settled space, where cattle ranches abut
open rangeland; it is a social borderlands, home to a range of highly

differentiated and dynamic identities."[47] Mourning Dove's model of American community rejects rigid binaries—civilization/wilderness, white/red, "American"/"Indian," tradition/modernity—in favor of adaptation, transformation, and identification. Mourning Dove's West is a home for those willing to work for the betterment of its land and its various peoples. In *Cogewea*, belonging is a matter of what you do, not merely who you are. The novel thus represents an alternative definition of identity that accounts for culture, traditions, beliefs, and behaviors, regardless of blood quantum. The H-B Ranch becomes a kind of model of community formation, reproducible throughout the United States. Indeed, Mourning Dove suggests that identity is constituted by multiple identifications and overlapping (rather than opposed) communities—the biological family, the intentional family, the tribal family, the national family.

The Cultural Construction of Race

As I have discussed, Mourning Dove repeatedly rejects the essentialist logic common to turn-of-the-twentieth-century racial discourse. To underscore this point, the author depicts her heroine reading a contemporary novel, Therese Broderick's *The Brand* (1910). Cogewea tosses it away, angrily rejecting its representation of half-breed identity as a "stigma in the blood" that needs to be diluted through marriage to whites (88). Mourning Dove's own novel repeatedly emphasizes the importance of culture in shaping identity. As Martha Viehmann describes, Mourning Dove "changes the terms of discourse from blood and biology to culture" by "treating race as a story arising from a social context."[48] For example, the narrator asserts that Cogewea's expert horsemanship and "wilful" nature are not, contrary to popular opinion, merely the expression of some essential Native American nature but rather the product of education and nurture; the narrator explains that "although having passed through the mill of social refinement, she was still—thanks to early training—whole hearted and a lover of nature" (16–17). Mourning Dove's emphasis on Cogewea's "early training" is a rebuke of popular fantasies of the innate affinity of Native Americans to animals and the outdoors, as is the scene when Cogewea shoots a rattlesnake to avoid being bitten.[49]

More importantly, *Cogewea* emphasizes the heterogeneity of cultural hybridity, that is, the variety of ways people experience identification and difference.[50] In the novel, each sister is revealed to be culturally hybrid, though in distinct ways. All three girls attended Catholic school, but only Cogewea went on to attend the Carlisle Indian School. As a result, it is Julia and Mary, we learn, who "had imbibed more of the primitive Indian nature, absorbed from the centuries-old legends as told them by the Stemteemä" than Cogewea.[51] Such moments in the text underscore Mourning Dove's insistence that everyone is shaped by multiple cultural inheritances, and each responds differently to his/her experiences. The novel suggests that racial identification is not a matter of wholesale reinvention (such as was attempted at boarding schools); rather, modern identity—which I read as synonymous with half-breed identity—emerges out a variety of experiences, influences, and historical conditions. By recognizing the full range of hybrid subjects in the novel, we avoid oversimplifying Mourning Dove's tale. As a result, Mary's marriage to a French cowboy, like Cogewea's to Jim, and Julia's to John Carter, suggest that all half-breeds, and by extension all modern Americans, must forge their identities out of several cultural strands, adapting to available opportunities.

Even Stemteemä, the novel's unequivocal representative of the Native American past, is, in Mourning Dove's depiction, not necessarily antithetical to modernity or U.S. culture. For example, it was she who inculcated in Julia and Mary their devout Catholicism, revealing the legacy of Christian missionaries in her own life, and their effect on Native American culture—not to mention Native American culture's influence on Catholicism.[52] Appropriately, Mourning Dove emphasizes the relevance of the grandmother's stories to the present, declaring, "Whether portraying the simple deductive ideals of a primitive mind delving into the shadowy past, or constructive of the hopes of a future yet unborn, the philosophy [of Native American legends] is a sacred one" (40). Mourning Dove here erects a racialized distinction between the "primitive" past and the modern future, only to efface it by asserting the modern significance of Native American stories. Stemteemä's stories speak to both a vanishing past and an arriving future. As Alanna Kathleen Brown explains, Cogewea, Jim, and Stemteemä all must learn "how to bridge the currents of change with integrity. For Stemteema it is to love those half-breed children and to pass on to them all she knows. For Cogewea and Jim, it is the recognition of their 'rightness' in their world of change."[53] In both cases, the Native American has much to contribute to the nation's future; Mourning Dove thus rejects the myth of the Vanishing Indian, which asserts that the Native American is incompatible with the modern age. Indeed, Cogewea predicts, "The day will dawn when the desolate, exiled bred will come into his own; when our vaunting 'superior' will appreciate our worth" (95).

The role of culture (that is, its heterogeneity and hybridity) is especially important, and overlooked, when it comes to reading the novel's various romances. Critics typically represent Cogewea and her sisters as stock types in a racial romance version of "Goldilocks and the Three Bears"—Julia is entirely white-identified ("too white"), Mary is the most "Indian" (perhaps "too Indian"?), and Cogewea is the half-breed who is "just right." Cathryn Halverson stakes out this position when she declares that, "apparently without inner conflict, her sister Julia has chosen to identify herself with her husband's white culture and her sister Mary with her grandmother's Okanogan one."[54] Similarly, Arnold Krupat describes John Carter as "the atypically 'good' white husband, [who] illustrates one possible choice available in the period"—that is, Julia's rejection of "Indian" identity in order to assimilate.[55] I disagree with these readings of Julia as a two-dimensional figure of assimilation, or of Mary as entirely Okanogan, since Mourning Dove complicates such schemas; moreover, such readings imply that each of the sisters should be judged by readers as making "good" or "bad," "right" or "wrong" marital-racial-political choices. To the contrary, Mourning Dove depicts all three sisters as marrying good men who make them happy and treat them well. In fact, these husbands are best understood as neither "atypical" nor "white" men. Carter and Frenchy are European immigrants who offer a more qualified and contingent sense of racial identity. As hard-working immigrants, both show themselves capable of adapting to new circumstances. As such, they are suitable husbands who are willing to adopt new culture(s) and welcome others into their families and communities, culminating in a hybrid, mixed-race family. This alliance of immigrants and American Indians emphasizes the marginal status of both groups as geographically internal to, yet politically and culturally outside of, the nation. The "Easterner" Densmore voices the elitism and snobbishness of the other coast, rejecting all of the H-B Ranch's residents as half-civilized subjects unworthy of serious consideration; yet it is he who turns out to be brutal, selfish, unfeeling, and immoral. The novel thus valorizes a western perspective on identity and community formation.

The novel's lack of full-blood Native American suitors for its half-breed heroines might suggest that Native Americans are, indeed, a vanishing race. Yet I believe such a reading is inconsistent with the novel's emphasis on culture over blood, for the half-breed is, Mourning Dove repeatedly insists, capable of passing on Native American tradition, albeit in changing forms. As Stemteemä repeatedly shows, tribal rituals are passed on through oral lore, not simply carried in the blood. Cogewea and her sisters are responsible for maintaining Okanogan traditions, no matter whom they marry. Refuting the assimilationist logic of the Dawes Act and Indian boarding schools, Mourning Dove makes clear that half-breeds will not simply become white; they remain tied to Native American culture, creating new, hybrid forms of identity that will be a model for an increasingly multicultural nation. Such a strategic deployment and redefinition of multiculturalism is particularly remarkable in an era when American Indians were the object of oppressive assimilation programs. Mourning Dove makes multiculturalism work *for* Native American subjects, and for European immigrants who embrace a pluralist model of U.S. culture.

The location of Mourning Dove's vision of an inclusive multiculturalism should not be overlooked. Land is a powerful symbol of Native American identity and agency in the age of allotment. Mourning Dove stakes her claims for half-breed identity in the half-wilderness, half-cultivated landscape of the American West. Just as Mourning Dove depicts the half-breed as culturally hybrid, she shows western *spaces* to be hybrid, shaped by white homesteading and Native American land management practices. Margaret Lukens emphasizes the role of the landscape to the novel's message, arguing that "Mourning Dove's novel not only redefines Native people and half-bloods in their own terms, but also establishes a permanent space, an American homeland chosen by the mixed-blood people who embody that connection."[56] It is vital that the three sisters are not forced to find new, "open" territory. Rather, the community forms around them and their ties to the land; it is the European immigrants who arrive, adapt, and adjust. The West becomes a multicultural space shaped by both Native American and U.S. American culture, while acknowledging Native American authority and agency. The H-B Ranch is geographically both Native American and U.S. American, a reminder of western expansion into Native American lands, while promising a home to the contemporary half-breed; as Mourning Dove explains, "although constructed on allotted Indian lands, it [the H-B Ranch] was typical of the pioneer homes of certain parts of the West, and at one time traceable across the continent" (31). Accordingly, the domestic interior of the ranch house is a warm and inviting place with "a pleasant homelike appearance," decorated with elements such as "leather upholstered chairs and divan" and "buffalo, bear and mountain lion skins scattered about" the floor (31). Aesthetically as well as socially, the H-B Ranch is a place where cultures combine in a uniquely "American" fashion.

Just as western spaces are culturally hybrid, so are western citizens. The novel shows that Cogewea and her sisters are surrounded by fellow half-breeds. Jim, "Celluloid Bill" Cameron, and "Rodeo Jack" Galvin are all "breed" ranch hands. In effect, the entire Horseshoe Bend Ranch— frequently shortened to H-B, suggesting "half-blood" or "half-breed"— is a collective of mixed-blood orphans. The new "American homeland" being created in the West is populated by an array of diverse citizens— half-breeds, immigrants, and various outsiders who prove themselves open-minded and flexible. Mourning Dove insists on the omnipresence of the half-breed, and of the importance of both Native American and white cultural inheritances to the American West, suggesting that the H-B Ranch is a model for a sustainable, intentional community.

Once again, *Cogewea* refuses the limitations of blood-logic, expanding "family" and "kinship" to include adopted and biological siblings, husbands and brothers-in-laws, Europeans and Native Americans.[57] Moreover, as I will discuss in greater detail in the next section, the novel makes functionally equivalent two different kinds of marriage: the quasi-incestuous marriage between Cogewea and her half-breed "brother" Jim, and the interracial (miscegenated) marriages of her sisters to their European immigrant husbands. Endogamy and exogamy become equivalent, even interchangeable, strategies toward the achievement of a multicultural American family. Whereas the Dawes Act associated miscegenation with assimilation and the extermination of Native American culture, Mourning Dove links miscegenation to cultural hybridity and the survival of Native American culture.

Read this way, the half-breed's alliance with European immigrants is not a capitulation to the miscegenation-as-extermination policy advocated by the U.S. government; rather, it is an alternative that effectively posits miscegenation as expansionist. Mourning Dove's literary strategy offers a modern means to maintain and even extend Native American identity by moving beyond the U.S. government's blood-based notion of culture. Mourning Dove's novelistic solution was also pragmatic and historically accurate, since most Native Americans did not abandon their tribal identities, despite U.S. government incentives to assimilation. While intermarriage rates did rise, they did not result in the wholesale dissolution of tribal affiliation. Rather than seeing the novels' half-breed marriages as capitulations to hegemony, we should read them as strategic alliances that ensure the survival of (some) Native American traditions and the creation of new ones.

Undeniably, *Cogewea*'s rejection of the myth of the Vanishing Indian and commitment to an alternative order is comedic in the sense of ending happily in marriage. Moreover, given the novel's insistence that what it means to be a Native American changes with the times, *Cogewea* might be understood as an early twentieth-century version of what Gerald Vizenor calls "survivance," despite Mourning Dove's lack of late twentieth-century irony.[58] All this is to say that the novel might productively be read as radical and visionary. As I have shown in my discussions of other turn-of-the-twentieth-century minority women writers, conservative generic forms frequently contain provocative political messages. The racial romance is thus a kind of Trojan horse, challenging domination through clever disguise.

The Winding Paths of Miscegenation and Incest

As with the other racial romances I have discussed in the previous chapters, *Cogewea* weaves together the miscegenation plot with the incest plot, showing the mutually constitutive relationship between exogamy and endogamy. The novel begins by insisting on the familial and familiar relationship between its heroine and her half-breed suitor, Jim. Jim acts "the role of a 'brother protectorate'" over Cogewea, consistently addressing her as "Sis" (19). Cogewea, in turn, repeatedly tells him, "I love you as a big brother and let it go at that" (30). Cogewea insists that their shared experience as half-breeds utterly defines their identities and relationship, effectively making them into blood siblings; the bond of common hybridity precludes romance, since it would be incestuous. Cogewea thus attempts to distinguish kinship (her sense of "family feeling" with Jim) from marriage, separating endogamy from exogamy.

Yet from the beginning, Jim's feelings exceed mere fraternity. Mourning Dove continually reminds readers that "he betrayed his love for her in his own simple way, which at times appeared to the other boys as not exactly brotherly" (19). Jim's longing for heterosexual romance with his "Sis" indicates a desire to transform family feeling into an actual family—to turn endogamy into exogamy—by creating a new nuclear family out of their shared sense of cultural kinship. The romantic (re)union is a marker of futurity. Ultimately, Mourning Dove endorses Jim's affection by transforming Cogewea's platonic love for her half-breed "brother" into romantic feeling after her ill-fated elopement with Densmore. Once her broken heart has mended, Cogewea confesses to Jim that her feelings toward him have changed, though she does so in the bantering way of a western tomboy: "I've tol' yo' that I would be yo' sister; but if yo' don't behave I'll quit likin' yo' as—as a *brother!* Savey? . . . Call me Cogewea! your own little Cogewea!" (283). Using the rough *lingua franca* of cowboy vernacular, Cogewea ultimately merges sibling affection with romance, uniting incest and miscegenation, endogamy and exogamy. The novel transforms the fraternal model of the miscegenated family into a fully erotic one. As in Winnifred Eaton's *The Heart of Hyacinth*, two culturally hybrid "siblings" become romantic partners, offering the possibility of an egalitarian marriage solution. Siblings become spouses, and racial/cultural ties become familial ones. Real incest is disavowed, as is the exploitation and domination associated with previous generations of miscegenation. Notably, however, Mourning Dove's Cogewea continues to sound like "one of the boys" while confessing her love for Jim. For one thing, Cogewea's language represents a gendered rebuke of the patriarchal logic of assimilation and romance, which demand submission to normative femininity and wifehood. For another, her rough talk is a refusal to redirect sibling affection entirely into romance; rather, both forms of eroticism remain present, expressing the multiple ties of kinship that bind them together. This further underscores that hybridity is not synonymous with assimilation.

At its most basic, Cogewea's marriage to Jim is a rejection of either/or affiliations, for she does not have to choose between her "white" and "red" identities, between U.S. culture and Native American tradition. But this view is incomplete, as it neglects two other marriages in the novel: Julia's marriage to John Carter and Mary's to Frenchy LaFleur. Cogewea's biological sisters make happy marriages of their own to European immigrants who, I argue, function as cultural half-breeds and adoptive family members. Supporting this view, the narrator describes John as "more of a father to Cogewea than otherwise," proving that he is not just a brother-in-law, but an adopted father-figure who replaces her own negligent parent (19). When all three sisters' marriages are considered together, it becomes clear that the kinship created by cultural hybridity links quasi-incest with miscegenation.

Just as Mourning Dove shows John to be a good husband to Julia, she depicts Frenchy as an honorable and appropriate suitor for Mary; presumably, Frenchy will likewise become an adoptive family member. In particular, Frenchy's exile from his homeland, loss of native language (his speech is comically rendered in dialect), and lack of class privileges in the United States place him in a position much like that of Mary and her sisters. As the narrator explains, "he had moved in the most exclusive circles of the Old World, but here, in Democratic America, he felt to be a social outcast" (209). The immigrant and the half-breed are alike in their isolation and disenfranchisement. Frenchy proves himself worthy of Mary, the most Native-identified of the three sisters—as well as of U.S. citizenship—through his response to these challenging conditions. He is supremely adaptable, learning horsemanship so well that the veteran cowpunchers are forced to admit, "He ain't no longer no tenderfoot!" (212). Frenchy's flexibility suggests that he will be similarly open-minded in his marriage. Whereas for Native American subjects, "marriage was one mechanism, among others, that could move land and individuals out of the tribal national into the settler national domestic," Mourning Dove insists that marriage for Cogewea and her sisters keeps them firmly in their lands and does not threaten their kinship ties.[59] Instead, marriage affects the geography and identification strategies of the homesteading European immigrants (representatives of the "settler national domestic" sphere). Moreover, Mourning Dove rejects the idea that interracial marriage is necessarily coercive and exploitative. If all three sisters' marriages are considered together, we can see that Mourning Dove aligns the immigrant with the Native American to model marriage based in equality and affection. In the context of the H-B Ranch's family of orphans and outsiders, quasi-incest and miscegenation are functionally equivalent and socially unifying.

Immigrants and Native Americans are further linked as settlers in and of the West, where they have transformed the wilderness into a habitable, domesticated landscape. The association of the Native American and the immigrant is reinforced when Jim asks Mary if she's "clearin' land a ready for you and Frenchy to homestead?" (238). Indeed, Mary is, and her union with Frenchy marks an alliance of the Old World and the New World to create a new hybrid western identity, unburdened by past hierarchies and divisions. The Horseshoe Bend Ranch becomes an intentional family of half-breeds and immigrants, consisting of those who have committed to creating new lives according to new and more egalitarian rules in the West. Accordingly, Silent Bob, another cowboy and an orphan, rushes to warn Jim of Cogewea's elopement because "he had learned to love [Cogewea] as a close friend. For her and her family ties, was he now dashing across the wastes, reckless of lurking badger holes. . . . As for himself, the word 'home' was almost unknown until, as a wanderer, he came among the breeds at the 'H-B.' There he had been taken in the family circle as one of them" (268). "Family ties" and "home," in Silent Bob's view, are no longer defined by blood, but by the kinship of mutual affection and shared values. Mourning Dove's fictional community serves as a model for collective identity in the borderlands. The H-B Ranch represents an idealized version of the U.S. nation: the place where a ragtag band of outsiders create a meaningful community.[60] As such, her novel is a rebuke to the assimilation and extermination policies of the Dawes Act, while speaking in the popular language of national familiality and emerging multiculturalism. *Cogewea* thus participates in the rhetoric of the racial romance, making it speak for Native American concerns.

Clearly, culture and adoption play crucial roles in Mourning Dove's sense of family, just as they do in many Native American tribes' kinship systems. Appropriately, Stemteemä, who stands for Native American tradition, and who repeatedly tells tragic stories of Native American women who marry white men, shows no prejudice against John Carter or Frenchy, suggesting that her warnings about Densmore were warnings about a particular white man who was unworthy of her granddaughter's trust and love. As Carol J. Batker explains with regard to the novel's depictions of white characters, "the text suggests that the Stemteemä's evaluation of colonial exploitation is not a form of racial determinism but, rather, an historical critique."[61] As immigrants and outsiders, the H-B cowboys are not implicated in the history of white domination. Indeed, to underscore this point, Mourning Dove tells readers how Frenchy abandoned his aristocratic family and elite academic job in France to become a western cowboy. He had been "struck by the American craze, eventually drifting to the Flathead in a quest of adventure" (152). Frenchy's romantic naïveté makes him a source of amusement for the other cowpunchers, yet these qualities also reveal an earnest and guileless heart (187). While Densmore also came west for adventure, the two men differ in material circumstances, as well as in character. Frenchy's wealth ensures that he will never need Mary's inheritance, a clear contrast to Densmore, who requires a pecuniary motivation—an "incentive"—to marry (161).[62]

The importance of cultural adaptation and transformation even applies to Jim, who learns to redefine gender roles for a new century. When Mary begins to build a sweat lodge so that Stemteemä may consult the Great Spirit about Cogewea's marital future, Jim offers to help, and Mary accepts. Mary warns him that in earlier times women were strictly forbidden from entering the sweat house of a warrior; "and if she did, he would never use it again. Neither would the man enter that of a woman, and each had to build their own" (240). Yet Mary accepts his help, suggesting that traditional gender divisions, which imply their own hierarchies and inequalities, are not relevant in the twentieth century. Underscoring that some traditions will change to reflect the modern age, Jim further volunteers to put stones on the fire, declaring, "Bein' as the old time rules was busted in the buildin' of this here cookin' oven, makin' it a sort of man and woman 'fair, the best rider of the Flathead [i.e., Jim himself] is a goin' to help with them there ash-biscuits" (241). By acknowledging the need to both honor tradition and adapt to changing conditions, Jim gains Mary's trust and affection to such an extent that "she now regarded him as one of her own kind" (241). At this moment, before his romantic reunion with Cogewea, Jim officially becomes a full member of the family. Before Cogewea accepts him as a husband, her sister acknowledges him as a member of the extended family.

Mourning Dove thus emphasizes the frontier as a site of hybridity of various types: of Native American and white, male and female, tradition and innovation. Rejecting the myth of the Vanishing Indian and Frederick Jackson Turner's "frontier thesis," which declared the West now closed, Mourning Dove insists that the nation's future may yet arise out of the cultural mixing that occurs on western ranches and reservations. As Halverson explains, Mourning Dove "contests the mythic version to assert that instead of a racially pure, exclusively masculine, bygone space, the frontier is a mixed space still very much present and home to women as well as men. . . . Mourning Dove presents its natural inhabitants as the 'breeds,' the mixed bloods who participate in both Native American and white cultures while at the same time creating cultures of their own."[63] Extending Halverson's argument to include those half-breed immigrants, and taking into account the various types of multiculturalism these characters' relationships represent, I argue that *Cogewea* expands the racial romance for the twentieth century, in terms of race, ethnicity, culture, and geography.

Kinship, not blood or race, is clearly the essential concept structuring Mourning Dove's novel of half-breed—which is to say, "American"— identity. *Cogewea*'s model of kinship is expansive, including husbands and wives, adopted brothers and sisters, parents and children, relatives and friends, half-breeds and immigrants. Yet Mourning Dove also suggests that kinship is created and extended through shared labor and the cultural ties of art. Just as work binds the various members of the H-B Ranch together into a productive community, stories are essential for maintaining and transforming culture. Thus, Stemteemä shares with her granddaughters the tales of earlier times in order to ensure the survival of Native American traditions, just as Mourning Dove's novel offers its readers a new version of the Sacagawea plot.

Early in the novel, Densmore insists (with the certainty and authority of white privilege) that legends are distinct from facts, that fiction is different than truth. But Cogewea responds: "Are oral impartations of mind-stored truths to be reckoned as naught? A fact, like the life germ of a seed, is no less a fact from having been stored for a time" (129). Stories *do* tell important truths. For Mourning Dove, those truths include the history of whites' exploitation of Native Americans, and of Native women's particular vulnerability. But the story of *Cogewea* also tells of possibilities for the future, of egalitarian marriages—among "half-breeds" but also between half-breeds and immigrants—and of multicultural community as a model for the nation. The romance of race, I have been arguing over the course of this book, is a peculiarly American (that is, based in the United States, but continental in its reach) story that is no less truthful for being fictional. *Cogewea*, like the other fictions I analyze in this book, is a window into an emerging national narrative that acknowledges past traumas while expressing hope for a more inclusive future.

Throughout the nineteenth and twentieth centuries, popular westerns reenacted the history of white domination over Native Americans—what Vizenor calls narratives of "manifest manners." Likewise, U.S. politicians and reformers sought to exterminate actual Native Americans while co-opting Native American culture (as at the Boston Tea Party or in the Boy Scouts) as a sign of authentic American values such as freedom and self-reliance. As Philip Deloria argues, "Playing Indian offered Americans a national fantasy—identities built not around synthesis and transformation, but around unresolved dualities themselves."[64] In contrast, Mourning Dove insists on the agency and cultural authority of her half-breed heroines and heroes. For Mourning Dove and the other writers of the racial romance, the mixed-race subject forces white readers to acknowledge the nation's history and redefine its future. Unlike narratives of "playing Indian," racial romances seek to synthesize and transform the nation, to resolve the dualities of multicultural identities into a new and unified whole. Mourning Dove thus offers a distinctive Native American take on the racial romance in order to refuse the assimilation and extermination policies of U.S. law.

This process is an avowedly literary one. Appropriately, Mourning Dove shows how the half-breed is uniquely positioned to collect and share racial romances for the next generation by putting them on paper. Few Native Americans have the English education to make this happen, the novel tells us, and no white person is capable of getting the truth since, due to widespread and well-earned distrust, Native Americans will lie to white people (94). This line echoes the authorship debates over Mourning Dove's collaboration with McWhorter, suggesting the difficulties for Native American truths to be said, heard, and understood within the white-dominated world of publishing. Yet hope remains for half-breed subjects to bridge the gap. According to Harry J. Brown, Mourning Dove anticipates contemporary Native American novelists like M. Scott Momaday, Leslie Marmon Silko, and Louise Erdrich, in that "the hybrid subject occupies a unique position" to be able to "mediate" between white and Indian communities, serving as a cultural interpreter.[65] At the novel's end, Cogewea becomes a stand-in for the novel's author(s) by promising to transform Stemteemä's stories into a book: "Recognizing the new order of things, Cogewea realized that these threads in the woof of her people's philosophy must be irretrievably lost unless speedily placed on record" (33). *Cogewea* thus ends by positing the half-breed as a potential archivist and translator of Native American tradition for the contemporary age.

Significantly, this line describes stories in the language of textiles ("threads in the woof") to communicate their role as the material stuff of culture. The link between text and textile is deeply meaningful, expressing both the importance of stories in the fabric of a community, and of the role of women in creating and maintaining that community. In the next chapter, I take up this relationship between stories and fabric when I discuss the meaning and utility of cultural traditions in a textile museum, Jane Addams's Hull-House Labor Museum. In that space, the relationship between immigrants and Native Americans is profound and fraught, revealing the permeable boundary between the fictional and the material, the figurative and the literal, inclusion and exclusion. The racial romance is, once more, where the nation's realities and fantasies, its past and its future, converge.

5 / Blood and Blankets: Americanizing European Immigrants through Cultural Miscegenation and Textile Reproduction

In the previous chapters I have explored the common ground between incest and miscegenation in North American fictions by minority writers who sought to expose the racial and gender inequalities between white men and racialized women. But where do European immigrants fit within the racial romance? How does the racial romance work for ethnic minorities who were legally identified as "white," yet were not accepted as fully, authentically "American"?[1] How did women reformers adapt the racial romance in order to argue for the inclusion of these provisional "white folks"? In this chapter, I study Progressive Era reformer Jane Addams's Hull-House Labor Museum, a popular Chicago attraction that put ethnic difference on display in order to present a new model of interracial familiality. Addams's museum emphasized the idea that European immigrants might be uniquely, even quintessential U.S. subjects, in contrast to common complaints that mass immigration threatened American culture and civilization.[2] However, as I will show, the Labor Museum modeled the inclusion of European "ethnics" through a desexualized model of the racial romance and at the expense of African Americans, Asian Americans, Mexican Americans, and Native Americans. Unlike the previous chapters, all of which centered on fiction, this chapter focuses on a museum. While formally distinct, the Hull-House Labor Museum illustrates the imaginative power of cultural institutions, and the fantasies upon which they are based. The gap between text and textile, fiction and "performance," authenticity and authority is remarkably narrow. In its commitment to making visitors into participants, and performers into representative Americans, the Labor Museum further eroded the line between a representation of the past and a fantasy of the future.

Jane Addams was the acknowledged spiritual and political head of the settlement house movement in the United States, and Chicago's Hull-House was its epicenter.[3] Founded in 1889 by Addams and Ellen Gates Starr with the aim of improving living conditions for Chicago's immigrant population, Hull-House was the nation's first settlement house. Over the next two decades, Hull-House expanded to thirteen buildings and extended its services to include housing, education, social services, citizenship and language courses, cultural and social activities, as well as institutions for health and safety. Aimed at immigrants, the working classes, as well as middle-class women in search of meaningful occupation, Hull-House programs effectively modeled new ways of living in, participating in, and imagining the nation: cross-class, coeducational, and multiethnic.

Among these programs, the Labor Museum was a particularly popular attraction that captured the attention of visitors—immigrant and native-born, young and old.[4] Founded in 1900, it remained a showpiece of the Hull-House settlement until the First World War, when public sentiment turned against mass immigration, and was finally dismantled in 1938.[5] The museum featured wall displays explaining the "evolution" of natural materials such as wool and flax into products like yarn and fabric. Illustrating the aesthetic diversity of the weaving tradition, the museum also included an array of textiles from around the world, as well as an assortment of spinning and weaving technologies, from the hand spindle to the spinning wheel to the fly-shuttle loom.[6] The museum created a seamless narrative of development, from early agriculture to contemporary factory labor, with ethnic women as the constant. However, the main attraction of the museum was the live demonstration of spinning performed by local immigrant women. As Addams describes: "Within one room a Syrian woman, a Greek, an Italian, a Russian, and an Irishwoman enabled even the most casual observer to see that there is no break in orderly evolution if we look at history from the industrial standpoint; that industry develops similarly and peacefully year by year among the workers of each nation, heedless of differences in language, religion, and political experiences."[7] Offered every Saturday evening, as well as by special arrangement during the week for groups, these demonstrations were the highlight of the museum, with immigrant women showing off their speed, dexterity, and aesthetic talents to appreciative audiences.[8] The Labor Museum's multicultural and multitemporal display offered audiences vivid evidence of technological progress and interethnic harmony through its display of working women.

Over the next several years, the Labor Museum expanded to include six departments: textiles, pottery, metals, wood, grain, and books.[9] Each department featured a corresponding manual training component, such as a cooking school (connected to the "grain" department) and hand bookbindery. While the expansion included the male-dominated trades of metalworking and woodworking, the textile department remained the most recognized and popular department in the museum.[10] In a long-standing act of metonymy, Addams and visitors alike referred to the textile department *as* the Labor Museum. Through its display of ethnic handicrafts and the immigrants who made them, and its message that these practices were the foundation of modern factory labor, the Labor Museum defined European immigrants as essential to the nation's origin story.[11] I argue that Jane Addams and the Hull-House Museum are central agents in the rise of multiculturalism, a link that scholars have failed to recognize. The Hull-House Labor Museum marks a crucial turning point in the nation's narrative of immigration and national identity. Through its multiethnic display of immigrants at work, the Labor Museum provided a living model for a uniquely American future defined by cultural diversity. In this way, the Labor Museum represents a decisive shift away from biological notions of ethnic/racial difference and toward a cultural model that emphasizes hybridity.

The Labor Museum was thus a vital agent in the institutionalization of multiculturalism as a national value, although its model of the multicultural national family depended upon certain strategic omissions and evasions. Addams's vision of interethnic harmony (her faith "that industry develops similarly and peacefully year by year among the workers of each nation, heedless of differences in language, religion, and political experiences") elides the history of racial inequality and labor exploitation evident in African American enslavement, Chinese "coolie" labor, and Native American dispossession and extermination. The Labor Museum avoids referencing racial exploitation (both sexual and labor) by omitting those who embodied its history.

Addams similarly avoids the titillation and taboo of interracial sex by transforming the biological family into a cultural "family" of immigrants and Americans. Whereas the fictions of Pauline Hopkins, Winnifred Eaton, María Cristina Mena, and Mourning Dove focus on the biological family—parents and children, brothers and sisters, husbands and wives—as the central metaphor of national belonging, the Labor Museum offered a nonsexual model of multiculturalism. Its vision of immigrant women and their Americanized daughters was doubtless more socially acceptable to her white, middle-class benefactors and settlement house workers, while still offering a newly expansive model of U.S. culture. By shifting the racial romance away from sexual reproduction and toward cultural reproduction—from the discourse of blood to blankets—the Labor Museum helped to redefine American identity as a process, rather than a substance. In this, I argue that Jane Addams is a direct ancestor of late twentieth-century multiculturalism, embodied in the United Colors of Benetton advertisements, which merges both strands—biological and cultural—in its vision of a radical multicultural world.

In placing immigrant women at the center of the American story, Addams's museum made various ethnicities into members of the national family, but did so through a desexed variation of the racial romance. The Labor Museum's model features incest and miscegenation without sex or marriage. In the museum, incestuous desire is redirected toward homosocial intimacy between mothers and daughters. Miscegenation, too, is transformed, becoming an aesthetic strategy rather than a sexual transgression: the museum featured multiethnic "families" of women and multicultural displays of ethnic handicrafts. I argue that this desexualization of multiculturalism shifts the language of kinship away from blood and biology, in favor of adoption and culture. Such a cultural model of ethnic difference accommodated white ethnics into the national family, but at the expense of other groups—including African Americans, Asian Americans, Mexican Americans, and Native Americans—whose racial, cultural, and historical experiences posed too great a threat to the nascent narrative of cultural assimilation. These racial Others remained outside Addams's model of cultural adoption, trapped in the logic of blood and intrinsic racial difference.

"More Meaning and a Sense of Relation"

During the Progressive Era (1890–1914) in the United States, reformers of all kinds sought to transform America's crowded, dangerous, dirty cities and their heterogeneous populations. The settlement house movement in particular explicitly linked public issues such as immigration, sanitation, and labor conditions to the private sphere of home, family, and domesticity.[12] Women led this movement, formed the majority of its workforce, and shaped its diverse programming in the feminized language of "municipal housekeeping."[13] Accordingly, the language of "sisterhood" was commonly used to describe social relations in the settlement house movement, as well as in other reform efforts like the Young Women's Christian Association and the Salvation Army.[14] While Hull-House settlement workers were called "residents" rather than "sisters," Addams's writings are nevertheless filled with familial analogies that extend kinship ties to disenfranchised populations.[15] For example, in her essays and speeches, Addams naturalizes women's activism as an extension of a daughter's filial duty[16] and repeatedly invokes the rhetoric of "brotherhood" to urge equality for immigrants and laborers.[17] Echoing Theodore Roosevelt's Corollary to the Monroe Doctrine, she even declares that Hull-House's relationship to the neighborhood "resembles that of the big brother whose mere presence on the playground protects the little ones from bullies."[18]

While sibling metaphors are common in Addams's writings, she was far more interested in the ties between parents and children as a model for civic responsibility and reciprocity. Indeed, the parent-child bond becomes the foundation of the Hull-House Labor Museum's model of the racial romance.[19] The failure of the family claim is nowhere so threatened as between Americanized children of immigrants and their "Old World" parents.[20] For twentieth-century immigrant families, biological ties were a weak force of attraction compared to the vast differences (of knowledge, experience, and history) that separated the generations. The child's rapid Americanization, particularly through the multiethnic environments of the public school, the workplace, and the neighborhood, weakened family ties, in turn threatening the foundational bonds of community. The children of immigrants defined themselves as fundamentally American, but did so by disavowing their "greenhorn" parents. As Sarah E. Chinn explains, "By enacting the generation gap, the children of immigrants dissolved the conflation of 'American' and 'Anglo-Saxon'—instead, to be American meant to be sophisticated, to be involved in industrial labor or commerce, to participate in commercial leisure and consumer spending, and to reject the 'Old World.'"[21] For the U.S.-born or -raised children of immigrants, the past was a foreign country, distant and incomprehensible. The Labor Museum embraced and extended the youths' capacious definition of American identity to incorporate those Old World parents who seemed to be the antithesis of cosmopolitan Americanism. In short, the Labor Museum asked both immigrant parents and children to see themselves in new ways—the parents as American, and their children as ethnic—in order to renew the affective bonds between them. Like other racial romances I have discussed, the Hull-House Labor Museum asked its audiences and performers to imagine new relationships between family members as a model for recognizing the ties linking white Americans to the nation's racial/ethnic Others.

The Labor Museum paralleled the relationship between immigrants and their children with the relationship between ethnic minorities and the larger body politic. As Addams explains in *Twenty Years at Hull-House* (1910), the genesis of the Labor Museum was familial: "It seemed to me that Hull-House ought to be able to devise some educational enterprise, which should build a bridge between European and American experiences in such wise as to give them both more meaning and a *sense of relation*. I meditated that perhaps the power to see life as a whole, is more needed in the immigrant quarter of a large city than anywhere else, and that the lack of this power is the most fruitful source of misunderstanding *between European immigrants and their children, as it is between them and their American neighbors*; and why should that chasm *between fathers and sons*, yawning at the feet of each generation, be made so unnecessarily cruel and impassable to these bewildered immigrants?"[22] Addams declares her mission is to give immigrants and native-born Americans a greater "sense of relation," healing the rift between immigrants and their children, ethnic communities and "American neighbors," "fathers and sons." The result is a deeply familial and multicultural social experiment. Addams analogizes the biological ties between parents and children to the cultural connections between immigrants and native-born populations. The modern immigrant family is itself now multicultural, being shaped by both ethnic tradition and American popular culture. That is to say, the modern American family is culturally hybrid, just like the United States. Consequently, the multicultural nuclear family becomes a microcosm of the increasingly diverse city and nation. The model of cultural mixing that we saw illustrated as miscegenation in minority literature is, in Addams's museum, the prototype for U.S. multiculturalism.

While avowedly multicultural, Addams's familial model was distinctly homosocial, uniting immigrant and Americanized women. Although Addams's rhetoric in the above quotation emphasizes "fathers and sons," the museum display was overwhelmingly feminine, focusing on mothers and daughters. Addams likewise exchanges the masculine rhetoric of building "bridges" for the feminized metaphor of spinning and weaving a new social fabric. The museum's focus on textiles promised its visitors that immigration would create new and beautiful patterns in the United

States, out of diverse ethnic strands, in order to create a stronger and more useful community fabric. This focus on textiles, as I will discuss, also signaled a shift away from biological definitions of American identity (embodied by Nativists' emphasis on Anglo-Saxon blood) toward cultural ones (symbolized by the handcrafted blanket).

In its emphasis on feminized forms of manual labor—work typically performed by women in the home—Addams created a homosocial world of ethnic variety. In its focus on immigrant mothers and daughters, the Hull-House Labor Museum evacuated sex, although not eroticism, from the racial romance. The museum posited women as the carriers of culture, with textile production as an essential form of cultural reproduction. This is made evident when Addams argues that the relationship between immigrant parents and children provides a necessary model for good parenting and good citizenship: "I do not believe that the children who have been cut off from their own parents are going to be those who, when they become parents themselves, will know how to hold the family together and to connect it with the state. I should begin to teach the girls to be good mothers by teaching them to be good daughters."[23] The family is, for Addams as it was for Hopkins, Eaton, Mourning Dove, and Mena, the Ur-model for socialization and acculturation. Emphasizing the ties of affection and culture between ethnic women was good for the nation. Indeed, the museum treated cultural bonds as indistinguishable from emotional ones.

The emotional appeal of multiculturalism is readily apparent in contemporary photographs of the museum's live demonstrations. In figure 4, an Irish woman spins wool using the comparatively sophisticated spinning wheel at the center of the image, with an Italian woman spinning by hand at the right. The two adult immigrant women represent European ethnic diversity on display, as do the objects that surround them: spinning wheels, looms, small tapestries, pottery, baskets, and photographs. Flanking these two women are two young girls, learning the handicrafts of these immigrant elders. The girl at right shyly refuses to engage the camera, but presses herself against the Italian woman, seeming to find comfort in the warmth of the older woman's body. At left, the older girl sits weaving a basket, proving that she has successfully absorbed the lesson. The museum display effectively offers a multiethnic and multigenerational model of family and domesticity based on adoption rather than blood. The American(ized) girls fulfill the role of dutiful daughters or granddaughters, intimately connected to the immigrant women and their craft. The museum provides a closed loop uniting

FIGURE 4. "Spinning with Wool Wheel." Jane Addams Hull-House Photographic Collection, Photo #JAMC_0000_0177_0475, University of Illinois at Chicago Library, Special Collections.

mothers and daughters in a shared love of ethnic variety. In this way, the Labor Museum features the key elements of racial romance—incest and miscegenation—but in desexualized terms. The erotics of Addams's racial romance are, instead, maternal and filial.[24]

There is further contemporary proof of Addams's success at forging familial ties between Americanized children and immigrant women. Hilda Polacheck, née Satt, was a young Jewish immigrant from Poland when she first visited the Labor Museum, a transformative moment in her American education. In her autobiography, she remembers being "fascinated" by the "deft hands" of the women in the museum and amazed to learn that her own work sewing cuffs in a factory bore a relationship to the work on display.[25] Polacheck describes the immigrant women she met decades earlier in loving terms, emphasizing the emotional bonds formed through the museum's display.[26] According to Polacheck, "Mrs. Brasnahan" [sic] was "a plump, good-natured Irish woman, whom I learned to love," who "used a spinning wheel with great skill."[27] While the Italian woman in the Labor Museum "did not understand English, we did carry on a friendship in sign language. Mrs. Molinari showed the type of spinning that was done before the spinning wheel was invented."[28] As Addams intended, Polacheck notes the women's ethnic differences and the evolution of labor methods. More importantly, the immigrant girl identifies with these women affectionately, speaking of Honora Brosnahan as a kind of surrogate mother, grandmother, or aunt ("whom [she] learned to love"). The Labor Museum thus not only united girls with their own mothers, but with "Old World" immigrants and their ethnic cultures more generally. Decades later, she still recalls the affective bond she forged with this immigrant Irish woman. Ultimately, the Hull-House Labor Museum inaugurates two more acts of adoption: of Addams as Polacheck's role model, and of America as her homeland. To this end, Polacheck titled her autobiography *I Came a Stranger: The Story of a Hull-House Girl*, an acknowledgment of the formative influence Addams had on her development, including her career as a labor organizer and her transformation from foreigner to American.

Conjoining kinship and craft production, the Labor Museum metaphorized American culture as both a multiethnic family and a multicultural fabric. Through its mixture of diverse ethnic cultures, manual labor methods, and textile patterns, the museum aimed to "knit together" immigrant mothers and daughters into a tighter social fabric. The mixing of metaphors makes sense in the context of Addams's pedagogical message: that recognizing one's connection to older, ethnic traditions is a learned skill, like weaving a basket or a blanket. Indeed, Hilda Satt Polacheck learned this lesson so well that she became one of those weaving women on display; a 1916 photograph (figure 5) features her at a spinning wheel, under the caption "Russian Spinning."[29] While Addams describes her intention to mitigate the gap between "fathers and sons," the museum more accurately modeled mothers and daughters, with visitors asked to link the two generations, to weave the past with the future, ethnic tradition with American modernity.[30] That the United States is now touted, at home and abroad, as a "nation of immigrants" speaks to the success of Addams's venture.

Miscegenation without Sex

The absence of men in the Labor Museum's model of the multicultural "family" is striking, especially since Addams was well aware of the threat that heterosexual romance held for unsupervised youth in Chicago. In *Twenty Years at Hull-House*, Addams details numerous cases

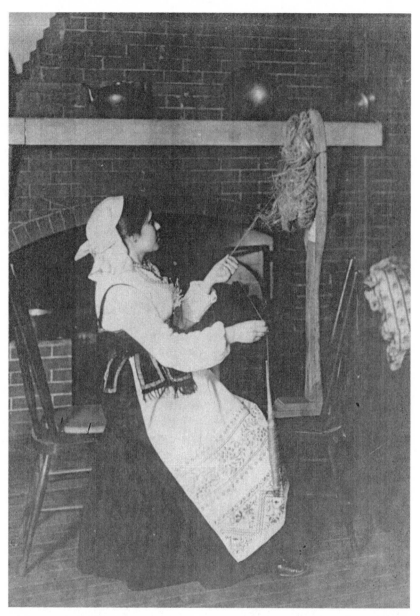

FIGURE 5. "Russian Spinning." Jane Addams Hull-House Photographic Collection, Photo #JAMC_0000_0177_0926, University of Illinois at Chicago Library, Special Collections.

of prostitution, disease, pregnancy, and other sex-based ills that she encountered among the city's immigrant and working-class girls.[31] In an unsentimental passage about cases of incest in immigrant neighborhoods, Addams blames crowded tenements for "the surprisingly large number of delinquent girls who have become criminally involved with their own fathers and uncles."[32] Addams wrote passionately about the social causes of juvenile delinquency and crime, urging for better education, improved housing, and more wholesome forms of entertainment. Nevertheless, popular discourse tended to blame the victims—particularly poor, immigrant women—for society's sexual ills. As Elizabeth Wilson explains, urban women were assumed to be sexually available: "It almost seems as though to be a woman—an individual, not part of a family or kin group—in the city, is to become a prostitute—a public woman."[33] To combat these problems, Hull-House offered a variety of cultural programs and chaperoned spaces for immigrant youth, and the Labor Museum focused its attention on providing "at-risk" girls with a sense of meaningful and appropriate familial connection.

The Labor Museum eased popular fears of immigrant sexuality by depicting a nonthreatening, nonsexual vision of immigrant femininity. The museum's tableau of homosocial familiality was a positive alternative to the narrative of sexual deviancy and moral degradation. The Labor Museum presented a healthy model of intimacy and connection, of domesticity and familiality. By asserting immigrant girls' connection to—that is, kinship with—ethnic communities and to each other, Addams soothed public anxieties about the sexual threat of immigrant women. At the same time, for its youth audience, the museum modeled a sexless version of parent-child love (mothers and daughters weaving together) to combat actual cases of pathological family romance (fathers and daughters committing incest). Whereas writers such as Pauline Hopkins and Winnifred Eaton depict fictional scenes of incest or incestuous desire to expose a real history of racial exploitation, Addams creates a nostalgic fantasy of asexual family love as a model of multicultural harmony. The realism—that is, the apparent authenticity—of the Labor Museum's tableaux was thus a dramatic *fiction* designed to change the present and future of the city's poor. The absence of men in the museum removed all threat of exploitation, disease, incest, miscegenation, or other forms of sexual boundary-crossing. In this, the Labor Museum erased the stigma of deviancy, even if it did not solve all of its causes.

More troublingly, the absence of men also removed the promise of marriage and procreation for immigrant women. While avoiding the problems of urban sexuality, the Labor Museum absented legitimate heterosexual romance from its vision of the multicultural family. The museum's focus on women and their labor prioritized cultural reproduction (textiles, ethnic traditions) over sexual reproduction. Craft labor replaces the "labor" of childbirth as the means to pass on traditions and values. Cultural reproduction becomes a homosocial, multicultural alternative to heterosexual reproduction. I argue that in this respect, the Labor Museum represents a decisive turn away from biological notions of ethnic/racial difference and toward a cultural model, which emphasizes hybridity. Multiculturalism is thus redefined and redirected in Addams's museum, away from the threat of miscegenation and incest (which "taint" or "dilute" the blood) and toward a model of cultural hybridity, whereby citizens weave together multiple strands into a colorful, representative tapestry.

All of this is to say that in the Hull-House Labor Museum, the conjunction of endogamy and exogamy of the racial romance still applies, but in a distinctively nonsexual variant. Instead of addressing, for example, the rise in interracial, interethnic, or interfaith marriages, Addams's museum addresses exogamy solely through the display of multiethnic variety. Real-life examples of turn-of-the-twentieth-century exogamy— such as marriages among coreligionists like Irish and Italian Catholics, or between Jews and Gentiles, whites and Negroes, or white women and Chinese men—were growing more visible, but provoked widespread anxiety.[34] Uncomfortable with actual miscegenation, the Labor Museum's multicultural model of the nation is an intentional family rather than a biological one. In its display of Irish, Italian, and Greek women spinning alongside one another, each using the traditional method of her European motherland, the museum modeled a multicultural nation free of historical inequalities. Endogamy is similarly transformed in the museum, evacuated of sexual tension and taboo. Instead of expressing incestuous desire, endogamy in the museum occurs only as the reaffirmation of intraethnic ties, a celebration of the bonds between mothers and daughters. Instead of emphasizing heterosexual romance as a model for futurity, the museum consistently focused on parents passing down traditions to the next generation. Yet such a focus on the past is anything but atavistic; the museum turned the ethnic past into the basis of an American future.

Throughout the display, women were represented as carriers of culture, with immigrant women transmitting their knowledge to the younger generation. Addams describes the museum as allowing Americanized youth to "find a dramatic representation of the inherited resources of their daily occupation."[35] Addams thus prioritizes Americanized girls' *acquisition* of this legacy from the older generation, over its *transmission* into the next generation (as through marriage or motherhood). T.J. Jackson Lears reads the museum's investment in preindustrial methods as evidence of its fundamental "antimodernism."[36] While a certain amount of nostalgia is present in its celebration of craftwork, the Labor Museum's emphasis on culture over blood should, I argue, be understood as fundamentally forward-thinking. The Labor Museum united the generations through an appreciation of past traditions, but its multiethnic display provided a model for a uniquely American future defined by cultural diversity.

Cultural Miscegenation of Objects

The transformation of miscegenation into multiculturalism occurs through Addams's definition of a "sense of relation" as primarily cultural. Addams understood that people require context and significance in order to feel a strong sense of identity and connection. Culture is powerful, she writes, because it provides "a knowledge of those things which have been long cherished by men, the things which men have loved because thru [sic] generations they have softened and interpreted life, and have endowed it with value and meaning."[37] Addams astutely recognized the role that culture plays between generations, as between immigrants and "native born" citizens. These social relationships, Addams believed, were capable of being reformed and redefined through the instructive and entertainment capacities of the museum, which could provide a three-dimensional model of multiethnic, familial harmony. The Labor Museum reframed ethnic tradition as essential to contemporary American life and labor. Addams romanticizes ethnicity, making it central, not only to family history, but to the nation's history as well. In this way, the museum's display of cultural mixing established the United States as distinct from all other nations.

Indeed, in its display of various ethnic groups, the Labor Museum redefined the boundaries of inclusion and exclusion for the imagined community of the nation. The museum's appeal and novelty lay in the diversity of materials, methods, and people being displayed side by side, each one as fascinating as the next.[38] Like a modern department store, the Labor Museum awed visitors with its profusion.[39] Marion Foster Washburn, a visiting journalist and former president of the Indiana

State Federation of Women's Clubs, noted the Labor Museum's remarkable content and method of display in a 1904 article: "Here is a large wall case containing Navajo and Hindu handlooms: the East and the West cheek by jowl. A stocking loom stands next and bits of rare brocade and embroidery cover all available wall spaces. There are embroideries in gold and silk from Germany of the seventeenth century, beautiful Norwegian embroideries and fringes, Nuremberg and Italian embroideries, all manner of modern weaves, Mexican serapes, Venetian velvets from the fifteenth century, resplendent in gold, red, green, and yellow, upon a cloth-of-gold background, and even a framed fragment of mummy-wrapping."[40] Washburn's rhapsodic catalogue makes clear the appeal of the museum's geographic, temporal, aesthetic, and functional juxtapositions. In the Labor Museum's display, world geography was scrambled; cheap and prosaic were presented alongside rare and costly items; and aesthetic objects were displayed with their means of production. This profusion forces the viewer to imagine new relationships between the objects, finding links between European and North American cultures, the past and the present. This synchronic approach granted various ethnicities equality in the "heterotopic" space of the museum display.[41] Rejecting hierarchical models of racial and ethnic difference, the museum treated various cultures, nations, and technologies as equal. By rejecting rankings and instead celebrating variety and relationships, the Hull-House Labor Museum led the way to new forms of national identification. This newly expansive vision of American culture, however, would not extend to all of the nation's citizens.

Nevertheless, the Labor Museum was a crucial bridge between an older, hierarchical model of racial difference and what, in the latter decades of the twentieth century, came to be called "multiculturalism." In the older model, embodied by world's expositions and natural history museums, every nation was ranked according to its degree of "modernization," "civilization," or "primitivism."[42] In the Labor Museum, by contrast, different technologies and cultures existed simultaneously, both illustrating and undermining the teleological narrative of Spencerian evolution. The Labor Museum effectively transformed the imperialist narrative of the "Family of Man" into a multiethnic and intergenerational American Family of Weaving Women. Through its live demonstrations of spinning and weaving from various geographies and moments of industrial development, the Labor Museum created a synchronic multicultural present. The Labor Museum assimilated its representative ethnic groups into whiteness by representing them as the ancestors of all modern

Americans, and depicting immigrant methods as the foundation of U.S. industrialization.

Washburn's description of textiles from the East and West as lying "cheek by jowl" is a turn of phrase that suggests the "mongrel" character of the museum, and the miscegenated quality of its multiethnic display. Washburn's bestial language reveals the attraction of, as well as discomfort about, the unexpected intimacy between these geographies and temporalities in the museum.[43] Yet Addams has effectively stripped miscegenation of its biological basis in blood, emphasizing instead the *frisson* of cultural diversity.[44] Washburn succumbs to the museum's erotics of cultural miscegenation, swept up in the romance of textile plenitude. The weavings and tapestries substitute for actual mixed-race subjects ("mongrels") to become objects of admiration and fetishization. Yet while the textiles on display represent an incredible variety of world cultures—from North America, Europe, Africa, and Asia—the women who illustrated the manual methods were not nearly so diverse. The Labor Museum's human specimens were overwhelmingly European— from Greece, Italy, Ireland, Russia, and Syria—reflecting the immigrant populations who resided near Hull-House. As a result, the museum's model of multiculturalism was relatively narrow, revealing the limits of kinship. By excluding African Americans, Asian Americans, and other "racial" minority groups, the Labor Museum clarified the boundaries of the national family. It is more than coincidence that those who were absent from the museum had complicated labor and sexual histories in the United States, and whose sexuality had long been policed to prevent and discourage interracial marriage and sex.

The Limits of Inclusion

Despite the Labor Museum's emphasis on affective ties, it is possible to read it as objectifying the women on display. The immigrant women were, after all, presented as representative specimens, alongside textiles and outmoded technologies. Svetlana Alpers describes the "museum effect" as "the tendency to isolate something from its world, to offer it up for attentive looking and thus to transform it into art like our own."[45] While the Labor Museum did isolate its performers from their original context—such as a nineteenth-century village in Sicily—it provided them a new context, that of the multicultural American family. This shifting sense of relationship, which emphasizes likeness, was Addams's central goal. Unlike, for example, a natural history museum, the Labor Museum emphasized the subjectivity, agency, and creativity of its "specimens." As a result, viewers were forced to rethink what it meant to "objectify" in the museum.

Nevertheless, the Labor Museum could be, and frequently was, read in various ways by different audiences. Hilda Satt Polacheck felt kinship with the Irish and Italian women and recognized her connection to their labor methods. But Marion Foster Washburn, the visiting journalist who reveled in the wild profusion of textiles, saw racial differences and hierarchies when she witnessed the live display. Washburn's description of the performers reiterates turn-of-the-twentieth-century racial hierarchies, where physical differences reflect degrees of civilization: "This Italian woman, with big gold ear-rings swinging against her dark and scrawny neck, patiently twirling the hand spindle hanging at her side, and skillfully drawing out the woolen thread with her long fingers, unconsciously carries out the part."[46] Washburn portrays the Italian woman as underfed, her "scrawny" neck indicating the inferior methods of food production in southern Italy (the place of origin for most Italian immigrants to Chicago during this period), just as her dark skin and oversized jewelry represent cultural primitivism. The Italian woman's "patience," too, is less a virtue than proof that she exists out of time; she is, according to Washburn, "unconsciously carrying out the part" of an old-fashioned woman from a preindustrialized nation.

In contrast, Washburn emphasizes the seemingly natural contemporaneity of the Irish worker: "But the sweet-faced Irish woman near her, rocking the treadle of her spinning-wheel, with an invisible foot beneath a decent black skirt, her white Irish hands deftly twisting the thread, is altogether too respectable and modern to look her part."[47] Washburn understands perceived racial differences as temporal and moral: Mrs. Brasnahan's "white Irish hands" are superior to Mrs. Molinari's "dark and scrawny neck," proving that the former is "altogether too respectable and modern" to belong in the Labor Museum, the mere inclusion in which implies a low social position. Significantly, the Irish woman's claim to whiteness is itself historically contingent, for fewer than fifty years earlier, Irishness was synonymous with racial Otherness.[48]

The shifting boundaries of racial categories like whiteness, which first accommodated the Irish before including Italians (as well as Greeks, Poles, and Russians), is evidence of the importance of culture in defining seemingly biological traits. The sociologists Michael Omi and Howard Winant coined the term "racial formation" to describe "the process by which social, economic and political forces determine the content and importance of racial categories, and by which they are in turn shaped by racial meanings."[49] Far from being static, "race" shifts over time, as public attitudes are changed by historical events, political alliances, social protests, and cultural representations. The Labor Museum illustrates these shifting meanings. Despite her insistence on the Italian woman's racial differences from the Irish spinner, Washburn was on the losing side of history when it came to the whiteness of Italians. In the Labor Museum, virtually all European immigrants were recognized as culturally equal to each other, and as essential to modern American industrial labor. Addams's emphasis on the beauty of these European craft traditions, and the skill of their practitioners, made it possible to imagine the United States as a nation of (European) immigrants. This expansion of national identity was solidified in the popular imagination over the next several decades, as immigrants assimilated, had children, and became a significant (and permanent) proportion of the population.

James Clifford's description of museums' role in shaping one's sense of community is apropos: "When a community displays itself through spectacular collections and ceremonies, it constitutes an 'inside' and an 'outside.' The message of identity is directed differently to members and to outsiders—the former invited to share in the symbolic wealth, the latter maintained as onlookers, or partially integrated, whether connoisseurs or tourists."[50] The Labor Museum constituted one of the most ambitious attempts of its era to create an inside that could accommodate many of the nation's newest citizens while remaining legible (and acceptable) to its patrons. Yet the Labor Museum's expansive "inside" required a firm "outside." Accordingly, those minority groups whose history in the United States was more problematic—African Americans, Asian immigrants, Latinos, and Native Americans—were excluded.[51] For one thing, these populations contradicted the museum's narrative of labor, which emphasized "that industry develops similarly and peacefully year by year among the workers of each nation, heedless of differences in language, religion, and political experiences."[52] Addams's vision of harmonious evolution was deeply compromised by the history of slavery, indentured "coolie" labor, U.S. annexation of Mexican territory, and Native American dispossession and extermination.

These four groups' histories in the United States were incompatible with the image of the United States as a welcoming host nation, and, consequently, these minority populations were not transformed from "races" to "ethnicities," from blood-based identities to examples of "cultural" variation. Racial exclusivity was inherent in the Naturalization

Law of 1790, which limited naturalized citizenship to "free white persons," explicitly excluding Africans and Native Americans. The "one-drop" rule for black enslavement followed the same logic, continuing on in Jim Crow policies limiting black political participation.[53] As W.E.B. Du Bois predicted, the color line was the most intractable problem of the twentieth century. Asian immigrants were also the objects of racist legislation designed to manage the nation's political participation. In 1882, the Chinese were targeted for immigration restriction and barred from naturalized citizenship, with similar policies extending to Japanese immigrants and then to all immigrants from Asia.[54] Given these histories, as well as their small populations in the Hull-House neighborhood, it is not surprising that African Americans and Asian immigrants were excluded from the museum's live display.

Native Americans occupied a more ambiguous position, both in the United States generally and in the Hull-House Labor Museum in particular. Historically, Native Americans had been repeatedly moved off of their lands, pushed into reservations, and denied the rights of either independent nations or U.S. citizens. When Indians were officially granted U.S. citizenship in 1924, it was an act of incorporation that foreclosed *tribal* independence.[55] With the failure of exile and extermination strategies, the Progressive Era ushered in a new era in Native American policy. Native Americans became the target of aggressive assimilation campaigns designed to encourage intermarriage with whites, weaken tribal affiliations, and shift landholdings to individual owners. During the same period, the Indian was nostalgically depicted as a model for authentic "American" values being threatened by industrialization. An "Indian Craze" spurred middle-class, white Americans eagerly to collect Native American artifacts and handicrafts for display in the home.[56] The ambivalent status of Native Americans is visible in the Labor Museum, where Native Americans represented the boundary between "inside" and "outside."

Native Americans did not appear as performers in the Hull-House Labor Museum, but Indian craftwork was prominently displayed. Addams explained the absence of Native American women in practical terms: "Where it is impossible to have the actual process ably done the lack is made partly good by series of photographs and models as in the case of the Navajo Indian weavers."[57] Yet the elision of Native American subjectivity and agency has broader cultural implications. It is true that "Indian" was a category that could not easily be filled in the Labor Museum by living Native Americans, who didn't predominate in cities like Chicago. However, in the context of a museum devoted to the cultural incorporation of new Americans, Native Americans were not necessary because they were widely assumed to be heading toward extinction.

The in-between status of Native Americans is illustrated in photographs from the early years of the Hull-House Labor Museum. Most documentation features captions emphasizing the ethnicity of the women who performed in the museum. For example, the *First Report of the Labor Museum* included individual portraits titled "Italian Woman Spinning," "Irish Woman Spinning," "Russian Woman Spinning," and "Syrian Woman Spinning."[58] However, a photograph captioned "Weaving an Indian Blanket" (figure 6) emphasizes a different perspective. Here the textile, not the woman creating it, is the subject of visitor attention; viewers see only the weaver's back, forcing them to focus on the act of creation rather than the ethnicity of the actor.[59] Addams's pedagogical purpose for immigrant children's participation in the museum is evident in figure 6, for the unidentified girl makes a blanket too small to be used for anything but decorative or demonstration purposes. She sits cross-legged on the floor with her back to the viewer, obscuring her features, but her dark braided hair and seated position (so-called "Indian-style") suggest that she stands in for Native American-ness, just as the blanket she weaves is a metonymic object. The faceless city girl in the photograph literally takes the place of the original native-born American.[60]

The museum's emphasis on Native American arts, rather than Native American people, reveals the peculiar role of Indian culture at this time in U.S. history. In her autobiography, Hilda Satt Polacheck recalled being asked by the Labor Museum's docent "whether I would like to learn to weave something that was typically American. Yes, I was ready to learn almost anything. . . . [A]nd very soon I was weaving a small Navaho-style blanket."[61] The act of weaving brought the girl actively into the labor of the museum display, enabling her to participate in making something "typically American." The centrality of bodily comportment to the museum's educational mission is an example of what Shannon Jackson describes as the performative function of Hull-House programming.[62] Here, the process of *making* something "typically American" is an important step toward *becoming* a "typical American." Given Polacheck's identification with Hull-House and with the pluralist America it represented, the purpose of learning to weave an "Indian blanket" was less to appreciate contemporary Native culture than to transform oneself into a proper daughter and a good American. The museum positioned Navajo craft as

FIGURE 6. "Weaving an Indian Blanket." Jane Addams Hull-House Photographic Collection, Photo #JAMC_0000_0177_3019, University of Illinois at Chicago Library, Special Collections.

authentically, "typically American," but did not extend that designation to Native American people themselves. Instead, learning Native American craftwork serves as a model for European immigrant incorporation. Through the strategic co-optation of this one thread of American culture, immigrant children were woven into the fabric of America.

The immigrant child's educational lesson in weaving is a vivid model of the process of assimilation and adoption of U.S. culture. By physically learning a manual method of craft labor, the immigrant child carries on an older generation's traditions, completing the circle of homosocial familiality. By learning to weave an "Indian blanket" rather than, for example, an Irish tapestry or a Greek tablecloth, the immigrant identifies with a particularly North American ethnic tradition, cementing the multiethnic character of the nation going forward. Addams's version of the racial romance transforms identity into a process, moving away from blood and biology, toward blankets and culture. Thus, while ethnics enter into American culture through reference to Native American craftwork, the "Indian" is not represented as a viable modern identity. The Labor Museum was not unique in this assumption. Less than a decade earlier, Frederick Jackson Turner had declared that the American frontier was "closed," implying that Native Americans and their way of life no longer existed, having been supplanted by immigrant homesteaders and industrialization. In the Labor Museum, the Native American is likewise vanished, functioning primarily as a historic symbol of American history and values, rather than as a vibrant living identity.[63] As Philip J. Deloria explains, in U.S. culture, "acting Indian brought dialectical interplay to a standstill. It froze contradictions into equivalence."[64] Weaving an Indian blanket in the museum was a way for recent Americans to take up the contradictory mantle of authenticity and historicity carried by the American Indian. To *be* Native American was to be a relic of a dying race, but to weave an Indian blanket was to participate in authentic modern American culture.[65] In a way, the museum's future-oriented vision, which focused on incorporating millions of immigrants into Americans, made the erasure of Native Americans inevitable.

Clearly, the museum's depiction of Native Americans reveals more about whites' attitudes toward Native Americans than it does about actual Native Americans. By 1900, the Indian served, according to Susan Hegeman, as a "Janus-faced ideological function: as artifacts of the 'vanishing' past of native North America (and a kind of racial childhood of all Americans), they also marked Euro-America's present and future as the agent of Manifest Destiny."[66] In the Labor Museum, Native

Americans quite literally stood in for cultural "childhood" since the role of the Indian was filled by immigrant girls learning the craft ethic and the performativity of labor. Weaving a Native American–style blanket is the immigrant's initiation into American identity through narratives of progress and Manifest Destiny. By "playing Indian," the immigrant becomes ideologically American. Immigrants' own ethnic and historical subject positions are elided: the performance of generic Indian identity temporarily replaces Hilda Satt's Polish and Jewish heritage. In effect, by playing Indian she proves herself capable of shedding her own past and *adopting* American identity. Those who are willing and able to fit the vision of multicultural America will eventually become white citizens; meanwhile, actual Native Americans were once more vanished from American history.

Jane Addams's Hull-House Labor Museum was by far the most politically influential version of the racial romance, as it doubtless gained cultural legitimacy through her reputation as "Saint Jane." Its methods of display and systems of value participated in shifting the discourse of American citizenship and belonging. The Labor Museum celebrated immigrants' labor and cultures, defining European ethnic customs, clothing, and domestic methods as necessary precursors to American progress and ingenuity. Through its narratives of science, methods of display, and emphasis on ethnic aesthetics and women's labor, the Labor Museum established a set of terms for ethnicity that remain central to modern-day multiculturalism. But it did this by effectively taking sexuality out of the equation, and as a consequence, erasing the nation's history of exploitation of, domination over, and violence toward minorities. Instead, Addams offered an aesthetically pleasing version of difference, wrapping ethnic variation in a cloak of nonthreatening, nonsexual, and overwhelmingly "white" domesticity. The Labor Museum provided a template for inclusion and exclusion, extending American culture to millions of "ethnic" immigrants while denying that privilege to "racial" Others. In so doing, she unwittingly strengthened the color line in the United States. Not until the mid-twentieth century would progressive national leaders again work so publicly to redefine those boundaries, and this time explicitly in the language of multiculturalism.

Conclusion

The Romance of Race has illustrated the extent to which miscegenation and incest were dangerous and powerful tropes deployed in literature and popular culture as a means to reimagine racial and ethnic minorities as members of the national family. A remarkable array of U.S.-based women writers redefined African Americans, Asian Americans, Mexican Americans, Native Americans, and European immigrants as brothers and sisters, sons and daughters, fathers and mothers, husbands and wives through the common language of the racial romance. These compelling fictions reached national audiences in magazines, best-selling novels, newspapers, and a museum, nudging public opinion through their emotional stories of romantic unions and familial reunions.

This inclusivity had limits, however. As I discussed in the last chapter, Jane Addams's vision of U.S. multiculturalism made European immigrants central to American history and the nation's future, but did so by reifying the color line. In the Hull-House Labor Museum, a host of ethnic minorities effectively "became white," while other groups whose experiences in the United States troubled Addams's narrative of the peaceful evolution of labor practices—African Americans, Asian Americans, Mexican Americans, and Native Americans—were implicitly deemed Other and inassimilable. It was precisely this distinction between (white) citizens and "foreign" Others that racial romances sought to renegotiate. By utilizing the familiar and irrefutable language of shared blood, women writers challenged the United States' racial regime, demanding their readers expand their notions of both nation and family. And by confronting the dangerous sexualities that link various racial communities in a common lineage, these writers did not simply aestheticize and exoticize racial difference. Rather, they revealed the instability at the heart of the concept of Otherness.

Using the gendered language of family and domesticity, the African American magazine editor and novelist Pauline Hopkins, Asian American Oriental romance writer Onoto Watanna (Winnifred Eaton), Mexican American short story writer María Cristina Mena, Native American novelist Mourning Dove (Christine Quintasket), and Progressive reformer Jane Addams asserted a multicultural message *avant la lettre*. In their works, the United States is always already a mixed-race family, though its citizens too often fail to acknowledge that truth. Their stories are socially provocative and politically radical, demanding a reckoning with the nation's past in order to chart a more inclusive future. Through fictions featuring mixed-race heroes and heroines searching for their place within their families and seeking recognition as citizens, these writers established a script for twentieth-century American literature and culture. The racial romance is thus a crucial, heretofore unrecognized, element of the familiar narrative of the United States as a multicultural nation.

As I've illustrated throughout this book, racial romances expose the nation's anxieties and its countervailing fantasies about racial mixing, and about what we mean by "American" identity. These allegorical stories contextualize and naturalize racially and sexually "queer" or "deviant" families by showing their historical origins; thus, Pauline Hopkins shows incest to be the inevitable result of slavery's systemic denial of white paternity, refuting racist stereotypes of "oversexed" black women. Yet for all their criticisms of historical inequalities, these fictions also speak a common ambition for a more egalitarian social order. Accordingly, Mourning Dove promises equally happy futures for Cogewea, who marries another "half-breed," and her sisters, who marry European immigrants, while Winnifred Eaton's half-caste heroine Hyacinth weds her adopted brother Koma in a ceremony conjoining East and West, masculine and feminine. With their insistence that "they" are the same as "us," that difference is a kind of likeness, and that the Other is contained within the Self, racial romances challenge the binary logic structuring U.S. law and society. In all their variety, racial romances are founded on the axiom that the United States has been, is now, and always will be both multiracial and multicultural.

At the same time, racial romances illustrate for their readers the transnational dimensions of "American" culture. In an age of unprecedented expansion, these fictions highlight the impact of U.S. imperialism—cultural, economic, and military—on its neighbors, trading partners, and conquered subjects. For example, María Cristina Mena shows the effects of Spanish colonialism and contemporary U.S. capitalism on Mexico's younger generation, and Eaton illustrates the familial ties between Japan and the United States as a result of American intervention in the Pacific. In turn, racial romances illustrate how the United States has been dramatically altered by its encounters with minorities at home and around the world: Jane Addams's Labor Museum depicts American culture as a patchwork of immigrant and ethnic labor practices, and Mena's mestizo is a model of multiracial equality and cross-class solidarity for the United States to emulate. Racial romances remind us that if the United States has an exceptional history, it was not written in isolation. The late nineteenth and early twentieth centuries represent a transformative, transitional moment when the United States became a world power. By the late nineteenth century, all U.S. culture was international. As racial romances make clear, these political and economic shifts had immense social consequences.

The affective power of racial romances should not be underestimated. These stories expose the primal longings of minorities to belong in and to the United States, while also revealing secret histories in which "whites" have long desired (and had intimate relations with) those whom they ostracize. These interracial fictions express a desire to be wanted, with fantasies of whites drawn by invisible forces toward their long-lost racialized kin, alongside tales of mixed-race subjects attracted to white brothers, husbands, friends, and lovers: Eaton's white patriarch longs to be reunited with his half-caste daughter, while Hopkins's mulatto hero Reuel Briggs is inextricably drawn toward his "white" twin brother, Aubrey (Aubrey, in turn, seeks to possess their sister Dianthe). In short, turn-of-the-twentieth-century racial romances reveal what Anne Cheng calls "racial melancholia" to be a process that applies to all of the nation's citizens.[1]

As a kind of U.S. folktale, the racial romance provides a window into an emerging national narrative that ran counter to widespread nativism and racism. It is easy to criticize these works (as women's literature has long been criticized) for being conventional and emotionally manipulative. However, just as nineteenth-century sentimental fiction presumed that intense emotional responses—sorrow, anger, horror, joy—could inspire social change, racial romances depend upon their readers' "natural" responses to stories of family formation as a tool to change hearts and minds. Pathos could turn faceless readers into ardent allies and coconspirators. The intense emotional state of melancholia, Jonathan Flatley argues, brought together writer and reader, "facilitat[ing] the feeling that one is part of a collectivity."[2] Similarly, Lauren Berlant has shown how women's literature and popular culture has long functioned to create "intimate publics" that both challenge and reinforce mainstream politics.[3] As works written by and for women, racial romances granted cultural agency and political voice for a population not yet granted the franchise.

In addition, racial romances did important cultural work by asking their overwhelmingly white, middle-class, female readers to understand the pain of racial ostracism and the joy of recognition, to be outraged by injustice and buoyed by interracial (re)unions. Racial romances effectively guided their readers to a new American racial landscape, where equality was desirable and even inevitable. The formulaic quality of racial romances became a useful template for the development of a uniquely American multicultural aesthetics, one applicable to European immigrants, as well as Asian Americans, Mexican Americans, Native Americans, and African Americans. Based in desire at once exotic and familiar, the racial romance expanded the meaning of American identity. The popularity of these fictions in their day and their continuing relevance to contemporary U.S. culture attest to their effectiveness in extending sympathy across the color line. Indeed, turn-of-the-twentieth-century scenes of perversely cozy interracial familiality begat late twentieth-century multiculturalism, with its mix of progressive aesthetics and neoliberal politics.

Elements of the racial romance persist in the late twentieth and early twenty-first centuries, reappearing in texts as varied as literary novels and fast-food advertisements. During the 1990s, the rhetoric of multiculturalism reached its saturation point in the United States, becoming omnipresent in popular culture, and spurring a backlash against all things "politically correct." Since then, multiculturalism has acquired a bad reputation for style over substance and for internal incoherence. Coco Fusco derides the kind of "happy multiculturalism" that celebrates diversity while eliding the very real structural inequalities that marginalize minorities. Focusing on the tension between diversity and common culture, Scott Michaelsen criticizes multiculturalism's origins and basis in anthropology, which paradoxically "seeks to preserve, at one and the same time, 'difference' and 'equality'—the recognition of the right to and value of difference in a larger framework of national, regional, or world justice."[4] Underscoring these critiques is the question of how politics and aesthetics affect each other. So-called "strong multiculturalism" asserts that changing power relationships will have political consequences, and it's easy to envision how policies of redress, reparations, and redistribution could affect the status and representation of minorities in the United States; however, the reverse is not nearly so apparent. That is to say, it is unclear whether multicultural representations actually lead to transformative politics. And yet, much of late twentieth-century multiculturalism was based on that assumption. In the 1990s in particular, multiculturalism relied upon a politics of aesthetics that assumed the transformative power of images. According to this logic, merely seeing an array of nonwhite models or rainbow-hued children on television, in movies, and in print would, by itself, promote a shift toward inclusive political representation.

No company epitomizes the era's disconcerting blend of liberal and conservative politics, radical and regressive aesthetic strategies, more than the United Colors of Benetton. Centering on scenes of interracial and familial sexuality, their provocative print advertisements took the racial romance into the heart of the marketplace. The brand's edgy photographs by Oliviero Toscani featured models of various races in an array of sexualized configurations. Merging pop aesthetics, progressive politics, and global capitalism, the advertising campaign emphasized the taboos of interracial romance and homosexual erotics, while signifying universal human connections through family.

The image that best represents the brand's strategy is a 1990 print advertisement titled "Blanket" or "Wrapped in Blanket" that conjoins the trope of the interracial and incestuous/homosocial family with Jane Addams's visual metaphor of the nation as a multicultural textile.[5] This advertisement speaks the languages of blood and blankets in its tableau of the modern multicultural and queer family. The image features a pale, blond white woman and a dark-skinned black woman whose hands overlap on the torso of an Asian toddler. Though this is ostensibly an advertisement for a clothing company, all three figures are naked, save for a colorful green blanket, edged in purple, which envelops them. The women do not smile, but instead stare straight ahead, challenging viewers to question their right to model family bonds, to speak for the brand, and by extension to represent the contemporary globalized world. Provocatively, though ambivalently, sexual, this image epitomizes and challenges the aesthetic and political strategy of multiculturalism. "Blanket" fully realizes the radical ethics of the racial romance, with its insistence on the interracial origins of the nation and the world.

This advertisement updates the racial romance for the late twentieth century, shifting away from the radical politics that treats incest as inseparable from miscegenation. The Benetton photograph instead defines queerness as same-sex desire, transnational adoption, and interracial family-formation. In so doing, it retreats from the racial romance's message that what appears to be Other is, in fact, deeply familiar and familial; the image instead reifies visible difference as a commodity. In its service to consumerism and to the ethos of brand-loyalty as a marker of political engagement, the advertisement serves as little more than window dressing for transnational capital flows and global inequality.[6] As advertising, Toscani's image demands nothing of viewers except consumption and self-congratulation. Such work tapped into the zeitgeist's fascination with race, becoming one of the most widely recognized and discussed advertising campaigns of the twentieth century. More than two decades later, in the era of the Great Recession, the company returned to Toscani's formula in an effort to regain international attention and market-share. Benetton's 2011 advertising campaign, "unhate," featured digitally altered images of world leaders in homoerotic embraces, such as U.S. President Barack Obama kissing Venezuelan President Hugo Chavez, and Pope Benedict XVI lip-locking Sunni imam Ahmed el Tayyeb. By explicitly mixing contemporary politics and religion with its multicultural aesthetics, the United Colors of Benetton is doubling down on its bet that provocation sells. Yet in the current economic climate, such images seem desperate rather than progressive.

The truth is that these forms of multiculturalism fail when they presume that visibility is the primary indicator, method, and measure of political transformation. Perhaps the problem with turn-of-the-twenty-first-century multiculturalism is not its use of the racial romance, but rather its diversion from the core elements of the original formula. By emphasizing shocking images over intimate affects, by asking viewers to *see difference* rather than *feel likeness*, the United Colors of Benetton's brand of multiculturalism deradicalizes the racial romance. The racial romance may have been conventional in its generic contours, but its emotional demands were dangerous—lest we forget that for most of the twentieth century, miscegenation and incest were illegal in most states.

It is for this reason that, despite the apparent "failure" of multiculturalism, some of the late twentieth and early twenty-first centuries' most progressive and important writers continue to rely on the racial romance to stake their claims.[7] The racial romance remains a vital stock-in-trade for artists interested in exploring the United States' history of inequality and imagining an alternative future. From Toni Morrison to John Sayles, from Ruth Ozeki to Barack Obama, from Cherríe Moraga to Gish Jen, contemporary writers continue to deploy the racial romance as a means to illustrate viscerally the ways that the nation's people are part of a single national family, bound by a shared (if long-denied) past and united in a common future. For example, John Sayles's *Lone Star* (1995) updates the racial romance for the Texas borderlands in the latter half of the twentieth century. High-school sweethearts Sam Deeds and Pilár Cruz, separated for nearly two decades by the community's racism and their parents' disapproval, are reunited only to discover they share the same white father. Sayles's film is an elegiac portrait of the United States as a multiracial, multicultural, and incestuous nation shaped by centuries of contact between Anglos, Mexicans and Mexican Americans, African Americans, and Native Americans. In short, Sayles relies upon the racial romance to explain U.S. history and imagine new identificatory possibilities.

What has become an essential part of the United States' origin story—that we are a nation of immigrants, a mosaic, and a melting pot—should be credited not simply to the Founding Fathers who dreamed of "a more perfect union," but also to multiculturalism's literary mothers: those overlooked late nineteenth- and early twentieth-century writers who offered their readers an alternative family tree. Jane Addams, Mourning Dove, María Cristina Mena, Winnifred Eaton, and Pauline Hopkins all deserve recognition for their contributions to this familiar national narrative.

The role of affect in politics is as relevant today as it was a hundred years ago. As a result of globalization and the attacks of September 11, 2001, the public is again focused on the role of kinship and domesticity in popular nationalism. As Gore Vidal tellingly wrote in 2004, "we have ceased to be a nation under law but [have become] instead a homeland."[8] In this moment of heightened anxiety about the foreign—both immigrants in our midst and terrorists plotting against us from afar—affect has become more important to national identity than ever. The very language of "homeland" conjures up intimacy, allying the nation with the domestic sphere of family. Such language implies a threat from "outside," conjuring anxieties of racial Otherness: Mexicans "illegally" crossing the border, swarthy Islamists plotting "death to America." In this hothouse environment, the racial romance is more dangerous and radical than ever, for it challenges any whitewashed vision of the American family and offers affective alternatives to anxiety, hatred, and fear.

Notes

Introduction

1. Chesnutt, "The Wife of His Youth," 106.

2. Ibid., 108.

3. Mourning Dove, *Cogewea*, 41.

4. Dexter Fisher, in her introduction to the reprint of *Cogewea*, argues that her name was Christal, according to her correspondence, while "Christine" was likely a misprint in the Indian Bureau rolls. However, most critics identify her as Christine, and so I follow that tradition.

5. Werner Sollors, writing on Chesnutt's "The Wife of His Youth," argues that the idealized response features a character claiming a previously disavowed ethnic-racial identity, whereas a naturalistic ending would likely show the character continuing to refuse identification with the denigrated group (Sollors, *Beyond Ethnicity*, 161–62).

6. Ellison, *Invisible Man*; Faulkner, *Absalom, Absalom!*; Herron, *Thereafter Johnnie*; Jen, *The Love Wife*; Moraga, *Loving in the War Years*; *Lone Star*, dir. John Sayles.

7. *Studies in Hysteria* was published in 1895, followed by *The Interpretation of Dreams* (1900) and *Three Essays on Sexuality* (1905). Freud himself visited the United States only once, in 1909, when he lectured at Clark University in Worcester, Massachusetts, on the invitation of G. Stanley Hall. The same year, A. A. Brill began translating Freud's works into English.

8. Roosevelt, "True Americanism," 69.

9. Kallen, "Democracy versus the Melting-Pot," 78.

10. When I use the capitalized term "Progressive," I am indicating those, like Jane Addams or John Dewey, who identified with the Progressive movement in the United States, engaged in political activism to curb the ills wrought by unregulated capitalism, rapid industrialization, and urban poverty. When I use the lowercased term "progressive," I mean liberal policies more generally. I am not, however, invoking the eugenicist programs of "Progressives" in England in the early twentieth century.

11. Bourne, "*Trans-National America*," 105.

12. The *Oxford English Dictionary* marks the first appearance of "multicultural" in 1935 in the *American Journal of Sociology*. By 1941, the understanding of "multicultural" as fundamentally opposed to narrow racial or nationalist models of identity was clearly established; the *OED* credits a *New York Herald Tribune* book review with describing a new book as "A fervent sermon against nationalism, national prejudice and behavior in favor of a 'multicultural' way of life" (*Oxford English Dictionary Online*, 3rd ed. [September 2011], s.v. "multicultural," http://0-www.oed.com .maurice.bgsu.edu/view/Entry/123531).

13. See Brodkin, *How Jews Became White Folks*; Guglielmo, *White on Arrival*; Ignatiev, *How the Irish Became White*; Jacobson, *Whiteness of a Different Color*; Roediger, *Working Toward Whiteness*; and Rogin, *Blackface, White Noise*. The expansion of the category of whiteness was made possible, in part, by the scientific trend away from scientific racism (different races defined by physiognomic differences) and toward anthropology (which focused on "cultures" that, presumably, could be altered). For more on this idea, see Hegeman, *Patterns for America*.

14. This policy remained unchallenged until *Brown v. Board of Education of Topeka* (1954) declared segregation unconstitutional, marking the beginning of the civil rights movement.

15. California enacted the 1913 Alien Land Law to deprive Asian immigrants of the right to own property. The Chinese Exclusion Act was finally repealed in 1943. The Luce-Celler Act of 1946 returned the rights of naturalization and immigration (in very limited numbers) to Filipinos and Indians. The 1917 law would not be repealed until the McCarran-Walter Act of 1952, which returned naturalization rights to Koreans, Japanese, and other Asians, and created a new, comprehensive, and consistent immigration policy.

16. Goldberg, introduction to *Multiculturism: A Critical Reader*, 9.

17. The economic logic of multiculturalism is criticized by Walter Benn Michaels, who dismisses current multiculturalist/antiracist discourse that implies that the real problem with racism is that it "is arbitrary because it interferes with the efficiency of the market" (Michaels, "Plots Against America," 292).

18. Fusco, *English Is Broken Here*.

19. A *New York Times* article from August 14, 1898, highlights the correspondence between domestic labor of the home with domestic concerns of the nation. The columnist Cromwell Childe writes, "Like the traditional 'woman's work,' the labor of the Federal officers at the Barge Office is never done." A few sentences later, Childe continues the metaphor by emphasizing the similarity between women's labor such as sewing with the effort to incorporate immigrants from across the world into a national fabric. Thus, he describes the immigrant-laden steamers arriving in U.S. ports: "Now, all these entities, these shreds and patches from foreign shores, must be handled. . . . It is the part of the officials to examine each thread of this gay-tinted fabric" (Cromwell Childe, "The Arrival of the Immigrant," *New York Times (1857–1922)*, August 14, 1898, http://search.proquest.com/docview/95664019?accountid=26417).

20. *Cherokee Nation v. the State of Georgia* (1831) established the status of Native American tribes as "domestic, dependent" wards rather than independent nations with treaty-making authority.

21. See Murphy, *Hemispheric Imaginings*.

22. With economic and political conditions in the South worsening for poor African Americans, nearly 2 million would journey north between 1910 and 1930 in search of jobs and to escape racial terrorism. One result of the Great Migration was thus a massive demographic redistribution within the nation's borders, which would have a profound effect on the civil rights movement several decades later.

23. In 1898, Dr. Aleš Hrdlička, a preeminent Czech anthropologist who later founded and became the first curator of physical anthropology of the U.S. National Museum (now the Smithsonian Institution National Museum of Natural History), claimed that "the future of the North American Indian would be extinction as a separate race" through marriage with whites ("The Future of the Negro," *New York Times [1857–1922]*, December 28, 1898, http://search.proquest.com/docview/95582693?accountid=26417).

24. This statistic comes from Trachtenberg, *Shades of Hiawatha*, 32. Between 1820 and 1920, the number amounted to more than 35 million immigrants (see also Handlin, *The Uprooted*, 3).

25. Asian immigration spiked due to the gold rush, the building of the transcontinental railroad, and the need for migrant agricultural laborers and service industry workers. Anti-Chinese violence reached its apex in 1885–86, when there was a series of racially motivated acts of violence.

26. The "Gentlemen's Agreement" of 1907 ended Japanese contract labor; the 1917 Immigration and Naturalization Act created the " Asiatic Barred Zone" excluding immigrants from that continent.

27. "Greasers in New-Mexico," *New York Times (1857–1922)*, March 26, 1882, http://search.proquest.com/docview/94089916?accountid=26417.

28. A representative example is the following quotation from the *New York Times*: "Mexico is our sister, older in years though far younger in her present form of successful Government" ("The President of Mexico," *New York Times [1857–1922]*, May 14, 1899, http://search.proquest.com/docview/95687192?accountid=26417).

29. Taft is reported to have warned William McKinley that "Our little brown brothers' would need 'fifty or one hundred years' of close supervision 'to develop anything resembling Anglo-Saxon political principles and skills." Certainly, not everyone embraced the role of Big Brother to the world. Stanley Karnow discusses how U.S. soldiers in the Philippines rejected Taft's familial metaphor. A lyric in one of their marching songs goes: "They say I've got brown brothers here, / But still I draw the line. / He may be a brother of Big Bill Taft, / But he ain't no brother of mine" (Karnow, *In Our Image*, 174).

30. Throughout the nineteenth century, American literature and popular culture depicted the races of the world, and their representatives within the U.S. nation-state, in the language of the biological family. The dominant image was the "the Family of Man" racial classification system, which distinguished the world's races within the hierarchical model of a family tree, with white Anglo-Saxons as the highest, most advanced limbs. Based on Herbert Spencer's "social Darwinism," which applied Charles Darwin's theory of evolution to human societies, the "Family of Man" theory posited the "survival of the fittest" as a law of culture, not simply of genetics. According to this model, northern European (and U.S.) cultures were situated as the pinnacle of human achievement and progress, with less-industrialized cultures at various points "behind" on this spatio-temporal scale. Despite its patina of scientific logic, the

Family of Man theory was based on racial pseudoscience that assumed white, European cultures to be superior to Asian, African, or indigenous American societies.

Robert Rydell discusses how the 1876 Centennial International Exhibition in Philadelphia was organized according to race, with U.S. and northern European countries dominating, while the 1893 World's Columbian Exposition in Chicago shifted away from "race" and toward "culture" as the defining basis of difference. These world exhibitions, like natural history museums of the time, emphasized imperial accumulation and technological innovation as evidence of progress. Accordingly, every nation fit within a hierarchy of "modernization," "civilization," or "primitivism" that benefited Western imperial powers (Rydell, *World of Fairs*). Donna Haraway emphasizes the cult of masculinity, death, and racial difference that Teddy Roosevelt and the American Museum of Natural History represent, with its message of "the racial division of labor, the familial progress from youthful native to adult white man" (Haraway, "Teddy Bear Patriarchy," 24).

31. In the late eighteenth century, Quakers in England created the familial slogan of the Society for Effecting the Abolition of the Slave Trade, "Am I not a man and a brother?," which was followed by its female version, "Am I not a woman and a sister?" Both were popularized on Wedgwood medallions and in illustrations, which circulated in England and the United States. For more on the iconography and language of sisterhood in England and the United States, see Boulukos, *The Grateful Slave*; Egenolf, "Josiah Wedgwood's Goodwill Marketing"; Rappoport, *Giving Women*; and Yellin, *Women and Sisters*.

32. For more on the history of melodrama and race, see Gillman, *Blood Talk*; Lemire, *"Miscegenation"*; and Williams, *Playing the Race Card*. Jean Carol Griffith discusses how Edith Wharton, Willa Cather, and Ellen Glasgow articulate visions of democracy through appeals to the nation as a family or community, appeals that are enforced and challenged by the "local customs" governing the color line (Griffith, *The Color of Democracy*). Trent Watts makes a similar claim, showing how "dominant voices asserted that the South was essentially a well-ordered household whose integrity proceeded from natural, racialized imperatives" (Watts, *One Homogenous People*, xiv).

33. Charles Chesnutt writes that "Slavery was a rich soil for the production of a mixed race, and one need only read the literature and laws of the past two generations to see how steadily, albeit slowly and insidiously, the stream of dark blood has insinuated itself into the veins of the dominant, or, as a Southern critic recently described it in a paragraph that came under my eye, the 'domineering race'" (Chesnutt, "The Future American," 22).

34. Spillers, "Mama's Baby, Papa's Maybe," 74.

35. Davis, "Slavery's Shadow Families," 1.

36. Throughout the nineteenth century, the figure of the "tragic mulatta" was a staple of African American and abolitionist literature, illustrating the particular burdens of mixed-race women, and the political choices accompanying romantic object choice. For examples of the genre, see Lydia Maria Child's *A Romance of the Republic* (1867), Frances E. W. Harper's *Iola Leroy* (1892), and Pauline Hopkins's *Contending Forces* (1900).

37. "Mulatto" was the contemporary term for a person of mixed black and white parentage; "mestizo" refers to someone of Spanish (white) and Indian blood born in

the Americas; "half-caste" refers to a person of white and Asian descent; "half-breed" refers to a person of white and Native American descent; and "half-blood" usually was synonymous with "half-breed," although it could be used for other mixed-race identities.

38. Sommer, *Foundational Fictions*, xi.

39. Hughes, *Treatise on Sociology*, 239–40.

40. Eva Saks argues that both taboos depend upon a fundamental, structural relationship between the bodies in question. Saks argues that "the taboo of too different (amalgamation/miscegenation) is interchangeable with the taboo of too similar (incest), since both crimes rely on a pair of bodies which are mutually constitutive of each other's deviance, a pair of bodies in which each body is the signifier of the deviance of the other." According to Saks, the central issue in Hughes is not one of endogamy and exogamy, but rather the relationship between two bodies a priori deemed socially inappropriate as a couple. In this way, miscegenation and incest work according to the same structural logic, which defines sexual suitability in binary relational terms, as appropriate/inappropriate (Saks, "Representing Miscegenation Law," 11–12). Janice Doane and Devon Hodges describe Hughes's method of "making monsters" by conflating miscegenation and incest as revealing white patriarchy's responsibility for the violent sexual abuse of black women (Doane and Hodges, *Telling Incest*, 35).

41. The term "miscegenation" was coined in late 1863 or early 1864 in a hoax pamphlet entitled *Miscegenation: The Theory of the Blending of the Races, Applied to the American White Man and Negro*. The document was written by David Goodman Croly and George Wakemen, newspaper writers for the *New York World*, who hoped to damage the Republicans in the upcoming presidential election by linking emancipation with interracial sex (Wallenstein, *Tell the Court I Love My Wife*, 51–52). Prior to its coinage, other words for the (undesirable) mixing of the races had been in circulation, including "amalgamation" and "mongrelism." "Miscegenation" stuck, however, perhaps because of its pseudoscientific ring and racial specificity. With its origins in racist fantasy akin to *The Protocols of the Elders of Zion* a few decades later, "miscegenation" remained the collective nightmare of whites throughout the North and South.

42. Hence, the term "mulatto" for the offspring of two races.

43. "The Future of the Negro," *New York Times (1857–1922)*, December 28, 1898, http://search.proquest.com/docview/95582693?accountid=26417.

44. Adams explains: "How the country at large has carried itself in turn towards Indian, African, and Asiatic is matter of history. And yet it is equally matter of history that this carriage, term it what you will,—unchristian, brutal, exterminating,—has been the salvation of the race. It has saved the Anglo-Saxon stock from being a nation of half-breeds!—miscegenates, to coin a word expressive of an idea. The Canadian half-breed, the Mexican, the mulatto, say what men may, are not virile or enduring races; and that the Anglo-Saxon is none of these, and is essentially virile and enduring, is due to the fact that the less developed races perished before him. Nature is undeniably often brutal in its methods" (Adams, "Imperialism," 10–11).

45. Fiedler explains that "the man who screams in panic that some black buck is about to rape his sister is speaking of one who is, indeed, his brother, and whom secretly he loves" (Fiedler, *Love and Death*, 413). John T. Irwin reads Faulkner's recurring theme of incest and miscegenation as evidence that narrative itself is a compulsion to retell stories (Irwin, *Doubling and Incest*, 9). Eric Sundquist makes similar

claims about Faulkner's doubling of incest and miscegenation in *Absalom, Absalom!* (Sundquist, *Faulkner*, 111; see also Sollors, *Neither Black nor White Yet Both*, 334).

46. Michaels focuses on modernist and nativist American literature of the 1920s. His professed aim is to reveal pluralism as nationalism by another name, and thereby to debunk all racial identification as racism (Michaels, *Our America*).

47. Harkins, *Everybody's Family Romance*, 1.

48. Lévi-Strauss, *Elementary Structures of Kinship*, 46.

49. While antimiscegenation laws did not distinguish between white male/black female and black male/white female couples, national anxiety centered far more on the latter, since that particular partnering fed into fears about white male sexual inadequacy. In contrast, scenes of white men with racialized women evoked the misogynistic, patriarchal, phallocentric, and deeply Freudian belief that all women are as unknowable as the "dark continent" of Africa (Freud, "The Question of Lay Analysis," 1926e). White men involved with racialized women reiterated long-standing sexual practices under slavery and imperialism. For this reason, antimiscegenation laws primarily functioned to punish white men with racialized women for the taboo of *marrying* across the divide of race, rather than for the crime of sexual liaison. A white man might understandably desire an exotic woman for sex, but to marry her was to threaten the entire racial hierarchy on which the United States had been built.

50. In 1897, Indiana criminalized incest between parents and children, stepparents and stepchildren, grandparents and grandchildren, uncles and nieces, aunts and nephews (see Barrows, *New Legislation*, 101).

51. Ibid., 13.

52. These antimiscegenation laws affected small minority populations in unexpected ways. As Karen Leonard explains, in the 1910s, Punjabi men "who stayed permanently in California sought to marry local women but were hampered by the state's anti-miscegenation laws which made marriages with women of other 'races' difficult. In the Southern Valley, which lay inland from San Diego along the border with Mexico, however, the Punjabis were able to marry Mexican or Mexican-American women" (Leonard, "Ethnic Celebrations in Rural California," 146).

53. I am thinking of all of those "deviant" matriarchal black families that white male politicians claim threaten the nation, such as Daniel Patrick Moynihan's "pathological" Negro family and Ronald Reagan's "welfare queens."

54. Butler explains that the "postulate of a founding heterosexuality must also be read as part of the operation of power . . . such that we can begin to ask how the invocation of such a foundation works in the building of a certain fantasy of state and nation" (Butler, *Undoing Gender*, 124).

55. My title also, though inadvertently, echoes Gina Marchetti's study of orientalist films of the twentieth century (Marchetti, *Romance and the "Yellow Peril"*).

56. In another variant, Freud also hypothesizes that children fantasize that they might be the product of maternal infidelity.

57. In these "unconscious fantasmatic scenarios . . . a subject substitutes a primordial character from his family history, especially father, mother or grandparent, for a part of his ego or superego. This substitute is then made to live out a more or less important fragment of the subject's existence in his stead" (Mijolla, "Unconscious Identification Fantasies," 399).

58. Sedgwick, *Between Men*, 2.

59. The *Oxford English Dictionary* defines "romance" from the mid-nineteenth century onward as "love, esp. of an idealized or sentimental kind" and "a love affair" (*Oxford English Dictionary Online*, 3rd ed. [September 2011], s.v. "romance," http://0-www.oed.com.maurice.bgsu.edu/view/Entry/167065).

60. Moreover, a scenario is "a schematic plot . . . structured in a predictable, formulaic, hence repeatable fashion." While Taylor distinguishes the (literary) trope from the (theatrical) scenario, the racial romance bridges the divide between the two, being a literary mode put to highly theatrical use (Taylor, *The Archive and the Repertoire*, 13).

61. In Claudia Tate's study of domestic allegories by black women authors at the turn of the twentieth century, she defines "a *female text*" as "one in which the dominant discourse and their interpretations arise from woman-centered values, agency, indeed authority that seek distinctly female principles of narrative pleasure" (Tate, *Domestic Allegories*, 24).

62. This is not to say that male writers did not also employ the discourses of family and domesticity toward political ends. Figures like Charles Chesnutt, George Washington Cable, Luther Standing Bear, and others certainly did. But the majority of mainstream domestic writing in this vein was by women, and those women deserve recognition for their contribution.

63. The 1924 act that granted Native Americans U.S. citizenship was not a reversal of prior anti-Indian sentiment; rather, it was an acknowledgment of the failure of interracial marriage as the nation's unofficial strategy for assimilating Indian tribes. In any event, nearly two-thirds of Native Americans were already citizens prior to the act.

64. For the role of print culture in nationalism, see Anderson, *Imagined Communities*.

1 / Mulattos, Mysticism, and Marriage

1. For more on the "golden age of hysteria" and its most influential figures, see Beizer, *Ventriloquized Bodies*; Gelfand and Kerr, eds., *Freud and the History of Psychoanalysis*.

2. Hysteria was also associated with working-class men and "uncivilized" peoples. For the relationship between the discourses of femininity, class, and colonialism, see Beizer, *Ventriloquized Bodies*; and McClintock, *Imperial Leather*.

3. See Hanna Wallinger's biography of Hopkins, *Pauline E. Hopkins*, for more on the history and mission of the magazine.

4. The magazine continued to publish until 1909, but Hopkins left in 1904. By most accounts, Hopkins was pushed out due to political differences with Booker T. Washington, who had recently become the magazine's financial backer. For more on the political disagreement with Booker T. Washington that ended Hopkins's tenure at the magazine, see Bergman, "Everything We Hoped She'd Be," 181–99.

5. Hopkins's output was so great during this time that she resorted to the use of pen names to obscure the extent of her influence within the magazine. For more on her use of pen names, see Bergman, "Everything We Hoped She'd Be"; and Cordell, "'The Case Was Very Black Against' Her."

6. This venture folded after only two issues.

7. *Contending Forces* was first reprinted in 1978 by Southern Illinois University Press. In 1988, Oxford University Press published *Contending Forces* and *The Magazine Novels of Pauline Hopkins* in its Schomburg Library of Nineteenth-Century Black Women Writers, edited by Henry Louis Gates, Jr.

8. Tate, *Domestic Allegories*, 19.

9. Ibid., 198.

10. Unless otherwise noted, all citations of *Of One Blood* refer to the McDowell-edited reprint, and page numbers will appear parenthetically in the text.

11. In Faulkner's *Absalom, Absalom!*, incest and miscegenation are identical acts; in *The Sound and the Fury*, the drive to avoid miscegenation leads to incest. The Trueblood section of Ellison's *Invisible Man* illustrates whites' fascination/obsession with incest in the black family. Morrison's *The Bluest Eye* deals with incest that "derives from [the father's] own disempowerment through historical and material contravention"; for more on this variation, see Gwin, "'Hereisthehouse,'" 317. See also Walker, *The Color Purple*.

Hortense Spillers writes about incest and fatherhood (see the following chapter for more on her argument). Karen Sanchez-Eppler focuses on the hint of incest in (white) temperance fiction as redemptive domesticity (Sanchez-Eppler, "Temperance in the Bed of a Child," 33).

12. Randle, "Mates, Marriage, and Motherhood"; Berg, "Reconstructing Motherhood."

13. Sundquist, *To Wake the Nations*, 569.

14. Tate, "Pauline Hopkins," 62. She later revises this estimation in Tate, *Domestic Allegories*; and Tate, *Psychoanalysis and Black Novels*.

15. Luciano, "Passing Shadows," 149.

16. Gillman, *Blood Talk*, 24.

17. See Tate, *Domestic Allegories*; and Carby, *Reconstructing Womanhood*.

18. Cynthia D. Schrager argues that Reuel should be understood as a neurasthenic, the ultimate modern subject. Neurasthenia, in this view, is "both the sign of his professional status, however marginal, and the price of the sacrifice of his black identity that even such a tentative status exacts" (Schrager, "Pauline Hopkins and William James," 312).

19. Mary Ann Doane notes that "the theme of passing is not equivalent to the convention of the tragic mulatta (the mulatta may or may not choose to pass), [but] the two are intimately connected since passing always suggests the historical dimension of miscegenation" (Doane, *Femmes Fatales*, 233).

20. Otten, "Pauline Hopkins and the Hidden Self of Race," 228.

21. Eric Lott describes the Fisk Jubilee Singers' inclusion of "Jubilee" in their name as an effort to differentiate themselves from racist minstrel performances (Lott, *Love and Theft*, 236).

22. Hopkins herself performed as a soloist with the Hopkins Family Singers (see Wallinger, *Pauline E. Hopkins*, fn. 1).

23. For more on the particular formations of Hopkins's Egyptology, Pan-Africanism, and nationalism, see Gillman, *Blood Talk*, 48–50.

24. Hopkins's substitution of Candace for Dianthe, the replacement of American sibling for African look-alike, resonates with ancient Egyptian sibling marriages. According to Walter Scheidel, marriages between full siblings were extremely common in Roman-ruled Egypt. Whether or not Hopkins knew this fact is an open question. However, it does point to Hopkins's use of displacement in her novel. If Dianthe is an inappropriate partner for Reuel because she is his full sibling, her look-alike, Candace, can take her place as an African "sister." Dianthe is replaced by Candace, not

unlike the American Reuel being remade as the African king Ergamenes (Scheidel, "Ancient Egyptian Sibling Marriage").

25. Ammons, *Conflicting Stories*, 83.

26. In using the term "trauma," I refer to the work of critics such as Cathy Caruth, Shoshana Felman, Dori Laub, Judith Herman, Dominick LaCapra, and Ruth Leys, who join clinical studies of trauma with the study of its literatures, particularly with regard to traumatic events such as the Holocaust, sexual abuse, and slavery (Caruth, *Unclaimed Experience*; Felman, "Education and Crisis"; Herman, *Trauma and Recovery*; LaCapra, *Writing History, Writing Trauma*; Leys, *Trauma: A Genealogy*).

27. Brogan, *Cultural Haunting*, 29.

28. Luciano, "Passing Shadows," 149.

29. Flatley, "Reading into Henry James," 109.

30. Zamora, "Magical Romance/Magical Realism," 501.

31. Freud, "Uncanny," 241.

32. Valerie Rohy argues that such "gothic tropes are reminders of slavery's traumatic history. In the American literary tradition, the gothic is the language of slavery, inextricably linked to captivity and suffering, doomed perpetually to retell such brutal tales as the Cassy and Simon Legree story from *Uncle Tom's Cabin*" (Rohy, "Time Lines," 218–19). For more on the connection between sentimentalism and slavery, see also Stern, *The Plight of Feeling*. Charles Chesnutt masterfully evokes the Gothicism of slavery in *The Conjure Woman*, a tradition that Toni Morrison continues in *Beloved*.

33. In a different register, the manipulative puppet master also echoes the anti-Semitic caricature of Svengali in George Du Maurier's *Trilby* (1894).

34. Schrager, "Pauline Hopkins and William James," 317.

35. Freud and Breuer, *Studies in Hysteria*, 2.

36. Horvitz, "Hysteria and Trauma," 245.

37. For more on Hopkins's deployment of Jamesian psychology, see Schrager, "Pauline Hopkins and William James"; Otten, "Pauline Hopkins and the Hidden Self of Race"; and Horvitz, "Hysteria and Trauma."

38. W. James, "The Hidden Self," 364.

39. The trope of the double is exceedingly common, both in tragic-mulatto literature (as in *Iola Leroy*'s two couples) and in contemporary treatments of racial identity (Spike Lee's *School Daze*, set on a historically black college campus).

40. Late in the novel, as Aubrey witnesses Dianthe on her deathbed, the syntax and punctuation slip, and it seems as though Hopkins articulates Aubrey's desire for his friend: "There lay the peaceful form—spread with a drapery of soft, white gauze around her, and only the sad and livid, poisoned face was visible above it; and kneeling by the side of her, his first love and his last—was Reuel Briggs" (190). Whose "first love and his last" is being referred to? We might understand "her" to mean Dianthe, who is Aubrey's "first love and his last." But the sentence also suggests, due to the confusing combination of dashes and commas, that Reuel is Aubrey's "first love and his last." Considering Sedgwick's formulation in *Between Men*, this does not seem implausible.

41. Rohrbach, "To Be Continued," 493.

42. For more on Egypt's place in the American literary imagination, see Trafton, *Egypt Land*.

43. Reuel Briggs is the speaker of this passage, and his interlocutors are Professor Stone, the leader of the expedition, and Charlie Vance. Reuel is ironizing white dismay

at African civilization; this moment is one of the first in which Reuel separates himself from the privilege and bigotry of whites.

44. Otten, "Pauline Hopkins and the Hidden Self of Race," 229.

45. Schrager, "Pauline Hopkins and William James," 315.

46. Sundquist argues that Hopkins and Du Bois shared an interest in the philosophy of William James due to his theory of Ethiopianism: "James provided the key to a theory of diasporic consciousness that was capable of yoking together the conception of a split-off, perhaps hidden but in any case culturally oppositional 'personality' and the conceptions of race nationalism comprised by the ideological watchword 'African Personality'" (Sundquist, *To Wake the Nations,* 571).

47. Rohy, "Time Lines," 225. Martin Japtok argues that the novel falls into the "'Darwinist trap'" since "making the 'worth' of a people dependent on technological and cultural accomplishments means following the same quasi-Darwinian logic that served nineteenth- and twentieth-century imperialists to 'justify' their ventures." The novel does rely on Darwinian associations of Africa with origins, but it does so in service of a positive model of African progress (Japtok, "Pauline Hopkins," 403).

48. McDowell, introduction to *Of One Blood* (2004), xviii.

49. Schrager, "Pauline Hopkins and William James," 321.

50. Freud, "Question," 212.

51. Doane, *Femmes Fatales,* 212.

52. Hopkins's allegory of a national or international psyche is further emphasized in the use of names. Reuel was Moses's father-in-law in the Bible, who later appears as Jethro. Both Reuels undergo name changes, and both figure in the unification of two distinct cultures and communities: Euro-American and African national identities in *Of One Blood,* and the Tribes of Israel with the Canaanites in the Old Testament. Reuel's name is a homonym for his true "royal" nature (Luciano, "Passing Shadows," 159).

Furthermore, the prime minister's name, Ai, is a homonym for "I," equivalent to the ego that Reuel will be charged with managing on a world-psychic scale. Rohrbach argues that Ai/I "is also reminiscent of the Hebrew rendering of Yahweh, translated into the self-reflexive phrase: I am what I am" (Rohrbach, "To Be Continued," 494).

53. Some critics have argued that Reuel's conversion of the Telassarans to Christianity marks a capitulation to imperial discourses. Certainly to today's readers this conversion seems problematic, but to Hopkins's readers it no doubt represented a positive admission of Christian morality.

54. The slave's name is overdetermined by ironic literary allusions: to Huck's companion Jim, to the historical Roman emperor Titus, and/or Shakespeare's Titus Andronicus. This Jim's loyalty lies only with the villain Aubrey, and he is anything but royal. Indeed, he is like a minstrel slave, believing in the superiority of whites (501).

55. Gillman, "Pauline Hopkins and the Occult," 60.

56. Luciano, "Passing Shadows," 153.

57. This notion of a "black half" of the American literary imagination fits with what Toni Morrison describes as "playing in the dark" (Morrison, *Playing in the Dark).*

58. McDowell, introduction to *Of One Blood,* xx.

59. Condensation appears most vividly in relationship to gender: women like Dianthe are more passive, more thoroughly victimized, more damaged in the novel than in ordinary life.

60. In a work that otherwise dismisses Hopkins's African setting as escapist, Sundquist rightly credits Hopkins with deploying the African setting as a means to speak to contemporary American concerns: "What her protagonist, Reuel Briggs, finds in his journey back to Africa is not so much a geographic locale and a material history as a spiritual dimension of contemporary life. . . . Such a 'country' is both a figurative region—an unconscious reservoir of ideas, as the novel elaborates it—and the actual territory of Africa" (Sundquist, *To Wake the Nations*, 570).

61. Caruth, *Unclaimed Experience*, 4.

62. Tate, *Psychoanalysis and Black Novels*, 10.

63. Felman, "Education and Crisis," 53.

64. Like the ghost story about a tragic love affair that Molly Vance tells on Halloween, there can be no release from the past until guilt is confessed and heard by others (38).

65. For more on realist fiction and its creation of a world, see Kaplan, *The Social Construction of American Realism*.

66. The last paragraph of the novel argues that only God can solve these problems, and no one can understand His will. Hopkins ends with a promise/threat: "Caste prejudice, race pride, boundless wealth, scintillating intellects refined by all the arts of the intellectual world, are but puppets in His hand for His promises stand, and He will prove His words, 'Of one blood have I made all races of men'" (193).

67. The use of religious rhetoric recalls the Christian moralizing of antislavery novels like Harriet Beecher Stowe's *Uncle Tom's Cabin* (1852) but seems out of sync with the rest of the novel.

68. The political import of Hopkins's text is much more apparent in the context of the magazine, which surrounded the novel with nonfiction articles on "Ethiopians of the Twentieth Century" (6, no. 7, July 1903) and profiles of African Americans of influence in business, science, and the arts.

69. Gillman, "Pauline Hopkins and the Occult," 58.

2 / Half-Caste Family Romances

1. Unless otherwise noted, all citations to "A Half Caste" and to Eaton's other short fiction refer to the Rooney and Moser–edited reprint, and page numbers will appear parenthetically in the text. "A Contract" was originally published in *Frank Leslie's Popular Monthly* in 1902. Watanna, *"A Half Caste" and Other Writings*, 55.

2. Lowe, *Immigrant Acts*, 4.

3. According to the *Oxford English Dictionary*, a "half caste" is "one of a mixed race, a half-breed; *esp.*, in India, one born or descended from a European father and native mother." As I show throughout this essay, Eaton relied on popular attitudes toward the "exotic" East, even as she complicated assumptions about Asian American subjectivity (*Oxford English Dictionary Online*, 3rd ed. [September 2011], s.v. "half-caste," http://o-www.oed.com.maurice.bgsu.edu/view/Entry/83425).

4. Through her focus on the differences between narratives in written history (the archive) and as performed (the repertoire), Taylor highlights the primal plots of discovery and conquest that continue to shape history in and of the Americas (Taylor, *The Archive and the Repertoire*, 13).

5. Audiences in England and America had first loved Gilbert and Sullivan's *The Mikado* (1885), which used the exotic setting of Japan to satirize English class politics.

Pierre Loti's *Madame Chrysanthème* (first published in French in 1887) was a major influence on John Luther Long's stage play of *Madame Butterfly*. For more on the American mania for all things Japanese, see Meech and Weisberg, eds., *Japonisme Comes to America*. For a more recent treatment of the cultural work of *Japonisme*, see Halverson, "Typical Tokio Smile."

6. Some stories and novels feature British men. The bulk of Eaton's works, however, feature American men, and her stories, when not set in Japan, were predominantly set in cities in the United States.

7. Yuko Matsukawa suggestively argues that while "Onoto Watanna" is not a real Japanese name, the pen name "foreshadows Winnifred Eaton's career as a trickster-like figure who assumes multiple identities": "Watanna" consists of the two "Chinese ideograms (Japanese pronunciation) for 'to cross': *wata[ru]*, and 'name': *na*" (Matsukawa, "Cross-Dressing and Cross-Naming," 107). For the complete Eaton/Watanna biography, see Birchall, *Onoto Watanna*. Watanna's peripatetic existence makes her easily both the first Asian Canadian and the first Asian American novelist.

8. Jean Lee Cole describes such publicity photos as contributing to the commodification of Watanna herself (Cole, *The Literary Voices of Winnifred Eaton*).

9. The 1882 Chinese Exclusion Act ended contract labor and made Chinese immigrants ineligible for naturalized citizenship.

10. The ethnic comparison between Chinese and Japanese immigrants is well illustrated in a *New York Times* article from 1900, which declares: "Unlike the Chinese, the Japanese who come to this country come with the idea that there is something to learn here. They do not desire to keep by themselves, but mingle as much as possible with Americans, and eagerly adopt American dress and manners." Less than a decade later, the same criticisms would be leveled against Japanese immigrants, and eventually all Asian immigrants. Indeed, the anti-Japanese turn would return in 1942, resulting in Japanese internment camps ("The Japanese Immigration Bogey," *New York Times [1857–1922]*, July 24, 1900, http://search.proquest.com/docview/95993797?accountid=26417).

11. Watanna, *The Wooing of Wystaria* (1902); Watanna, *The Heart of Hyacinth* (1903); Watanna, *The Love of Azalea* (1904); Watanna, *A Japanese Blossom* (1906).

12. Ferens, *Edith and Winnifred Eaton*, 155.

13. Cole, *Literary Voices of Winnifred Eaton*, 33. Sharing this critical viewpoint, Annette White-Parks contrasts Eaton's use of a Japanese persona to her sister Edith Maude Eaton's (pen name Sui Sin Far) "loyalty to her Chinese descent" (White-Parks, *Sui Sin Far/Edith Maude Eaton*, 33).

14. Koshy, *Sexual Naturalization*, 13.

15. Okihiro, "When and Where I Enter"; Said, *Orientalism*; Eng, *Racial Castration*. Frank Chin's concern with Asian masculinity is well discussed in Li, *Imagining the Nation*, 21–62; and Cheung, "The Woman Warrior versus the Chinaman Pacific," 234–54.

16. Bow, *Betrayal and Other Acts of Subversion*, 3. Bow usefully illustrates the ways that Asian and Asian American women's sexual and romantic attachments signal their ethnic and/or national allegiance(s), revealing the male homosociality assumed for citizenship and community.

17. Watanna's first novel, *Miss Numè of Japan* (1898), ends with the white woman Cleo marrying her cousin Tom (who is more like a brother), after her Japanese lover

has committed suicide and her American fiancé has left her for a Japanese woman. Noreen Groover Lape argues that Cleo and Tom's marriage, "given their relationship throughout the novel, borders on incest." Lape reads this union "as an alternative to miscegenation" (Lape, *West of the Border*, 131–32). However, given the rest of Eaton's oeuvre, Lape's analysis is inadequate. *Miss Numè* prominently features another interracial couple, a white man and a Japanese woman; this relationship survives, beginning a pattern of white masculinity and Asian femininity that Eaton repeated throughout her career.

18. In *Miss Numè of Japan*, interracial romance and cousin-marriage are opposing romantic options, echoing Walter Benn Michaels's claim that literary marriages are a choice between endogamy and exogamy (Michaels, *Our America*). In *A Japanese Blossom* (1906), Eaton attempted a romance between a Japanese man and his white wife. The novel was a flop, revealing popular discomfort or disinterest in romances between Japanese men and white women.

19. In *The Heart of Hyacinth*, Eaton mocks the artificiality of Japanese makeup (Watanna, *Heart of Hyacinth*, 95–96).

20. Brooks, *The Melodramatic Imagination*, 26.

21. Sollors is referring to Charles Chesnutt's story "The Wife of His Youth," which similarly turns on bodily inscriptions of race and the revelation of affiliation (Sollors, *Beyond Ethnicity*, 161–62).

22. Ch'ien, *Weird English*, 5, 25.

23. In contrast to Ch'ien's celebration of nonstandard English, Cole describes dialect fiction as an attempt to control representations of the Other, even as it opened up space for contradictory meanings. For more on dialect, see Jones, *Strange Talk*; and Favor, *Authentic Blackness*.

24. Fuss, *Identification Papers*, 116.

25. In "A Father," a cherished photograph of the long-absent father precipitates the daughter's recognition of her American father. In that story, the daughter reads her father's body for signs of likeness (Watanna, "A Father").

26. Robyn Wiegman usefully warns that the perceptions (and perceptibility) of race are inextricable from historically situated power relations (Wiegman, *American Anatomies*, 4).

27. For more on the interdeterminations of race, class, and gender, see McClintock, *Imperial Leather*.

28. Even the color of his gray eyes indicates his hazy morality and emphasizes the theme of racial ambiguity.

29. Klein, "A Contribution to the Psychogenesis of Manic-Depressive States," 1:264.

30. For more on African American fictions of race and family as they relate to slavery, see chapter 1. Carby, *Reconstructing Womanhood*; Hartman, *Scenes of Subjection*; Smith, *Where I'm Bound*; Spillers, "Mama's Baby, Papa's Maybe," 203–29.

31. Spillers, "The Permanent Obliquity,"128.

32. Seduction is also present in African American slavery narratives, as in Harriet Jacobs's *Incidents in the Life of a Slave Girl* (1861; repr., Cambridge: Harvard University Press, 1987), when "Dr. Flint" seeks "Linda Brent's" sexual consent. Thanks to Susan Fraiman for calling my attention to this important moment. The connection between incest, miscegenation, and coercion is far more common in tragic-mulatta narratives, in which the light-skinned heroine's relative class privilege, yet tenuous

position within racial taxonomies, exerts more powerful pressure than brute force; the half-caste romance shares this convention.

33. Cheng, *The Melancholy of Race*, 10.

34. Shimikawa, *National Abjection*, 3.

35. Michael Omi and Howard Winant coined the term "racial formation" to highlight how ideas about race change through history and in relation to contemporary political and social developments (Omi and Winant, *Racial Formation*).

36. See, for example, Pauline Hopkins, *Of One Blood* (1902–3), which highlights physical markers and psychological illness (melancholia, madness, hysteria) in mixed-race characters.

37. "The Half Caste" was published in *Conkey's Home Journal* in November 1898.

38. This is a version of what Eric Lott refers to as the twin practices of "love and theft" upon which racial mimicry (such as in the minstrel show) is based (Lott, *Love and Theft*).

39. Rody, *The Daughter's Return*, 3.

40. Blount further tells Koma: "You have been brought up to speak the [English] language. It is intelligible, but *queer—wrong*, somehow. You speak your father's language like a foreigner" (59, emphasis mine). Such racist logic demands the half-caste disavow his/her relationship to mother/land to avoid being "queer" or "wrong."

41. Berlant, *The Queen of America*, 3.

3 / The Mexican Mestizo/a in the Mexican American Imaginary

1. "The President of Mexico," *New York Times (1857–1922)*, May 14, 1899, http://search.proquest.com/docview/95687192?accountid=26417.

2. Fascinatingly, and weirdly, Mena published an essay in March 1915 in *Century* magazine describing the Mexican composer Julián Carrillo as "the herald of a musical Monroe Doctrine." The essay depicts Carrillo as the idealized future of Mexican music, shaped by European classical tradition, U.S. innovation, and Mexican experience. Mena thus reads the Monroe Doctrine as the template for Pan-American identity, distinct from European influence; this may reflect her years in the United States, since Latin Americans typically took a dimmer view of the Doctrine.

3. The Gadsden Purchase (1853) added another parcel of territory, completing the United States' acquisitions in the Southwest.

4. According to Ricardo Salvatore, from 1890 to 1930, "Pan-Americanism" replaced the Monroe Doctrine, emphasizing "an ideology of mutual cooperation among American states"; Pan-Americanism "activated a new imagined scenario where the possibility of cultural assimilation of South Americans depended upon the diffusion of U.S. products . . . and where better relations between North and South depended on expanded knowledge, the concern of both science and business" (Salvatore, "The Enterprise of Knowledge," 80, 93–94).

5. Murphy, *Hemispheric Imaginings*, 30.

6. Villa had led a raid on Columbus, New Mexico, that killed sixteen U.S. citizens. Moreover, his guerilla attacks across the Mexican countryside undermined the Carranza government.

7. Mena is given this epithet in a blurb introducing a story published in *Household Magazine* in January 1931 (reprinted in Mena, *The Collected Stories of María Cristina Mena*, 137).

8. Edward Said describes orientalism as "a Western style for dominating, restructuring, and having authority over the Orient"; orientalism does not reflect the reality of the East (or Middle East), but rather the West's *idea* of the East and its subordination to the West (Said, *Orientalism,* 3). Jesse Alemán describes Mexico as the United States' gothic double in nineteenth-century U.S. literature: "The US and Mexico share the same revolutionary spirit and hemispheric, republican ideals. Yet, the *translatio studii* assimilates Mexico's past and rearticulates it as Anglo-America's hemispheric story in a literary act that sets the stage for the US's continental colonization of the Americas." In contrast to the U.S. literature on which Alemán focuses, Mena's fiction posits Mexico as the origination of the hemisphere's revolutionary future (Alemán, "The Other Country," 408).

9. *Oxford English Dictionary Online,* 3rd ed. (September 2011), s.v. "mestizo," http://o–www.oed.com.maurice.bgsu.edu/view/Entry/117138.

10. For more on casta paintings, see Ilona Katzew, *Casta Painting: Images of Race in Eighteenth-Century Mexico* (New Haven: Yale University Press, 2004).

11. Other terms included: *Castizo,* offspring of a Mestizo/a and a Spaniard; *Cholo* or *Coyote,* offspring of an Indian and a Mestizo/a; *Mulatto* or *Pardo,* offspring of a Spaniard and a Negro/a (black); *Zambo,* person of mixed Indian and black ancestry; *Morisco/a,* offspring of a Mulato and a Spaniard; *Chino/a* or *Albino/a,* offspring of a Morisco and a Spaniard, etc.

12. These categories, and their effect on social identity, varied greatly depending on geography. In urban areas, Spanish hierarchies predominated, while in rural locales, older ethnic ties continued to be an important influence on identity. For more on rural/urban differences, see Cope, *Limits of Racial Domination,* 6.

In addition, the relationship between *indigenismo* and *mestizaje* was variable across Latin America. In some times and places, the two terms were mutually exclusive, while in others they were aligned (see Earle, *Return of the Native*).

13. To further confuse the meaning of the term, since the 1847 Caste War of Yucatán, "mestizo" also has been applied to indigenous Yucatecans.

14. Stavans, "The United States of Mestizo," 28–32.

15. *Historia de la revolución,* 2:301, cited in Brading, *The Origins of Mexican Nationalism,* 54 n. 113.

16. Brading argues that Mier et al. typically articulated the cause of Mexican nationalism in "an idiosyncratic blend of Marian devotion, anti-españolismo, and neo-Aztecism" embodied by the Virgin of Guadalupe (see Brading, *The Origins of Mexican Nationalism,* 55).

17. A *New York Times* article from 1899 notes: "Like many of the truest sons of Mexico, Diaz is an Indian, of Oaxaca. That he loves his birthplace is known to all who know him well" ("The President of Mexico," *New York Times [1857–1922],* May 14, 1899, http://search.proquest.com/docview/95687192?accountid=26417).

18. As the historian Enrique Krauze explains, "Porfirio Díaz saw himself as an immense father figure, the father of a flock of ambitious, dependant, and irresponsible children" (*Porfirio Díaz: Místico de la autoridad* [México: Fondo de Cultura Económica, 1987], 80, translated and cited in Guerrero, *Confronting History* 155 n. 10).

Accordingly, in a 1908 interview with American journalist James Creelman in *Pearson's Magazine,* Díaz described Mexico's indigenous population as "unprepared for the exercise" of democracy, resulting in his very undemocratic three-decades-long rule (230). In this fawning interview, Díaz describes his administration as having "adopted a patriarchal policy in the actual administration of the nation's affairs, guiding and restraining popular tendencies, with full faith that an enforced peace would allow education, industry and commerce to develop elements of stability and unity in a naturally intelligent, gentle and affectionate people" (Creelman, "President Diaz: Hero of the Americas," 237).

19. Fallaw, "Bartolomé García Correa," 556.

20. Further complicating things, Zapata (the Indian-identified revolutionary) is credited as the champion of revolutionary ideals, while Villa's (the mestizo) aims and tactics are far more troubling.

21. Anne McClintock warns of the dangers of the term "postcolonial" as it situates history in relationship to European conquest: "In other words, the world's multitudinous cultures are marked, not positively by what distinguishes them but by a subordinate, retrospective relation to linear, European time" (McClintock, *Imperial Leather*, 11). I would argue that a term like "mestizo" acknowledges the history of colonization without overwriting Latin America's prior racial history.

22. In stories such as "The Gold Vanity Set," Mena depicts Indians sympathetically, yet paternalistically, as emotional, superstitious, and childish. As a Mexican planter explains to an American tourist: "The ways of the Indito are past conjecture, except that he is always governed by emotion.... With their passion, their melancholy, their music and their superstition they have passed without transition from the feudalism of the Aztecs into the world of today, which ignores them" (10). Mena is careful to suggest middle-class Mexicans' corroboration of U.S. citizens' assumptions, noting that during this speech the planter "was nervous, sensitively anxious about the impressions of his guest from the North"; nevertheless, she does not offer much of a challenge to the image of Indians as backward.

23. Chance, "On the Mexican Mestizo," 165.

24. For more on Molina Enriquez's book *Los grandes problemas nacionales* (1909; 1978), see de la Peña, "A New Mexican Nationalism?"

25. Alonso credits Gamio's *Forjando patria* (1916) with articulating this view (Alonso, "Conforming Disconformity," 121).

26. Vasconcelos, *La raza cósmica*, 82–83.

27. Mexico's university system adopted the Vasconcelos-inspired slogan, "My spirit will speak through my race."

28. De la Peña discusses how these writers spoke of *mestizaje* primarily in cultural terms, while largely excluding actual indigenous peoples. He explains: "The failure of this strategy [Gamio's policy of *indigenismo*] was to a large extent caused by the government's gradual abdication of the revolutionary ideals of social justice and democracy. But ... it was also a consequence of the vision of Mexican citizenship as a function of cultural homogeneity, which ignored the demands of Indian peoples for cultural and political recognition, thus thwarting their participation in the public sphere. In practice, the ideal of *mestizaje* functioned as a mechanism of exclusion" (de la Peña, "A New Mexican Nationalism," 281).

29. Anzaldúa, *Borderlands/La Frontera*, 79.

30. Mena here follows the U.S. perspective on which nation is older, emphasizing the date of independence rather than of colonization. No doubt Mexicans

would reverse the "birth order" of the two nations. Unless otherwise noted, all citations to Mena's short fiction refer to the reprint edited by Amy Doherty, and page numbers will appear parenthetically in the text. Mena, *The Collected Stories,* 56.

31. "The Emotions of Maria Concepción" presents the same generation conflict in the relationship between Maria and her *papa,* who expects his daughter to relinquish her own future in order to be "the companion and consolation of my remaining years on earth." In response, she has fits of hysteria that render her incapacitated. Needless to say, this is not a healthy or viable future (Mena, *The Collected Stories,* 31).

32. Sommer, *Foundational Fictions,* 14.

33. Sommer writes that "these novels were part of a general bourgeois project to hegemonize a culture in formation. It would ideally be a cozy, almost airless culture that bridged public and private spheres in a way that made a place for everyone, as long as everyone knew his or her place" (ibid., 29).

34. Mena's irony is further evident in Popo's name, which (in addition to Prospero) is suggestive of Popocatépetl, an active volcano outside of Mexico City that, with an adjacent dormant volcano named Iztaccíhuatl (Sleeping Woman), figures in a Náhuatl version of *Romeo and Juliet.* Popo, like his namesake volcano, is dormant.

35. Another allusion to Shakespeare occurs in Mena's names for the Cherry family: her father is Montague Cherry, an ironic reference to the star-crossed lovers of *Romeo and Juliet,* with Alicia in the male role. I wish to thank Amy Robinson at Bowling Green State University for her insightful suggestions regarding the significance of the *Tempest* in Latin American literature.

36. Taylor, *The Archive and the Repertoire,* 58.

37. In 1971, the Cuban revolutionary poet and philosopher Roberto Fernández Retamar drew upon turn-of-the-twentieth-century Cuban revolutionary José Martí's celebration of the mestizo culture of the Americas in his work *Caliban.* Retamar's essay depicts Latin America as the West's Caliban, a figure of both marginality and political potential.

38. Simmen, "The Mountain Came Long Ago to Mohammed," 148.

39. Although the casting agency of this name did not appear until 1925, the idea fits. Ned Winterbottom is an all-American archetype, not a realistic human being.

40. Mena seems also to be mocking the stereotype of the Mexican macho, as Popo is anything but.

41. *Pace* Anderson, *Imagined Communities.*

42. It should be noted that the indigenous civilizations were also hierarchical, however not in racial terms.

43. Peralta might allude to Ángela Peralta, the late nineteenth-century opera singer known throughout Europe as the "Mexican Nightingale." Peralta died during a yellow fever epidemic in Mazatlán in 1883, and her husband went mad (like Jesús María) and died in a Parisian mental hospital. Lending credence to the theory, "The Soul of Hilda Brunel," another of Mena's *Century* magazine stories, features a main character who is an opera singer.

44. Ixtlán is a Toltec name, and the Oaxacan town of Ixtlán was founded before Spanish conquest.

45. Here Mena suggests the colonial continuities among nationalist revolutions, as Mexican nationalism tied to anti-French invasion directly led to new forms of neo-imperialism under Díaz.

46. She gets him to admit his love affair and then tries to insinuate herself into his revolutionary fervor: "Having thus converted her dead rival into a powerful ally, she turned a cautious front toward her living rival, whose formidable name was Patria, and soon she was giving hospitable ear to her son's dreams for the regeneration of his unhappy country" (77).

47. Mena considers these terms interchangeable: according to the story's narrator, "the unregarded persons of *rebozo* (*los enredados* are literally 'the wrapped-ups')." Moreover, they are rural folk: "They do not live in cities, these, but a few straggle in from neighboring pueblos with great baskets of country produce, which they sing in the patios in haunting, minor cadences" (73).

48. Underscoring the commonalities between Popo and Jesús María as mestizos of the Mexican Revolution, Popo is described by Alicia Cherry, when he spurns her, as "a regular young bandit" (61).

49. Mena's description echoes John Reed's profile of Pancho Villa in *Metropolitan* magazine in the United States in the fall of 1913 (reprinted in *Insurgent Mexico* in 1914), in which Reed describes Villa's attacks against mine owners, cattle ranchers, and other Mexican elites. Reed reiterates contemporary epithets for Villa, such as "The Friend of the Poor" (Reed, *Insurgent Mexico*, 118).

50. When seduction fails, Doña Rita fakes a sudden illness to regain his exclusive attention (75). However, her son has gone away during her "illness." When he returns, her first impulse is coquettish: "Praised by the Holy Name! Quick, *nana,* my face-powder, the compress on my brow!" (76).

51. In the postrevolutionary period, the government co-opted the language of solidarity popularized by the revolution, though its leaders eventually re-created Porfirian-era social hierarchies.

52. In 1910, the wealthiest 20 percent of American households held 46.2 percent of national personal income. Moreover, the wealthiest 10 percent had a larger income than the bottom 50 percent of the population (Schwarz, "American Inequality," A25).

53. Doña Rita even manipulates religious tradition in service of her unholy desire to return to the past: "Doña Rita, between her moans, caused a lamp to be filled with blessed oil, and to be burned significantly before a picture of the Virgin of the Remedies" (75). She uses Catholic ritual to add a patina of piety to her selfish and unhealthy attentions. In contrast to her son's authentic devotion to cause, the falsity of Doña Rita's religion is made apparent by the fact that her beleaguered, old Indian servant (*nana*) actually lights the lamp. Doña Rita doesn't even condescend to pray for her son; she has her servants do it. Moreover, Doña Rita worships the Spanish virgin, not the Mexican Virgin of Guadalupe. Clearly, Mena's message is that a healthy, vigorous future will require a new relationship to the Spanish colonial past and the North American neocolonial present. Doña Rita's obsession with the past—Jesús María's infancy and Spanish colonial-era hierarchy—is a pall over the nation, and its citizens', future.

54. Significantly, Mena suggests that Jesús María's early revolutionary fervor was underdeveloped, still tainted by elitism and racism, as evident by his membership in

the "Young Scientifics." "Los científicos" were a group of intellectuals associated with Díaz and his philosophy of positivism, who proposed applying the scientific method to the operations of government. The Young Scientifics were dubious about the role of the indigenous in Mexico's future. Jesús María's membership suggests that he had hitherto remained somewhat allied with the bourgeoisie and upper classes against the indigenous, despite his enthusiasm for the revolution. After his expulsion from the Young Scientifics, Jesús María experiences a more complete political awakening.

55. García Canclini, *Hybrid Cultures*, 10.

56. Mena here suggests a correlation between Jesús María's musical contribution to the Mexican Revolution and *corridos*, the popular folk songs that told the history of the revolution in ballad form.

57. Mena returns to the revolution in several other stories published in *Century* magazine, including "The Sorcerer and General Bisco" (April 1915), which depicts the confrontation between a violent despot—feudal landlord Don Baltazar Rascón, a "sorcerer" due to his expertise in hypnosis—and the guerilla leader determined to bring him down. Yet another national romance, this story centers on thwarted lovers Carmelita and Aquiles, whose fates lie in the hands of the lord and the general, in an allegorical contest between the feudal past and the revolutionary future. As with "Doña Rita's Rivals," his story moves away from the pathological family romance toward a nonsexual model of identity and cultural unity.

In "The Sorcerer and General Bisco," the Don is a cartoon villain, a murderer, thief, and rapist who perverts all family ties: he killed his wife, stole his brother-in-law Aquiles's money, and then forcibly married Aquiles's wife Carmelita (an act of incest). The Don represents the power and privilege of the Porfirian elite: "the son of a Spanish usurer, he had set himself up in the style of a born *caballero del campo,* and dared to oppress honest Mexicans" (103). In contrast, El Bisco is a cross-eyed "sometime bandit" who was a "terror to the rich and an idol to the poor" (100–101). A general who "would have been much more comfortable squatting on a mat, like most of his lieutenants," El Bisco is clearly modeled on Pancho Villa (102). The story ends happily after Carmelita and Aquiles help El Bisco escape the Don's powers of mesmerism, and the bandit kills the villain.

This story shows evidence of both Mexican and U.S. influence. El Bisco's rebels follow his rule that "all non-combatant prisoners were to be presented with consideration before General Bisco, in the name of God and the constitution" (100). Conjoining religion and law, moral and legal authority, and emphasizing citizens' rights and responsibilities, the revolutionaries seem to articulate a hybrid order distinct from either Catholic oligarchy or ethnic nationalism. Mexican readers would likely understand El Bisco's men to refer to the *Constitución Federal de los Estados Unidos Mexicanos de 1857,* which was notable for major liberal reforms, including the separation of church and state. There is a profound irony in El Bisco's unification of "God and the constitution," since such a conjunction is incompatible with the principles of the 1857 constitution. However, I believe this tension between "God and the constitution" makes more sense when seen from the perspective of Mena's U.S. audience, for whom constitutionalism suggests Thomas Jefferson and the other Founding Fathers. Given her readership, Mena's vagueness with regard to *which* constitution El Bisco honors suggests the influence of the U.S. Constitution as a model of democratic rebellion. In this light, the fusion of faith and reason, "domestic" and "imported" models of democracy, becomes another example of the new political "mixture" Mena is endorsing: an original, syncretic, multicultural, multiracial, transnational model for twentieth-century transformation.

Mena's optimism while the revolution rages on might suggest her alienation from the day-to-day realities in Mexico. As I have argued, her fiction tells us more about the Mexican Revolution's resonance for her U.S. readers than it reveals about living conditions in Mexico at the time. However, when she returns to the subject of the revolution more than fifteen years later, she takes a very different attitude. "A Son of the Tropics" (1931) exhibits deep pessimism about reform in Mexico as compared with her earlier stories of revolutionary leaders based on Pancho Villa and Emiliano Zapata. Don Rómulo, a feudal lord modeled on Porfirio Díaz, returns from a decadent life in the capital to his ancestral estate, finding it in disarray and poverty. He learns that a homegrown revolutionary, Rosario, is leading the peons in rebellion and acts of terrorism, and that Rosario is his illegitimate son by a servant. Meanwhile, Don Rómulo's daughter Dorotea has been captured by the rebels while out riding her horse. Upon finding her and Rosario, Don Rómulo promises to recognize Rosario as a legitimate heir, and to grant concessions regarding the peons' rights to work the land. However, Rosario is horrified by this revelation of his parentage, and he believes Don Rómulo's paternity irrevocably undermines his authority as rebel leader. Rosario commits suicide when he learns that he has the blood of a tyrant within him. This family drama is clearly an allegory for Mexico, whereby feudalism and revolution are born of the same family. In Mena's final published story for adults, the revolution is doomed as the fruit of a poisoned tree.

58. Pérez-Torres, *Mestizaje*, 39.

59. Fuentes, Prologue to *Ariel*, by José Enrique Rodó. 19.

4 / Half-Breeds and Homesteaders

1. Dexter Fisher, Mourning Dove's biographer, discovered that she had used the name Christal in some of her early correspondence. However, most critics refer to her as Christine Quintasket, which was the name on the tribal rolls, and I follow that precedent (Fisher, introduction to *Cogewea*, xvii). Jay Miller, who edited Mourning Dove's autobiography, claims that Mourning Dove was merely a pen name, first used in 1912 as she began writing *Cogewea* (Miller, introduction to *Mourning Dove: A Salishan Autobiography*, xvii). Henceforth all citations refer to the 1981 reprint of *Cogewea* edited by Fisher, and are included parenthetically in the text.

2. In her autobiography, Mourning Dove claims her paternal grandfather was a Scot, but, according to Jay Miller, census records and family history contradict this. Miller speculates that Mourning Dove invented a white grandfather to appeal to readers, though she did have an adopted white brother named Jimmy Ryan. By contrast, Dexter Fisher and Alanna K. Brown identify her paternal grandfather as an Irish employee of the Hudson Bay Company named Haines, who married, and quickly abandoned, his Indian wife (Miller, introduction to *Mourning Dove: A Salishan Autobiography*, xvi; Fisher, introduction to *Cogewea*, vii; Brown, "Mourning Dove's Voice in *Cogewea*," 4).

3. Viehmann, "My People ... My Kind," 205.

4. In addition, McWhorter did his own editing of the novel in 1922 (Krupat, "From 'Half-Blood' to 'Mixedblood,'" 121). Cathryn Halverson offers an astute reading of

McWhorter's epigraphs, claiming that they "contradict Mourning Dove by affirming popular understanding of the frontier as extant only in memory, an erstwhile kingdom . . . of the white cowboy" (Halverson, "Redefining the Frontier," 109). Harry J. Brown usefully cautions that "attempting to differentiate McWhorter's voice from Mourning Dove's voice similarly seeks to efface the hybrid characteristics of Mourning Dove's writing and to deny . . . at least part of the book as inauthentic" (Brown, *Injun Joe's Ghost*, 199).

5. S. Alice Callahan's *Wynema: A Child of the Forest* (1891) is recognized as the first novel by a woman of Native American heritage (Fisher, introduction to *Cogewea*, xii).

6. A. K. Brown, "Mourning Dove's Voice in *Cogewea*," 9.

7. Melissa L. Meyer discusses how the term "half-breed" was first coined in English to identify siblings who did not share both biological parents (Meyer, "Blood Is Thicker Than Family," 238).

8. Densmore is a Canadian, from eastern Ontario (50), as if to suggest that the ideology of white supremacy and western expansion into native lands is of continental concern. Margaret Lukens compellingly argues that Mourning Dove deliberately evokes the western border between the United States and Canada, particularly the movement of refugee Métis in Manitoba to Montana in the 1870s (Lukens, "Mourning Dove and Mixed Blood," 411–14).

9. Mourning Dove tells us that Cogewea's recovery and change of heart took two years, though the time is covered in mere pages in the novel, suggesting the inevitability of her recognition that Jim is her true love. However, for readers, their romance lacks the *frisson* of her encounters with the wicked Densmore.

10. Piatote, "Domestic Trials," 96.

11. Krupat, *Red Matters*, 88.

12. Owens, *Other Destinies*, 48.

13. Cannata, "Generic Power Plays in *Co-ge-we-a*, 711.

14. Krupat, "From 'Half-Blood' to 'Mixedblood,'"134.

15. Deloria, *Playing Indian*; Huhndorf, *Going Native*.

16. Piatote emphasizes the key differences between immigrants' and Native Americans' histories of "national domestication," noting that "immigrants joining the new national family were expected to *leave behind* their nations of origin, but not to *destroy* them" as indigenous subjects were (Piatote, "Domestic Trials," 98).

17. His tendency toward depression comes out after Cogewea agrees to marry Densmore; Jim sings a song featuring the lines, "There's a sadness in the moanin' / Of the pine tree in the gale; / There's a melancholia callin' / From the darkness of the plain" (236).

18. Hopkins, *Of One Blood*, 3.

19. Watanna, "The Half Caste," 150.

20. Mourning Dove repeatedly invokes familiar patriotic language to highlight the gap between U.S. ideals and its policies, such as when Cogewea rails at the injustice of "the land of the free-booter, and the home of the slave!" (142). Cogewea also describes the Indian Bureau as "a child of unnatural parentage, fostered by undemocratic principles, it has no legitimate place under a flag claimed to stand for all that is embodied in the word 'Liberty'" (145).

21. Cogewea distinguishes the simplicity of the Indian ceremony with the legal duplicity of U.S. marriage law. She wonders whether the Indian marriage is not superior

to the United States' "double-standard of morals and its *Reno* hackle. . . . [For] in this day, it requires but a few dollars in some crafty lawyer's pocket to sunder the 'holy bonds' which united as 'one' in the sight of God and the angels" (101). The problem, according to Mourning Dove, lies not in the technicalities of Indian and Christian marriage ceremonies, but in the hearts of those who say "I do." Among various tribes, marriages often could be easily dissolved, though the end of a marriage was not the end of familial responsibilities or community relationships.

22. Treat, "Writing Culture and Performing Race," 203.

23. Cogewea later declares: "The true American courses my veins and *never* will I cast aside my ancestral traditions. I was born to them!" (160).

24. Mourning Dove directly confronts the myth of the vanishing Indian when she has Cogewea think, "True, she reasoned, those poor settlers must live, the wild places subdued; but should it be at the expense of the helplessly weak? The unalterable edict had gone forth: 'Civilize or go under!' but where had there ever been a primitive hunter-race, able, ultimately to survive a sudden and violent contact with a highly developed agricultural civilization? The native American could be no exception to this most inexorable of nature's laws. . . . A few more generations at most, and the full-blooded Indian shall have followed the Buffalo" (139–40). Invoking Herbert Spencer's determinist philosophy, Cogewea apparently dooms full-blood Native Americans to extinction, just like the mighty buffalo who once roamed the West. Yet, she reveals, this is not a natural process, but something monstrous and perverse. According to Mourning Dove's logic, the half-breed may be the only hope for the continuation of Native American culture.

25. Sollors, *Beyond Ethnicity.*

26. In 1705, the Virginia colony denied civil rights to any "negro, mulatto, or Indian," who was defined as "the child of an Indian, and the child, grandchild, or great grandchild of a negro shall be deemed accounted, held, and taken to be a mulatto."

27. While Negroes and Indians were similarly targeted, the "taint" of Indian blood was assumed to pertain only to the next generation, while "negro" blood persisted through the generations. One explanation for the difference in this attitude toward race was each minority's relationship to property; Harry J. Brown explains that "while blacks *were* potentially property that might be possessed, Indians *occupied* property that might be possessed, and in vast quantity" (Brown, *Injun Joe's Ghost*, 23).

28. "The Future of the Negro," *New York Times* (1857–1922), December 28, 1898, http://search.proquest.com/docview/95582693?accountid=26417.

29. Trachtenberg, *Shades of Hiawatha*. 38.

30. See Otis, *The Dawes Act and the Allotment of Indian Lands,* 83. The U.S. government's role in regulating Indian identity continued with the Burke Act of 1906, which gave the secretary of the interior sole authority to grant citizenship and title to land for Native Americans. In 1907, Congress gave the Indian commissioner the authority to sell allotments belonging to Native Americans judged "noncompetent" to work them.

31. Under John Collier, the Bureau of Indian Affairs reversed the assimilationist policies of the Dawes era. The Indian Reorganization Act (the Indian New Deal) of 1934 restored tribal authority, and defined tribal members and nonenrolled Indians through a combination of blood quantum, residency, and descent.

32. Melissa L. Meyer explains how mixed-bloods were the first to be listed on federal tribal rolls, revealing how "record-keeping would be tied to allocations of private property" (Meyer, "Blood Is Thicker Than Family," 232).

33. McDonnell, *The Dispossession of the American Indian.*

34. Pfister, *Individuality Incorporated,* 25.

35. More than ten thousand children entered the crucible of Pratt's educational experiment in its thirty-nine years of operation, including future Native American leaders such as Luther Standing Bear, Zitkala-Ša, Mourning Dove, and Jim Thorpe. Pratt was pushed out of leadership in 1904, after which the school embraced a somewhat more pluralistic educational policy. The school finally closed in 1918.

36. "Some Reclaimed Indians," *New York Times (1857-1922),* July 16, 1887, http://search.proquest.com/docview/94489561?accountid=26417.

37. McBeth, *Ethnic Identity and the Boarding School Experience,* 141. For more on boarding schools and resisting assimilation, see Child, *Boarding School Seasons;* and Coleman, *American Indian Children at School.*

38. Dexter Fisher attributes this passage to McWhorter, due to its elevated tone (Fisher, introduction to *Cogewea,* xvii). However, the message of this passage, that the Indian Bureau perverted the natural ties between white and Native Americans, is thoroughly consistent with the ideas expressed in the novel.

39. *Cherokee Nation v. the State of Georgia* (1831). In 1871, Congress officially ended the practice of treaty making with Native American tribes by declaring all tribes "wards" of the federal government.

40. It is worth noting that the 1862 Homestead Act guaranteed women the right of property ownership. *Cogewea* makes clear that good men do not attempt to take control of their wives' money or property in the western territories. To the contrary, it is a place of uncommon sexual equality, as John Carter teasingly proposes making Cogewea his foreman once Jim becomes his partner (39).

41. The "one-drop" rule would, in 1914, be used to particular effect to apply to Native Americans: any amount of white ancestry, no matter how distant, would transform an Indian into a mixed-blood (Meyer, "Blood Is Thicker Than Family," 240).

42. Strong and Van Winkle, "Indian Blood," 558.

43. Terry P. Wilson, "Blood Quantum," cited in Waters, "Biometrics in Indian Country," 30-41.

44. For more on the history of blood quantum and its application, see Garroutte, "The Racial Formation of American Indians, 224-39. The issue of blood quantum has been brought vividly to life recently, as black Cherokees in Oklahoma who have been expelled from the official tribal rolls for lack of "Indian blood" use the federal courts to defend their standing as tribal members.

45. Waters, "Biometrics in Indian Country." As Jack D. Forbes explains, "The recording of blood quantum is both a product of white racism and of white social science theories of a racist nature, and also a product of a plan wherein Native nations are expected to vanish when the white blood quantum reaches a certain level (above three-fourths, for example)" (Forbes, "Blood Quantum").

46. Michaels, *Our America,* 32.

47. Fresonke and Spence, *Lewis & Clark,* 189.

48. Viehmann, "My People . . . My Kind," 209. See also Beidler, who argues that Mourning Dove's novel depicts "Cogewea's self-involved misreading of *The Brand,*" which reveals her own internalized racism (rather than Broderick's racism in *The Brand*) (Beidler, "Literary Criticism in *Cogewea,*" 58).

49. Sidonie Smith makes a similar claim about Zitkala-Ša's *Impressions of an Indian Childhood,* arguing that the wildness of the Indian child is a product of her fear and alienation at boarding school (see Smith, "Cheesecake, Nymphs, and 'We the People'").

50. I deliberately echo Lisa Lowe's language of "heterogeneity, hybridity, and multiplicity" to describe Asian American identities and experiences in the United States (Lowe, *Immigrant Acts*).

51. Mourning Dove's use of the term "primitive" must be understood as a product of her time, reflecting the association of urban living and technology with "civilization," "modernity," and "progress."

52. The importance of religion recurs when Cogewea's grandmother insists that Cogewea's marriage be performed by a Catholic priest, and not be done according to the traditional "Indian fashion." She has religious, as well as practical reasons, for such a marriage would ensure full legal rights and responsibilities.

53. A. K. Brown, "Mourning Dove's Voice in 'Cogewea,'" 12.

54. Halverson, "Redefining the Frontier," 111.

55. Krupat, "From 'Half-Blood' to 'Mixedblood,'" 129.

56. Lukens, "Mourning Dove and Mixed Blood," 411.

57. As Joel Pfister explains, the psychological dramas of western culture do not apply to Native American familiality, for "the elastic clan, kinship, and extended family system that ventilated life in close quarters—one could always stay with other loved ones—did not breed the White middle-class sentimental hothouse family with concentrated psychological dependencies, tensions, and possessiveness" (Pfister, *Individuality Incorporated,* 104).

58. Vizenor writes of ironic, postmodern texts, a category into which *Cogewea* certainly does not fit. Yet his emphasis on "postindian warriors" as those who reject tragedy and show the living (and therefore changing) nature of authentic Indian culture can be applied to Mourning Dove's novel (Vizenor, *Manifest Manners*).

59. Piatote, *Domestic Trials,* 98.

60. Toni Morrison's novel *A Mercy* (2008) depicts a seventeenth-century farm as a microcosm of the nation, created by an assortment of orphans from various ethnic and racial backgrounds: Dutch, English, Portuguese, Native American, and African.

61. Batker, *Reforming Fictions,* 48.

62. The financial language is echoed in one of Jim's declarations of love. He warns Cogewea that Densmore will "steal" her heart; she assures him that she prefers "*giving* her heart away rather than have some one sneak in and take it" (201).

63. Halverson, "Redefining the Frontier," 107.

64. Deloria, *Playing Indian,* 185.

65. H. J. Brown, *Injun Joe's Ghost,* 196.

5 / Blood and Blankets

1. I use the term "race" to denote those groups who, by the end of the nineteenth century, were defined as "nonwhite." Such informal distinctions continue to be commonplace. For more on the preference for "ethnicity" as a category for all racial and cultural difference, see Spickard, *Mixed Blood*; and Sollors, *Beyond Ethnicity.*

2. I will refer to both "immigrant" and "ethnic" throughout this chapter. By "immigrant," I mean those who were born elsewhere and came to America, either as children or adults; I use the term "ethnic" to refer much more generally to those

who identified with, or were identified by others as belonging to, a non-U.S. culture. Ethnicity is a vexed terminology that encompasses both racial typologies and cultural patterns (from foodways to clothing to speech patterns).

3. Although Addams was one of the most influential figures of the Progressive Era, her public reputation as "Saint Jane" was severely damaged by her uncompromising antiwar stance during the First World War. She was belatedly recognized for her achievements with the Nobel Peace Prize in 1931, and was honored with national attention at her death a year later. Thereafter, Addams's role in modern American reform has been eclipsed by male figures of the period, such as Theodore Roosevelt and Jacob Riis, and by the shift toward "social welfare" as a governmental responsibility. In the past decade, Jane Addams and Hull-House have been given renewed attention by biographers, historians, and literary critics such as V. B. Brown, *The Education of Jane Addams*; Diliberto, *A Useful Woman: The Early Life of Jane Addams*; Jean Bethke Elshtain, *Jane Addams and the Dream of American Democracy: A Life*; and Katherine Joslin, *Jane Addams, A Writer's Life*.

4. The museum remained part of Hull-House until shortly after Addams's death, when new management reduced the number and variety of Hull-House programs. Even with Jane Addams, Hull-House could afford to offer its services only with the help of wealthy donors; after her death and with the Great Depression, Hull-House could not depend on the same generosity.

5. In 1914, Americans shifted their attention from the "battle with the slum," in the phrase of the reformer-photographer Jacob Riis, to military battles in Europe. *The Battle with the Slum* (1902) was the title of Riis's account of improvements to tenement and working conditions in New York City. After Addams died in 1934, Hull-House went through a period of upheaval, with leadership changes, financial problems, and shifting priorities.

6. The Labor Museum received an early donation of Norwegian weavings from Lillian Wald, cofounder of the Henry Street Settlement in New York City. However, the majority of the textile collection came in 1902 from the Field Museum of natural history; Field's specimens had been famously displayed during the 1893 World's Columbian Exposition in Chicago (Jane Addams to Lillian Wald, 19 November 1900, *The Jane Addams Papers, 1860–1960* [microform]).

7. Addams, *Twenty Years at Hull-House*, 157.

8. On Saturday evenings, the performers, like the majority of their audience, were free from work in nearby factories and sweatshops. Despite its popularity, the museum, like most Hull-House programs, was not financially solvent, in part because there was no admission fee, in order to encourage local residents to visit. Anita McCormick Blaine was an early and reliable supporter of the museum (Jane Addams to Anita McCormick Blaine, November 27, 1900, and February 12, 1902, *The Jane Addams Papers, 1860–1960* [microform]). In an 1908 draft of a letter, Addams estimated that the "present cost of maintaining the Labor Museum with its allied classes in dressmaking, millinery, cooking and other subjects is $2500 a year." The letter sought an endowment of $5,000 per year to expand classes, for a total endowment of $100,000. As a means of revenue generation, the museum also sold objects created in its workshops (Jane Addams to unknown recipient, 18 May 1908, *The Jane Addams Papers, 1860–1960* [microform]).

9. In November 1901, the Labor Museum moved into larger quarters in the new Gymnasium Building. Textiles, bookbinding, and grains each had their own rooms;

metal, woodworking, and pottery shared a single space (see Jane Addams Hull-House Museum, "Urban Experience in Chicago").

10. Only after World War I and the 1924 Immigration Exclusion Act dramatically curtailed European immigration did the museum shift away from textiles. From 1927 to 1937, a growing community of Mexican immigrants energized the ceramics department with their skill and artistry (and no doubt brought in a much-needed dose of novelty).

11. Even longtime Addams historians such as Kathryn Kish Sklar and Christopher Lasch have devoted scant attention to the Hull-House Labor Museum (see Sklar, "Hull-House in the 1890s"; and Lasch, *The New Radicalism in America*).

12. For more on the centrality of domesticity and private spaces for a variety of women's reform organizations, including settlement houses, the Salvation Army, YWCA, and the NACW (National Association of Colored Women), see Spain, *How Women Saved the City*; and Hayden, *The Grand Domestic Revolution*.

13. The term seems to have been coined in the 1880s. In 1896, the Ladies' Health Protective Association held a convention in New York to discuss "municipal housekeeping hygiene." The president of the association, Mary Trautmann, reportedly told her audience of women reformers that this was their fight: "Men had tried to do the work before us, but they had failed; we are not so much surprised at that, because they are the breadwinners, and cannot give their time and attention to the details, nor do they so well understand housekeeping, with its numerous duties. We consider the city's housekeeping next in importance to our own" ("Women in Convention," *New York Times [1857–1922]*, May 15, 1896, http://search.proquest.com/docview/95362542? accountid=26417).

14. As Daphne Spain explains, reform organizations "depended on familial imagery to justify their interaction with strangers: their clients were 'daughters,' 'sisters,' or 'brothers'" (Spain, *How Women Saved the City*, 118). Jill Rappoport discusses the centrality of "sisterhood" to nineteenth-century reform movements in England (Rappoport, *Giving Women*).

15. Shannon Jackson describes how Hull-House residents referred to each other by an array of familiar terms of endearment (including "Sister"), a phenomenon she interprets as an "intimate habit" that "was also a performative utterance that reiterated their shared identity as an alternative 'family'" (Jackson, *Lines of Activity*, 171).

16. Addams advocates "an adaptation of our code of family ethics to modern conditions" (Addams, "Filial Relations," 80).

17. Addams urges teachers to encourage children to embrace their immigrant parents' cultural traditions, for the child "will in turn lead his family, and bring them with him into the brotherhood for which they are longing" (Addams, "The Public School," 239). In "A Modern Lear," she praises the labor movement's concern for "brotherhood, sacrifice, the subordination of individual and trade interests to the good of the working class" (Addams, "A Modern Lear," 135). In "Filial Relations," Addams credits college with teaching women "the recognition of the claims of human brotherhood" (82).

18. Addams here depicts Hull-House as a fraternal protector, transforming the (female-dominated) settlement house movement into a powerful (masculine) proxy for state interests (Addams, *Twenty Years at Hull-House*, 113).

19. She uses the parent-child relationship to describe labor relations, as well, as when, in a speech about the Pullman labor strike of 1894, she describes George

Pullman as a modern King Lear and criticizes his failure to recognize "the family claim" of his workers, whom she likens to Lear's daughter Cordelia (Addams, "A Modern Lear," 132).

20. In a 1908 article, Addams identifies the cause of this schism with the public school, which "too often separates the child from his parents and widens that old gulf between fathers and sons." Addams continues, "Can we not say, perhaps, that the schools ought to do more to connect these children with the best things of the past, to make them realize something of the beauty and charm of the language, the history, and the traditions which their parents represent" (Addams, "The Public School," 235–36).

21. Chinn, *Inventing Modern Adolescence*, 78.

22. Addams, *Twenty Years at Hull-House*, 155–156 (emphasis mine).

23. Addams, "The Public School," 237.

24. There are two images in the *First Report* that include a man. "Colonial Loom" features the Irish woman at front left, with a teen and preteen girl. An older white man stands at rear left. The man's presence, and the technological advancement, broadcast that we have entered the age of mass production. Yet this image lacks the emotional connection between all the participants that was evident in the homosocial scenes. "Fly Shuttle Loom" features a young girl at a spinning wheel, and the same elderly man from "Colonial Loom" at the loom. The dramatic age disparity and lack of eye contact, let alone physical contact, make these photographs so different from the images of immigrant women and girls. There is no threat of inappropriate sex, but neither is there a sense of familiality and relation between the young girl and the old man (Addams, *First Report*, 14).

25. Polacheck, *I Came a Stranger*, 64. The book's title is an allusion to the biblical story of Exodus. This association of immigration with exile was common in literature of the period (see Mary Antin's use of this trope in her autobiography *The Promised Land* [1912]). The story of Exodus was also deeply resonant for African Americans (see W.E.B. Du Bois, *The Souls of Black Folk*).

26. I am assuming that the women Polacheck describes in her autobiography are the same as those in the photographs from the *First Report of the Labor Museum*. Dena J. Polacheck Epstein, the editor of Hilda Satt Polacheck's memoir and her daughter, makes the same assumption.

27. Ibid., 64.

28. Ibid., 64–65.

29. This photograph was reprinted in Polacheck's autobiography. The ethnic distinctions blur over time, for Polacheck was a Polish Jew who had learned to spin in the museum. Yet perhaps this caption reveals the priorities of the museum; bridging the generation gap took precedence over ethnic specificity ("Russian Spinning," Jane Addams Memorial Collection, Department of Special Collections, University Library, University of Illinois at Chicago, JAMC 247).

30. Lynn Y. Weiner's introduction notes Hilda's estranged relationship to her own mother, and her mother's failure to learn English, suggesting that biological relationships were not always so easily repaired as cultural or metaphoric ones (Weiner, introduction to *I Came a Stranger*, xviii).

31. Prostitution: Addams, *Twenty Years at Hull-House*, 98–99, 112, 136, 141, 229; diseases transmitted via sweatshops and tenements: ibid., 140, 194; father-daughter incest: ibid., 194.

32. Ibid., 194.

33. Wilson, *The Sphinx in the City*, 8.The perceived threat represented by immigrant women's sexuality and reproduction is well documented. Sexuality was a growing concern in American culture more generally, as sexual mores were changing. See also Gilman, *Difference and Pathology*; Showalter, *Sexual Anarchy*; and Deutsch, *Women and the City*.

34. Such intermarriages were infrequent, but well publicized. Paul Spickard cites the statistic that in New York between 1908 and 1912, less than 1 percent of Jewish immigrants married those outside their faith, although that rose to 5–7 percent among second-generation immigrants (180, 182). Regardless of the numbers, Keren McGinity shows the outsized effect that just a few high-profile intermarriages between Jewish women and non-Jewish men had on the community (McGinity, *Still Jewish*; Sollors, ed., *Interracialism*; and Spickard, *Mixed Blood*).

35. Addams, *Twenty Years at Hull-House*, 156. Washburn echoes Addams's language, crediting the museum with providing meaning "in the midst of a foreign population largely wrenched away from its hereditary occupations" (Washburn, "A Labor Museum," 79).

36. Lears, *No Place of Grace*.

37. Addams, "The Public School," 235.

38. In this image, an Irish woman works at the spinning wheel, while an Italian woman illustrates hand spinning; their ethnicities are identified in other photographs from *First Report of the Labor Museum*.

39. Barbara Kirshenblatt-Gimblett calls this format a "jewel box" display (Kirshenblatt-Gimblett, *Destination Culture*, 28).

40. Washburn, "A Labor Museum," 79.

41. Addam's museum thus challenged the prevailing progress narratives with her radical equivalence. For more on the heterotopia, see Foucault, "Of Other Spaces," 22–27. For the ways that space is temporalized, with some nations relegated to an "earlier" stage of industrial and/or technological development, see Lefebvre, *The Production of Space*, 65.

42. The 1893 World's Columbian Exposition in Chicago, out of which the American Museum of Natural History was born, is commonly credited with initiating the shift from "race" to "culture," promising that "backward" nations could learn to become more modern. For more on racial hierarchies in world's fairs and natural history museums, see Bederman, *Manliness and Civilization*; Bennett, *The Birth of the Museum*; Booth, *How to Make It as a Woman*; Haraway, "Teddy Bear Patriarchy"; Rydell, *World of Fairs*; and Trachtenberg, *The Incorporation of America*.

43. Washburn described the domesticity of the Labor Museum in nostalgic terms: "A low window-seat to the right, and a big table before it, covered with a blue and white homespun cloth, make one wish that one could go back at once to the old colonial days, and make apply dowdy and mulled cider in this picture-booky place." She adds, however, that the illusion is destroyed by "laboratory samples" on display, which indicate up-to-date scientific insights on nutrition (Washburn, "A Labor Museum," 80).

44. Addams does talk about blood on at least one occasion, describing the difficulties immigrant parents have in adjusting to urban life as being akin to a wound "which leaves them bleeding and sensitive" (Addams, "The Public School," 238). This notion of blood is quite distinct from mainstream representations of racial taint.

45. Alpers, "The Museum as a Way of Seeing," 27.

46. Washburn, "A Labor Museum," 81.

47. Ibid.

48. See Ignatiev, *How the Irish Became White.* Stephen Steinberg shows how many perceived ethnic traits were, in fact, produced after arrival in the United States by the social conditions of emigration and adaptation (Steinberg, *The Ethnic Myth*).

49. Omi and Winant, *Racial Formation in the United States*, 61.

50. Clifford, "Museums as Contact Zones," 454.

51. Addams herself acknowledges the racial divisions, for she credits the Greek immigrants with being more responsive than other immigrant groups when W.E.B. Du Bois spoke at Hull-House on the anniversary of Lincoln's birthday (Addams, *Twenty Years at Hull-House*, 168).

Addams was involved in the NAACP, brought in major black public intellectuals, and integrated summer programs for children, but Hull-House remained more diverse and inclusive in terms of immigrants than African Americans. For more on the contradictions of race at Hull-House and other settlement houses, see Elshtain, *Jane Addams and the Dream of American Democracy*; and Elizabeth Lasch-Quinn, *Black Neighbors*.

52. Addams, *Twenty Years at Hull-House*, 157.

53. After the Civil War, African Americans were granted citizenship and voting rights by the Fourteenth and Fifteenth Amendments (1868 and 1870), but these rights were not enforced until the Voting Rights Act of 1965.

54. The Chinese Exclusion Act was only repealed in 1943. The "Gentlemen's Agreement" (1907) ended Japanese contract labor, while the 1917 Immigration Act created a "barred zone" prohibiting immigration and naturalization for those in nations situated "East of the Urals." Japanese internment during World War II was similarly based on the biological essentialist belief that Japanese Americans were incapable of assimilation or loyalty.

55. Blood quantum requirements for tribal membership asserted that Native American identity was biological rather than cultural. Such federal legislation often went against a tribal understanding of identity.

56. Hutchinson, *The Indian Craze.*

57. "The Labor Museum," *Hull-House Bulletin*, 8.

58. These images appeared in the *First Report of the Labor Museum* (1902), which was circulated to philanthropists and journalists to drum up interest and financial support. The report was a sixteen-page document with photographs, some of which were reprinted in Davis and McCree, eds., *Eighty Years at Hull-House.*

59. "Weaving with Navajo Loom," 6. This photograph is not unlike Jack Hillers's staged photographs of Native Americans in Utah in the 1870s and 1880s. Hillers, working with the explorer John Wesley Powell, dressed Utah tribespeople in buckskins, bowler hats, and feathered headdresses in order to gain the sympathy (and financial resources) of Congress.

60. The weaver in the photograph is possibly Hilda Satt, for Satt became the Labor Museum's Navajo weaving demonstrator during the 1910s, according to Jackie Petkewicz in "Contextualizing Craft: The Labor Museum and Immigrant Acculturation," Urban Experience in Chicago: Hull-House and its Neighborhoods, 1889–1963, University of Illinois, Chicago, http://tigger.uic.edu/htbin/cgiwrap/bin/urbanexp/main .cgi?file=img/show_image_in_gallery.ptt&gallery=19&image=244.

61. Polacheck, *I Came a Stranger*, 64.

62. Jackson, *Lines of Activity*.

63. This is yet another moment in the long history of the simultaneous co-optation of Indianness as a value and the destructions of Indians. The Carlisle School (the U.S. Training and Industrial School in Carlisle, Pennsylvania), opened in 1879, taught total assimilation and the denial of Native language and culture in order to achieve its goal of transforming "savage" Indians into "civilized" Americans. In 1893 at the World's Columbian Exposition in Chicago, the historian Frederick Jackson Turner famously announced the closing of the American frontier and thus the end of the Indian. According to these popular attitudes, Native American culture was salvageable and valuable only insofar as it could be "domesticated," remade in the image of middle-class white America. More recently, Michael D. McNally has shown how early twentieth-century theatrical productions of Longfellow's *Hiawatha* (performed in native languages by Native American actors) turned the romanticized Indian of American imagination into "the real one," while also critiquing white co-optation of Indian identity (see McNally, "The Indian Passion Play," 105–36).

64. Deloria, *Playing Indian*, 185.

65. See Hutchinson, *The Indian Craze*, for more on the contradictory relationship between Indian artifacts and modernism.

66. Hegeman, *Patterns for America*, 29.

Conclusion

1. Cheng, *The Melancholy of Race*.

2. Flatley, "Reading into Henry James," 109.

3. Berlant, *The Queen of America*; Berlant, *The Female Complaint*.

4. Michaelsen, "The Grounds and Limits of Multiculturalism," 660.

5. As of December 2011, the United Colors of Benetton no longer allows its old advertisements to be republished in any form. These images have also been removed from its website, which once proudly displayed the company's history of provocative ads.

6. Toscani did the photography for Benetton's advertisements from 1982 until 2000. His work for Benetton grew increasingly radical, culminating in a prison-themed campaign that ended his relationship with the company. Fundamentally, Toscani's personal politics were at odds with Benetton's desire for brand awareness and clothing sales.

7. On October 16, 2010, in response to growing anti-immigration sentiment, Angela Merkel, the chancellor of Germany, declared that multiculturalism in Germany had "utterly failed."

8. Gore Vidal, "State of the Union, 2004," *Nation*, September 13, 2004.

BIBLIOGRAPHY

Adams, Charles Francis, Jr. "Imperialism" and "The Tracks of Our Forefathers": A Paper Read before the Lexington, Massachusetts Historical Society, Tuesday, December 20, 1898. Boston: Dana Estes, 1899.

Addams, Jane. "Filial Relations." 1902. Reprinted in *The Jane Addams Reader,* edited by Jean Bethke Elshtain, 76–87. New York: Basic, 2002.

———. *First Report of the Labor Museum at Hull House, Chicago, 1901–1902.* Chicago: Hull-House, 1902: 1–16. Urban Experience in Chicago: Hull-House and Its Neighborhoods, 1889–1963. http://tigger.uic.edu/htbin/cgiwrap/bin/urbanexp/main.cgi?file=new/show_doc_search.ptt&doc=293.

———. *The Jane Addams Papers, 1860–1960.* Microform. Edited by Mary Lynn McCree Bryan. Ann Arbor, Mich.: University Microfilms International, 1984.

———. "Labor Museum at Hull House." *Commons* 47 (June 30, 1900): 1–4. Available online at the University of Illinois at Chicago web archive, "Urban Experience in Chicago: Hull-House and Its Neighborhoods, 1889–1963." www.uic.edu/jaddams/hull/urbanexp/.

———. "A Modern Lear." *Survey* 29, no. 5 (November 2, 1912): 131–37. Reprinted in *The Jane Addams Reader,* edited by Jean Bethke Elshtain, 163–76. New York: Basic, 2002.

———. "The Public School and the Immigrant Child." *Journal of Proceedings and Addresses* (National Education Association, 1908). Reprinted in *The Jane Addams Reader,* edited by Jean Bethke Elshtain, 235–39. New York: Basic, 2002.

———. *Twenty Years at Hull-House.* 1910. New York: Penguin, 1998.

Alemán, Jesse. "The Other Country: Mexico, the United States, and the Gothic

History of Conquest." *American Literary History* 18, no. 3 (Fall 2006): 406–26.

Alonso, Ana María, "Conforming Disconformity: "Mestizaje," Hybridity, and the Aesthetics of Mexican Nationalism." *Cultural Anthropology* 19, no. 4 (November 2004): 459–90.

Alpers, Svetlana. "The Museum as a Way of Seeing." In *Exhibiting Cultures: The Poetics and Politics of Museum Display,* edited by Ivan Karp and Steven D. Lavine, 25–32. Washington, D.C.: Smithsonian Institution Press, 1991.

Ammons, Elizabeth. *Conflicting Stories: American Women Writers at the Turn into the Twentieth Century.* New York and Oxford: Oxford University Press, 1992.

Anderson, Benedict. *Imagined Communities: Reflections on the Origin and Spread of Nationalism.* New York: Verso, 1983.

Antin, Mary. *The Promised Land.* 1912. Introduction by Werner Sollors. New York: Penguin, 1997.

Anzaldúa, Gloria. *Borderlands/La Frontera: The New Mestiza.* San Francisco: Aunt Lute, 1987.

Barrows, Samuel J. *New Legislation Concerning Crimes, Misdemeanors, and Penalties: Compiled from the Laws of the Fifty-Fifth Congress and from the Session Laws of the States and Territories for 1897 and 1898.* Washington, D.C.: Government Printing Office, 1900.

Batker, Carol J. *Reforming Fictions.* New York: Columbia University Press, 2000.

Bederman, Gail. *Manliness and Civilization.* Chicago: University of Chicago Press, 1995.

Beidler, Peter G. "Literary Criticism in *Cogewea:* Mourning Dove's Protagonist Reads *The Brand.*" *American Indian Culture and Research Journal* 19, no. 2 (1995): 45–65.

Beizer, Janet. *Ventriloquized Bodies: Narratives of Hysteria in Nineteenth-Century France.* Ithaca, N.Y.: Cornell University Press, 1994.

Bennett, Tony. *The Birth of the Museum: History, Theory, Politics.* New York: Routledge, 1995.

Berg, Allison. "Reconstructing Motherhood: Pauline Hopkins' *Contending Forces.*" *Studies in American Fiction* 24, no. 2 (Autumn 1996): 131–50.

Bergman, Jill. "'Everything We Hoped She'd Be': Contending Forces in Hopkins Scholarship." *African American Review* 38, no. 2 (Summer 2004): 181–99.

Berlant, Lauren. *The Female Complaint: The Unfinished Business of Sentimentality in American Culture.* Durham, N.C.: Duke University Press, 2008.

———. *The Queen of America Goes to Washington City: Essays on Sex and Citizenship.* Durham, N.C.: Duke University Press, 1997.

Birchall, Diana. *Onoto Watanna: The Story of Winnifred Eaton.* Urbana and Chicago: University of Illinois Press, 2001.

Booth, Alison. *How to Make It as a Woman: Collective Biographical History from Victoria to the Present.* Chicago: University of Chicago Press, 2004.

Boulukos, George. *The Grateful Slave: The Emergence of Race in Eighteenth-Century British and American Culture.* Cambridge: Cambridge University Press, 2008.

Bourne, Randolph. "Trans-National America." *Atlantic Monthly* 118 (July 1916): 86–97. Reprinted in *Theories of Ethnicity,* edited by Werner Sollors, 93–108. New York: New York University Press, 1996.

Bow, Leslie. *Betrayal and Other Acts of Subversion: Feminism, Sexual Politics, Asian American Women's Literature.* Princeton: Princeton University Press, 2001.

Brading, D. A. *The Origins of Mexican Nationalism.* Latin American Miniatures, Centre of Latin American Studies, University of Cambridge. Cambridge: Cambridge University Press, 1985.

Broderick, Therese. *The Brand: A Tale of the Flathead Reservation.* Seattle: Alice Harriman, 1910.

Brodkin, Karen. *How Jews Became White Folks: And What That Says about Race in America.* New Brunswick, N.J.: Rutgers University Press, 1998.

Brogan, Kathleen. *Cultural Haunting: Ghosts and Ethnicity in Recent American Literature.* Charlottesville: University Press of Virginia, 1998.

Brooks, Peter. *The Melodramatic Imagination: Balzac, Henry James, Melodrama, and the Mode of Excess.* 1976. New Haven: Yale University Press, 1995.

Brown, Alanna Kathleen. "Mourning Dove's Voice in *Cogewea.*" *Wicazo Sa Review* 4, no. 2 (Autumn 1988): 2–15.

Brown, Harry J. *Injun Joe's Ghost: The Indian Mixed-Blood in American Writing.* Columbia: University of Missouri Press, 2004.

Brown, Victoria Bissell. *The Education of Jane Addams.* Philadelphia: University of Pennsylvania Press, 2003.

Butler, Judith. *Undoing Gender.* New York: Routledge, 2004.

Cannata, Susan M. "Generic Power Plays in *Co-ge-we-a.*" *American Indian Quarterly* 21, no. 4 (Autumn 1997): 703–12.

Carby, Hazel V. *Reconstructing Womanhood: The Emergence of the Afro-American Woman Novelist.* New York: Oxford University Press, 1989.

Caruth, Cathy. *Unclaimed Experience: Trauma, Narrative, and History.* Baltimore: Johns Hopkins University Press, 1996.

Chance, John K. "On the Mexican Mestizo." *Latin American Research Review* 14, no. 3 (1979): 153–68.

Cheng, Anne Anlin. *The Melancholy of Race: Psychoanalysis, Assimilation, and Hidden Grief.* New York: Oxford University Press, 2001.

Chesnutt, Charles. "The Future American." In *Theories of Ethnicity: A Classical Reader,* edited by Werner Sollors, 17–36. New York: New York University Press, 1996.

———. *The House behind the Cedars.* Boston and New York: Houghton, Mifflin, 1900.

———. "The Wife of His Youth." 1899. Reprinted in *Conjure Tales and Stories of the Color Line*, 103–14. New York: Penguin, 1992.

Cheung, King-kok. "The Woman Warrior versus the Chinaman Pacific: Must a Chinese American Critic Choose between Feminism and Heroism?" In *Conflicts in Feminism*, edited by Marianne Hirsch and Evelyn Fox Keller, 234–54. New York: Routledge, 1990.

Ch'ien, Evelyn Nien-Ming. *Weird English.* Cambridge: Harvard University Press, 2004.

Child, Brenda. *Boarding School Seasons: American Indian Families, 1900–1940.* Lincoln: University of Nebraska Press, 1998.

Child, Lydia Maria. *A Romance of the Republic.* Boston: Ticknor and Fields, 1867.

Chinn, Sarah E. *Inventing Modern Adolescence: The Children of Immigrants in Turn-of-the-Century America.* New Brunswick, N.J.: Rutgers University Press, 2009.

Clifford, James. "Museums as Contact Zones." In *Representing the Nation: A Reader: Histories, Heritage and Museums*, edited by David Boswell and Jessica Evans, 435–57. New York: Routledge, 1999.

Cole, Jean Lee. *The Literary Voices of Winnifred Eaton: Redefining Ethnicity and Authenticity.* New Brunswick, N.J.: Rutgers University Press, 2002.

Coleman, Michael. *American Indian Children at School, 1850–1930.* Jackson: University Press of Mississippi, 1993.

Cope, R. Douglas. *The Limits of Racial Domination: Plebeian Society in Colonial Mexico City, 1660–1720.* Madison: University of Wisconsin Press, 1994.

Cordell, Sigrid Anderson. "'The Case Was Very Black Against' Her: Pauline Hopkins and the Politics of Racial Ambiguity at the *Colored American Magazine*." *American Periodicals: A Journal of History, Criticism, and Bibliography* 16, no. 1 (2006): 52–73.

Creelman, James. "President Diaz: Hero of the Americas." *Pearson's Magazine* 19, no. 3 (March 1908): 237.

Davis, Adrienne. "Slavery's Shadow Families: Rethinking Miscegenation Regulation." *Conference Papers—Law & Society* (2007 Annual Meeting 2007): 1. *Academic Search Complete*, EBSCOhost.

Davis, Allan F., and Mary Lynn McCree, eds. *Eighty Years at Hull-House.* New York: Quadrangle, 1969.

De la Peña, Guillermo. "A New Mexican Nationalism? Indigenous Rights, Constitutional Reform and the Conflicting Meanings of Multiculturalism." *Nations and Nationalism* 12, no. 2 (2006): 279–302.

Deloria, Philip J. *Playing Indian.* New Haven: Yale University Press, 1998.

Deutsch, Sara. *Women and the City: Gender, Space, and Power in Boston, 1870–1940.* New York: Oxford University Press, 2000.

Diliberto, Gioia. *A Useful Woman: The Early Life of Jane Addams.* New York: Scribner, 1999.

Doane, Mary Ann. *Femmes Fatales: Feminism, Film Theory, Psychoanalysis.* New York: Routledge, 1991.

Doane, Janice, and Devon Hodges. *Telling Incest: Narratives of Dangerous Remembering from Stein to Sapphire.* Ann Arbor: University of Michigan Press, 2001.

Du Bois, W.E.B. *The Souls of Black Folk.* 1903. New York: Vintage/Library of America, 1990.

Earle, Rebecca. *Return of the Native: Indians and Myth-Making in Spanish America, 1810–1930.* Durham: Duke University Press, 2007.

Eaton, Winnifred. See "Watanna, Onoto."

Egenolf, Susan B. "Josiah Wedgwood's Goodwill Marketing." In *The Culture of the Gift in Eighteenth-Century England,* edited by Linda Zionkowski and Cynthia Klekar, 197–213. New York and Houndmills: Palgrave Macmillan, 2009.

Ellison, Ralph. *Invisible Man.* New York: Random House, 1952.

Elshtain, Jean Bethke. *Jane Addams and the Dream of American Democracy: A Life.* New York: Basic, 2002.

Eng, David. *Racial Castration: Managing Masculinity in Asian America.* Durham, N.C.: Duke University Press, 2001.

Fallaw, Ben. "Bartolomé García Correa and the Politics of Maya Identity in Postrevolutionary Yucatán, 1911–1933." *Ethnohistory* 55, no. 4 (Fall 2008): 553–78. *Academic Search Complete,* EBSCOhost.

Faulkner, William. *Absalom, Absalom!* New York: Random House, 1936.

———. *The Sound and the Fury.* New York: Jonathan Cape and Harrison Smith, 1931.

Favor, Martin J. *Authentic Blackness: The Folk in the New Negro Renaissance.* Durham, N.C.: Duke University Press, 1999.

Felman, Shoshanna. "Education and Crisis, or the Vicissitudes of Teaching." In *Trauma: Explorations in Memory,* edited by Cathy Caruth, 13–60. Baltimore: Johns Hopkins University Press, 1995.

Ferens, Dominika. *Edith and Winnifred Eaton: Chinatown Missions and Japanese Romances.* Urbana and Chicago: University of Illinois Press, 2002.

Fernández Retamar, Roberto. *Caliban and Other Essays.* 1971. Translated by Edward Baker. Minneapolis: University of Minnesota Press, 1989.

Fiedler, Leslie. *Love and Death in the American Novel.* New York: Criterion, 1960.

Fisher, Dexter. Introduction to *Cogewea: The Half Blood,* by Mourning Dove, v–xxix. Lincoln: University of Nebraska Press, 1981.

Flatley, Jonathan. "Reading into Henry James." *Criticism* 46, no. 1 (2004): 103–23.

Forbes, Jack D. "Blood Quantum: A Relic of Racism and Termination." In "Native Intelligence: A Column," in *People's Voice,* November 27, 2000, www.weyanoke.org/reading/jdf-BloodQuantum.html.

Foucault, Michel. "Of Other Spaces: Utopias and Heterotopias." *Diacritics* 16 (Spring 1986): 22–27.

Fresonke, Kris, and Mark Spence. *Lewis & Clark: Legacies, Memories, and New Perspectives.* Berkeley: University of California Press, 2004.

Freud, Sigmund. "Fragment of an Analysis of a Case of Hysteria ('Dora')." 1905. In *The Freud Reader,* edited by Peter Gay, 172–239. New York: Norton, 1989.

———. *Group Psychology and the Analysis of the Ego.* 1921. Translated and edited by James Strachey. New York: Norton, 1959.

———. *Inhibitions, Symptoms and Anxiety.* 1926. Translated by Alix Strachey. Revised and edited by James Strachey. New York: Norton, 1959.

———. "Mourning and Melancholia." 1917. In *The Freud Reader,* edited by Peter Gay, 584–89. New York: Norton, 1989.

———. "The Question of Lay Analysis." 1926. *The Standard Edition of the Complete Psychological Works of Sigmund Freud*, edited by James Strachey, 20:179–260. London: Hogarth Press and the Institute of Psycho-Analysis, 1955.

———. "Repression." 1915. In *The Freud Reader,* edited by Peter Gay, 568–72. New York: Norton, 1989.

———. "The Uncanny." 1919. *The Standard Edition of the Complete Psychological Works of Sigmund Freud*, edited by James Strachey, 17:218–52. London: Hogarth Press and the Institute of Psycho-Analysis, 1955.

Freud, Sigmund, and Joseph Breuer. *Studies in Hysteria.* 1895. Translated by A. A. Brill. Boston: Beacon, 1937.

Fuentes, Carlos. Prologue to *Ariel,* by José Enrique Rodó, 7–28. Austin: University of Texas Press, 1988.

Fusco, Coco. *English Is Broken Here: Notes on Cultural Fusion in the Americas.* New York: New Press, 1995.

Fuss, Diana. *Identification Papers.* New York: Routledge, 1995.

Gamio, Manuel. *Forjando patria (pro nacionalismo).* México: Porrúa Hermanos, 1916.

García Canclini, Néstor. *Hybrid Cultures: Strategies for Entering and Leaving Modernity.* Minneapolis: University of Minnesota Press, 1995.

Garroutte, Eva Marie. "The Racial Formation of American Indians: Negotiating Legitimate Identities within Tribal and Federal Law." *American Indian Quarterly* 25, no. 2 (Spring 2001): 224–239. JSTOR http://www.jstor.org /stable/1185951.

Gelfand, Toby, and John Kerr, eds. *Freud and the History of Psychoanalysis.* New York: Routledge, 1992.

Gillman, Susan K. *Blood Talk: American Race Melodrama and the Culture of the Occult.* Chicago: University of Chicago Press, 2003.

———. "Pauline Hopkins and the Occult: African-American Revisions of Nineteenth-Century Sciences." *American Literary History* 8, no. 1 (1996): 57–82.

Gilman, Sander L. *Difference and Pathology: Stereotypes of Sexuality, Race, and Madness.* Ithaca, N.Y.: Cornell University Press, 1985.

Goldberg, David Theo. Introduction to *Multiculturalism: A Critical Reader.* Oxford: Blackwell, 1994.

Griffith, Jean Carol. *The Color of Democracy in Women's Regional Writing.* Tuscaloosa: University of Alabama Press, 2009.

Guerrero, Elisabeth. *Confronting History and Modernity in Mexican Narrative.* New York: Palgrave Macmillan, 2008.

Guglielmo, Thomas A. *White on Arrival: Italians, Race, Color, and Power in Chicago, 1890–1945.* New York: Oxford University Press, 2003.

Gwin, Minrose C. "'Hereisthehouse': Cultural Spaces of Incest in *The Bluest Eye.*" In *Incest and the Literary Imagination,* edited by Elizabeth L. Barnes, 316–28. Gainesville: University Press of Florida, 2002.

Halverson, Cathryn. "Redefining the Frontier: Mourning Dove's *Cogewea, The Half-Blood: A Depiction of the Great Montana Cattle Range.*" *American Indian Culture and Research Journal* 21, no. 4 (1997): 105–24.

———. "'Typical Tokio Smile': Bad American Books and Bewitching Japanese Girls." *Arizona Quarterly* 63, no. 1 (Spring 2007): 49–80.

Handlin, Oscar. *The Uprooted: The Epic Story of the Great Migrations That Made the American People.* 1951. 2nd ed. Boston: Little, Brown, 1973.

Haraway, Donna. "Teddy Bear Patriarchy: Taxidermy in the Garden of Eden, New York City, 1908–1936." *Social Text* 11 (Winter 1984/85): 19–64.

Harper, Frances E. W. *Iola Leroy, Or Shadows Uplifted.* Philadelphia: Garrigues, 1892.

Harkins, Gillian. *Everybody's Family Romance: Reading Incest in Neoliberal America.* Minneapolis: University of Minnesota Press, 2009.

Hartman, Saidiya. *Scenes of Subjection: Terror, Slavery, and Self-Making in Nineteenth-Century America.* New York: Oxford University Press, 1997.

Hayden, Dolores. *The Grand Domestic Revolution: A History of Feminist Designs for American Homes, Neighborhoods, and Cities.* Cambridge: MIT Press, 1981.

Hegeman, Susan. *Patterns for America: Modernism and the Concept of Culture.* Princeton: Princeton University Press, 1999.

Herman, Judith. *Trauma and Recovery.* New York: Basic, 1992.

Herron, Carolivia. *Thereafter Johnnie.* New York: Random House, 1991.

Hopkins, Pauline. *Contending Forces: A Romance Illustrative of Negro Life North and South.* 1900. Introduction by Richard Yarborough. New York: Oxford University Press, 1988.

———. *Hagar's Daughter: A Story of Southern Caste Prejudice.* 1901. Reprinted in *The Magazine Novels of Pauline Hopkins.* New York: Oxford University Press, 1988.

———. *Of One Blood: Or, The Hidden Self.* 1903. Introduction by Deborah McDowell. New York: Washington Square Press, 2004.

———. *Winona: A Tale of Negro Life in the South and Southwest.* 1902. Reprinted in *The Magazine Novels of Pauline Hopkins.* New York: Oxford University Press, 1988.

Horvitz, Deborah. "Hysteria and Trauma in Pauline Hopkins' *Of One Blood; or, The Hidden Self. African American Review* 33, no. 2 (1999): 245–60.

Hughes, Henry. *Treatise on Sociology: Theoretical and Practical.* Philadelphia: Lippincott, Grambo, 1854.

Huhndorf, Shari M. *Going Native: Indians in the American Cultural Imagination.* Ithaca, N.Y.: Cornell University Press, 2001.

Hutchinson, Elizabeth. *The Indian Craze: Primitivism, Modernism, and Transculturation in American Art, 1890–1915.* Durham, N.C.: Duke University Press, 2009.

Ignatiev, Noel. *How the Irish Became White.* New York: Routledge, 1995.

Irwin, John T. *Doubling and Incest/Repetition and Revenge: A Speculative Reading of Faulkner.* Baltimore: Johns Hopkins University Press, 1975. Jackson, Helen Hunt. *Ramona: A Story.* Boston: Roberts Brothers, 1884.

Jackson, Shannon. *Lines of Activity: Performance, Historiography, Hull-House Domesticity.* Ann Arbor: University of Michigan Press, 2000.

Jacobs, Harriet. *Incidents in the Life of a Slave Girl.* 1861. Introduction by Jean Fagan Yellin. Cambridge: Harvard University Press, 1987.

Jacobson, Matthew Frye. *Whiteness of a Different Color: European Immigrants and the Alchemy of Race.* Cambridge: Harvard University Press, 1999.

James, William. "The Hidden Self." *Scribner's Magazine* 7, no. 3 (March 1890): 361–73.

Jane Addams Hull-House Museum and the College of Architecture and the Arts at the University of Illinois at Chicago. "Urban Experience in Chicago: Hull-House and its Neighborhoods, 1889–1963." Edited by Rima Lunin Schultz. July 10, 2005. www.uic.edu/jaddams/hull/urbanexp/index.htm.

Jane Addams Memorial Collection. Department of Special Collections. University Library. University of Illinois at Chicago.

Japtok, Martin. "Pauline Hopkins' *Of One Blood,* Africa, and the 'Darwinist Trap.'" *African American Review* 36, no. 3 (Fall 2002): 403–16.

Jen, Gish. *The Love Wife.* New York: Knopf, 2004.

Jones, Gavin. *Strange Talk: The Politics of Dialect Literature in Gilded Age America.* Berkeley: University of California Press, 1999.

Joslin, Katherine. *Jane Addams, A Writer's Life.* Urbana and Chicago: University of Illinois Press, 2004.

Kallen, Horace. "Democracy versus the Melting-Pot: A Study of American Nationality." *Nation,* February 25, 1915. Reprinted in *Theories of Ethnicity,* edited by Werner Sollors, 67–92. New York: New York University Press, 1996.

Kaplan, Amy. *The Social Construction of American Realism.* Chicago: University of Chicago Press, 1988.

Karnow, Stanley. *In Our Image: America's Empire in the Philippines*. New York: Random House, 1989.

Kirshenblatt-Gimbett, Barbara. *Destination Culture: Tourism, Museums, and Heritage*. Berkeley: University of California Press, 1998.

Klein, Melanie. "A Contribution to the Psychogenesis of Manic-Depressive States." In *Love, Guilt and Reparation and Other Works, 1921–1945*, 262–89. New York: Free Press, 1975.

Koshy, Susan. *Sexual Naturalization: Asian Americans and Miscegenation*. Stanford, Calif.: Stanford University Press, 2004.

Krupat, Arnold. "From 'Half-Blood' to 'Mixedblood': *Cogewea* and the 'Discourse of Indian Blood.'" *Modern Fiction Studies* 45, no. 1 (1999): 120–45.

———. *Red Matters: Native American Studies*. Philadelphia: University of Pennsylvania Press, 2002.

"The Labor Museum," *Hull-House Bulletin* 4, no. 3 (Autumn 1900): 8. Quoted in Jackie Petkewicz, "Contextualizing Craft: The Labor Museum and Immigrant Acculturation." Urban Experience in Chicago: Hull-House and Its Neighborhoods, 1889–1963. University of Illinois at Chicago, College of Architecture and the Arts, Jane Addams Hull-House Museum. http://tigger. uic.edu/htbin/cgiwrap/bin/urbanexp/main.cgi?file=img/show_image_in_ gallery.ptt&image=254&gallery=19.

Lacan, Jacques. *The Seminar of Jacques Lacan, Book II: The Ego in Freud's Theory and in the Technique of Psychoanalysis 1954–1955*. 1978, 1988. Edited by Jacques-Alain Miller. Translated by Sylvana Tomaselli. New York: Norton, 1991.

Lape, Noreen Groover. *West of the Border: The Multicultural Literature of the Western American Frontiers*. Athens: Ohio University Press, 2000.

Lasch, Christopher. *The New Radicalism in America, 1889–1963: The Intellectual as a Social Type*. New York: Norton, 1965.

Lasch-Quinn, Elizabeth. *Black Neighbors: Race and the Limits of Reform*. Chapel Hill: University of North Carolina Press, 1993.

Lears, T. J. Jackson. *No Place of Grace: Antimodernism and the Transformation of American Culture, 1880–1920*. New York: Pantheon, 1981.

Lefebvre, Henri. *The Production of Space*. Oxford: Blackwell, 1991.

Lemire, Elise. *"Miscegenation": Making Race in America*. Philadelphia: University of Pennsylvania Press, 2002.

Leonard, Karen. "Ethnic Celebrations in Rural California: Punjabi-Mexicans and Others." In *Celebrations of Identity: Multiple Voices in American Ritual Performance*, edited by Pamela R. Frese, 145–60. Westport, Conn.: Greenwood, 1993.

Lévi-Strauss, Claude. *Elementary Structures of Kinship*. 1949, 1967. Translated by James Harle Bell, John Richard Von Sturmer, and Rodney Needham, 1969. Boston: Beacon, 1971.

Leys, Ruth. *Trauma: A Genealogy*. Chicago: University of Chicago Press, 2000.

Li, David. *Imagining the Nation: Asian American Literature and Cultural Consent.* Stanford, Calif.: Stanford University Press, 1998.

Lone Star. Directed by John Sayles. 1995. DVD. Burbank, Calif.: Warner Home Video, 1999.

Long, John Luther. *Madame Butterfly: Purple Eyes; A Gentleman of Japan and a Lady; Kito; Glory.* New York: Century, 1898.

Lott, Eric. *Love and Theft: Blackface Minstrelsy and the American Working Class.* New York: Oxford University Press, 1993.

Lowe, Lisa. *Immigrant Acts: On Asian American Cultural Politics.* Durham, N.C.: Duke University Press, 1996.

Luciano, Dana. "Passing Shadows: Melancholic Nationality and Black Critical Publicity in Pauline E. Hopkins's *Of One Blood*." In *Loss: The Politics of Mourning,* edited by David L. Eng and David Kazanjian, 148–87. Berkeley: University of California Press, 2003.

Lukens, Margaret A. "Mourning Dove and Mixed Blood: Cultural and Historical Pressures on Aesthetic Choice and Authorial Identity." *American Indian Quarterly* 21, no. 3 (Summer 1997): 409–22.

Marchetti, Gina. *Romance and the "Yellow Peril": Race, Sex, and Discursive Strategies of Hollywood Fiction.* Berkeley: University of California Press, 1994.

Matsukawa, Yuko. "Cross-Dressing and Cross-Naming: Decoding Onoto Watanna." In *Tricksterism in Turn-of-the-Century American Literature: A Multicultural Perspective,* ed. Elizabeth Ammons and Annette White-Parks. Hanover, N.H.: Tufts University/ University Press of New England, 1994.

McBeth, Sally. *Ethnic Identity and the Boarding School Experience of West-Central Oklahoma Indians.* Washington, D.C.: University Press of America, 1982.

McClintock, Anne. *Imperial Leather: Race, Gender, and Sexuality in the Colonial Contest.* New York: Routledge, 1995.

McCree, Mary Lynn, and Allen F. Davis. *Eighty Years at Hull-House.* Chicago: Quadrangle, 1969.

McDonnell, Janet A. *The Dispossession of the American Indian, 1887–1934.* Bloomington: Indiana University Press, 1991.

McDowell, Deborah. Introduction to *Of One Blood: Or, The Hidden Self,* by Pauline Hopkins, v–xxi. New York: Washington Square Press, 2004.

McGinity, Keren. *Still Jewish: A History of Women and Intermarriage.* New York: New York University Press, 2009.

McNally, Michael D. "The Indian Passion Play: Contesting the Real Indian in *Song of Hiawatha* Pageants, 1901–1965." *American Quarterly* 58, no. 1 (March 2006): 105–36.

Meech, Julia, and Gabriel P. Weisberg, eds. *Japonisme Comes to America: The Japanese Impact on the Graphic Arts, 1876–1925.* New York: Abrams, 1990.

Mena, María Cristina. *The Collected Stories of María Cristina Mena.* Edited by Amy Doherty. Houston: Arte Público, 1997.

———. "Julián Carrillo: The Herald of a Musical Monroe Doctrine." *Century,* March 1915, 753–59.

Meyer, Melissa L. "Blood Is Thicker Than Family." In *Over the Edge: Remapping the American West,* edited by Valerie J. Matsumoto and Blake Allmendinger, 231–49. Berkeley: University of California Press, 1999.

Michaels, Walter Benn. *Our America: Nativism, Modernism, and Pluralism.* Durham, N.C.: Duke University Press, 1995.

———. "Plots against America: Neoliberalism and Antiracism." *American Literary History* 18, no. 2 (Summer 2006): 288–302.

Michaelsen, Scott. "The Grounds and Limits of Multiculturalism." *Centennial Review* 42, no. 3 (Fall 1998): 649–66.

Mijolla, Alain de. "Unconscious Identification Fantasies and Family Prehistory." *International Journal of Psychoanalysis* 68 (1987): 397–403.

Miller, Jay. Introduction to *Mourning Dove: A Salishan Autobiography,* by Mourning Dove, ix–xxxix. Lincoln: University of Nebraska Press, 1990.

Molina Enriquez, Andrés. *Los grandes problemas nacionales.* Mexico City: Impr. de A. Carranza e Hijos, 1909.

Moraga, Cherríe. *Loving in the War Years: Lo que nunca pasó por sus labios.* Boston: South End, 1983.

Morrison, Toni. *Beloved.* New York: Knopf, 1987.

———. *The Bluest Eye.* New York: Knopf, 1970.

———. *Playing in the Dark: Whiteness and the Literary Imagination.* Cambridge: Harvard University Press, 1992.

Mourning Dove. *Cogewea: The Half Blood.* 1927. Edited by Dexter Fisher. Lincoln: University of Nebraska Press, 1981.

———. *Mourning Dove: A Salishan Autobiography.* Edited by Jay Miller. Lincoln: University of Nebraska Press, 1990.

Murphy, Gretchen. *Hemispheric Imaginings: The Monroe Doctrine and Narratives of U.S. Empire.* Durham, N.C.: Duke University Press, 2005.

Okihiro, Gary. "When and Where I Enter." In *Contemporary Asian America: A Multidisciplinary Reader,* ed. Min Zhou and James V. Gatewood. New York: New York University Press, 2000.

Omi, Michael, and Howard Winant. *Racial Formation in the United States: From the 1960s to the 1980s.* New York: Routledge, 1986.

Otis, D. S. *The Dawes Act and the Allotment of Indian Land.* Norman: University of Oklahoma Press, 1983.

Otten, Thomas J. "Pauline Hopkins and the Hidden Self of Race." *ELH* 59, no. 1 (Spring 1992): 227–56.

Owens, Louis. *Other Destinies: Understanding the American Indian Novel.* Norman: University of Oklahoma Press, 1992.

Pérez-Torres, Rafael. *Mestizaje.* Minneapolis: University of Minnesota Press, 2006.

Petkewicz, Jackie. "Contextualizing Craft: The Labor Museum and Immigrant Acculturation." Urban Experience in Chicago: Hull-House and its Neighborhoods, 1889–1963. University of Illinois at Chicago. http://tigger.uic.edu /htbin/cgiwrap/bin/urbanexp/main.cgi?file=img/show_image_in_gallery .ptt&gallery=19&image=244.

Pfister, Joel. *Individuality Incorporated: Indians and the Multicultural Modern.* Durham, N.C.: Duke University Press, 2004.

Piatote, Beth H. "Domestic Trials: Indian Rights and National Belonging in Works by E. Pauline Johnson and John M. Oskison." *American Quarterly* 63, no. 1 (March 2011): 95–116.

Polacheck, Hilda Satt. *I Came a Stranger: The Story of a Hull-House Girl.* Urbana and Chicago: University of Illinois Press, 1989.

Radway, Janice A. *Reading the Romance: Women, Patriarchy, and Popular Literature.* 1984. Chapel Hill: University of North Carolina Press, 1991.

Randle, Gloria T. "Mates, Marriage, and Motherhood: Feminist Visions in Pauline Hopkins's *Contending Forces.*" *Tulsa Studies in Women's Literature* 18, no. 2 (Autumn 1999): 193–214.

Rappoport, Jill. *Giving Women: Alliance and Exchange in Victorian Culture.* New York: Oxford University Press, 2011.

Reed, John. *Insurgent Mexico.* New York: Appleton, 1914.

Reid-Pharr, Robert. *Conjugal Union: The Body, the House, and the Black American.* New York: Oxford University Press, 1999.

Riis, Jacob. *The Battle with the Slum.* New York: Macmillan, 1902.

Rodó, José Enrique. *Ariel.* Translated by Margaret Sayers Peden. Austin: University of Texas Press, 1988.

Rody, Caroline. *The Daughter's Return: African-American and Caribbean Women's Fictions of History.* New York: Oxford University Press, 2001.

Roediger, David. *The Wages of Whiteness: Race and the Making of the American Working Class.* New York: Verso, 1991.

———. *Working toward Whiteness: How America's Immigrants Become White: The Strange Journey from Ellis Island to the Suburbs.* New York: Basic, 2005.

Rogin, Michael. *Blackface, White Noise: Jewish Immigrants in the Hollywood Melting Pot.* Berkeley: University of California Press, 1996.

Rohrbach, Augusta. "To Be Continued: Double Identity, Multiplicity and Antigenealogy as Narrative Strategies in Pauline Hopkins' Magazine Fiction." *Callaloo* 22, no. 2 (Spring 1999): 483–98.

Rohy, Valerie. "Time Lines: Pauline Hopkins' Literary History." *American Literary Realism* 34, no. 1 (Fall 2001): 212–32.

Roosevelt, Theodore. "True Americanism." 1894. Reprinted in *American Ideals, and Other Essays, Social and Political.* New York: G. P. Putnam and Sons, 1897.

Rydell, Robert. *World of Fairs: the Century-of-Progress Expositions.* Chicago: University of Chicago Press, 1993.

Said, Edward. *Orientalism.* New York: Pantheon, 1978.

Saks, Eva. "Representing Miscegenation Law." In *Mixed Race America and the Law: A Reader,* edited by Kevin R. Johnson, 11–12. New York: New York University Press, 2003.

Salvatore, Ricardo D. "The Enterprise of Knowledge: Representational Machines of Informal Empire." In *Close Encounters of Empire: Writing the Cultural History of U.S.-Latin American Relations,* edited by Gilbert M. Joseph, Catherine C. LeGrand, and Salvatore, 69–104. Durham, N.C.: Duke University Press, 1998.

Sanchez-Eppler, Karen. "Temperance in the Bed of a Child: Incest and Social Order in Nineteenth-Century America." *American Quarterly* 47, no. 1 (Spring 1995): 1–33.

Scheidel, Walter. "Ancient Egyptian Sibling Marriage and the Westermarck Effect." In *Inbreeding, Incest, and the Incest Taboo: The State of Knowledge at the Turn of the Century,* edited by Arthur P. Wolf and William H. Durham, 93–108. Stanford, Calif.: Stanford University Press, 2005.

Schrager, Cynthia. "Pauline Hopkins and William James: The New Psychology and the Politics of Race." In *Female Subjects in Black and White: Race, Psychoanalysis, Feminism,* edited by Elizabeth Abel, Barbara Christian, and Helene Moglen, 307–29. Berkeley: University of California Press, 1997.

Sedgwick, Eve Kosofsky. *Between Men: English Literature and Male Homosocial Desire.* New York: Columbia University Press, 1985.

Shimikawa, Karen. *National Abjection.* Durham, N.C.: Duke University Press, 2002.

Showalter, Elaine. *Sexual Anarchy: Gender and Culture at the Fin de Siècle.* New York: Viking, 1990.

Simmen, Edward. "The Mountain Came Long Ago to Mohammed: The American Cultural Invasion of Mexico as Seen in the Short Fiction of María Cristina Mena." *Journal of American Culture* 20, no. 2 (Summer 1997): 147–52.

Sklar, Kathryn Kish. "Hull-House in the 1890s: A Community of Women Reformers," *Signs* 10, no. 4 (Summer 1985): 658–77.

Smith, Sidonie. "Cheesecake, Nymphs, and 'We the People': Un/National Subjects about 1900." *Prose Studies: History, Theory, Criticism* 17, no. 1 (April 1994): 120–40. Available from: MLA International Bibliography, Ipswich, Mass.

———. *Where I'm Bound: Patterns of Slavery and Freedom in Black American Autobiography.* Westport, Conn.: Greenwood, 1974.

Sollors, Werner. *Beyond Ethnicity: Consent and Descent in American Culture.* New York: Oxford University Press, 1986.

———. *Neither Black nor White Yet Both: Thematic Explorations of Interracial Literature.* New York: Oxford University Press, 1997.

———, ed. *The Invention of Ethnicity.* New York: Oxford University Press, 1989.

———, ed. *Interracialism: Black-White Intermarriage in American History, Literature, and Law.* New York: Oxford University Press, 2000.

Sommer, Doris. *Foundational Fictions: The National Romances of Latin America.* Berkeley: University of California Press, 1991.

Spain, Daphne. *How Women Saved the City.* Minneapolis: University of Minnesota Press, 2001.

Spickard, Paul R. *Mixed Blood: Intermarriage and Ethnic Identity in Twentieth-Century America.* Madison: University of Wisconsin Press, 1989.

Spillers, Hortense. "Mama's Baby, Papa's Maybe: An American Grammar Book." *Diacritics* 17, no. 2 (Summer 1987): 64–81.

———. "'The Permanent Obliquity of an In(pha)llibly Straight': In the Time of the Daughters and the Fathers." In *Changing Our Own Words: Essays on Criticism, Theory, and Writing by Black Women,* edited by Cheryl A. Wall, 127–49. New Brunswick, N.J.: Rutgers University Press, 1989.

Stavans, Ilan. "The United States of Mestizo." *Humanities* 31, no. 5 (2010): 28–32.

Steinberg, Stephen. *The Ethnic Myth: Race, Ethnicity, and Class in America.* 3rd ed. Boston: Beacon, 2001.

Stern, Julia. *The Plight of Feeling: Sympathy and Dissent in the Early American Novel.* Chicago: University of Chicago Press, 1997.

Stowe, Harriet Beecher. *Uncle Tom's Cabin, or, Life among the Lowly.* Boston: John P. Jewett, 1852.

Strong, Pauline Turner, and Barrik Van Winkle. "'Indian Blood': Reflections on the Reckoning and Refiguring of Native North American Identity." In "Resisting Identities," special issue, *Cultural Anthropology* 11, no. 4 (November 1996): 547–76. JSTOR.

Sundquist, Eric. *Faulkner: The House Divided.* Baltimore: Johns Hopkins University Press, 1983.

———. *To Wake the Nations: Race in the Making of American Literature.* Cambridge: Belknap Press of Harvard University Press, 1993.

Tate, Claudia. *Domestic Allegories of Political Desire: The Black Heroine's Text at the Turn of the Century.* New York: Oxford University Press, 1992.

———. "Pauline Hopkins: Our Literary Foremother." In *Conjuring: Black Women, Fiction, and Literary Tradition,* edited by Marjorie Pryse and Hortense J. Spillers, 53–66. Bloomington: Indiana University Press, 1985.

———. *Psychoanalysis and Black Novels: Desire and the Protocols of Race.* New York: Oxford University Press, 1998.

Taylor, Diana. *The Archive and the Repertoire: Performing Cultural Memory in the Americas.* Durham, N.C.: Duke University Press, 2001.

Trachtenberg, Alan. *The Incorporation of America: Culture and Society in the Gilded Age.* New York: Hill and Wang, 1982.

———. *Shades of Hiawatha: Staging Indians, Making Americans, 1880–1930.* New York: Hill and Wang, 2004.

Trafton, Scott. *Egypt Land: Race and Nineteenth-Century American Egyptomania.* Durham, N.C.: Duke University Press, 2004.

Treat, Rita Keresztesi. "Writing Culture and Performing Race in Mourning Dove's *Cogewea, the Half Blood* (1927)." In *Literature and Racial Ambiguity,* edited by Neil Brooks and Teresa Hubel, 187–208. Amsterdam and New York: Rodopi, 2002.

Vasconcelos, José. *La raza cósmica: misión de la raza iberoamericana: Notas de viajes a la América del Sud.* Paris: Agencia Mundial de Librería, 1925.

Vidal, Gore. "State of the Union, 2004." *Nation,* September 13, 2004, 23–29.

Viehmann, Martha. "'My People . . . My Kind': Mourning Dove's *Cogewea, The Half Blood* as a Narrative of Mixed Descent." In *Early Native American Writing: New Critical Essays,* edited by Helen Jaskoki, 204–22. Cambridge: Cambridge University Press, 1996.

Vizenor, Gerald. *Manifest Manners: Postindian Warriors of Survivance.* Hanover, N.H.: University Press of New England, 1994.

Wade, Nicholas. *Psychologists in Word and Image.* Cambridge: MIT Press, 1995.

Walker, Alice. *The Color Purple.* New York: Harcourt Brace Jovanovich, 1982.

Wallenstein, Peter. *Tell the Court I Love My Wife: Race, Marriage, and Law: An American History.* New York: Palgrave Macmillan, 2002.

Wallinger, Hanna. *Pauline E. Hopkins: A Literary Biography.* Athens: University of Georgia Press, 2005.

Washburn, Marion Foster. "A Labor Museum." *Craftsman,* September 1904, 570–79.

Watanna, Onoto [Winnifred Eaton]. *The Diary of Delia: Being a Veracious Chronicle of the Kitchen with Some Side-Lights on the Parlour.* New York: Doubleday, Page, 1907.

———. "A Father." 1900. *The Winnifred Eaton Digital Archive.* Edited by Jean Lee Cole. Electronic Text Center, University of Virginia Library. http://etext.lib.virginia.edu/users/cole/.

———. "A Half Caste" and Other Writings. Edited by Linda Trinh Moser and Elizabeth Rooney. Urbana and Chicago: University of Illinois Press, 2003.

———. *The Heart of Hyacinth.* New York, London: Harper and Brothers, 1903.

———. *A Japanese Blossom.* New York: Harper, 1906.

———. *A Japanese Nightingale.* New York, London: Harper and Brothers, 1901.

———. *The Love of Azalea.* New York: Dodd, Mead, 1904.

———. *Miss Numè of Japan.* Chicago: Rand, McNally, 1898.

———. *The Wooing of Wystaria.* New York and London: Harper and Brothers, 1902.

Waters, Tiffany. "Biometrics in Indian Country: The Bloody Fight for Authenticity." *Fourth World Journal* 6, no. 1 (October 2005): 30–41. www.cwis.org/fwj/61/quantities_of_blood.htm.

Watts, Trent. *One Homogenous People: Narratives of White Southern Identity, 1890–1920*. Knoxville: University of Tennessee Press, 2010.

"Weaving with Navajo Loom." In Jessie Luther, "The Labor Museum at Hull House," *Commons* 70, no. 7 (May 1902): 6. Included in "Contextualizing Craft: The Labor Museum and Immigrant Acculturation." Urban Experience in Chicago: Hull-House and its Neighborhoods, 1889–1963, University of Illinois at Chicago, http://tigger.uic.edu/htbin/cgiwrap/bin/urbanexp/main.cgi?file=img/show_image_in_gallery.ptt&gallery=19&image=241.

Weiner, Lynn. Introduction to *I Came a Stranger: The Diary of a Hull-House Girl*, by Hilda Satt Polacheck, xi–xx. Urbana and Chicago: University of Illinois Press, 1989.

White-Parks, Annette. *Sui Sin Far/Edith Maude Eaton: A Literary Biography*. Urbana and Chicago: University of Illinois Press, 1995.

Wiegman, Robyn. *American Anatomies: Theorizing Race and Gender*. Durham, N.C.: Duke University Press, 1995.

Williams, Linda. *Playing the Race Card: Melodramas of Black and White from Uncle Tom to O. J. Simpson*. Princeton: Princeton University Press, 2001.

Wilson, Elizabeth. *The Sphinx in the City: Urban Life, the Control of Disorder, and Women*. Berkeley: University of California Press, 1992.

Wilson, Terry P. "Blood Quantum: Native American Mixed Bloods." In *Racially Mixed People in America*, edited by Maria P. P. Root, 108–25. Newbury Park, Calif.: Sage, 1992. Cited in Tiffany Waters, "Biometrics in Indian Country: The Bloody Fight for Authenticity." *Fourth World Journal* 6, no. 1 (October 2005): 30–41.

Yellin, Jean Fagin. *Women and Sisters: The Antislavery Feminists in American Culture*. New Haven: Yale University Press, 1989.

Yezierska, Anzia. *Bread Givers*. 1925. Introduction by Alice Kessler Harris. New York: Persea, 1975.

Zamora, Lois Parkinson. "Magical Romance/Magical Realism: Ghosts in U.S. and Latin American Fiction." In *Magical Realism: Theory, History, Community*, edited by Lois Parkinson Zamora and Wendy B. Faris, 497–550. Durham, N.C.: Duke University Press, 1995.

Index

Page numbers in bold type refer to figures.

acknowledgment of past, 35–36, 126, 147; historic accuracy and, 37

Adams, Charles Francis, Jr., 15–16, 183n44

Addams, Jane, 4, 10, 18, 24–25, 43; on blood, 206n44; culture and, 161; death, 203nn4–5; familial model, 153–54; limits of inclusion and, 171–73; as "Saint Jane," 170, 203n3; works by, 154, 157, 159, 204n17; *see also Hull-House Labor Museum; Twenty Years at Hull-House*

adoption, 169, 170; cultural hybridity and, 79–90

affirmative action, 9

Africa: femininity of, 44–45; Hopkins's portrayal of, 46; return to, 46–48, 51, 189n60

African Americans, 25, 27–54; future, 45; Hull-House Labor Museum and, 165–66, 171–72; incest in fiction, 68, 69; male citizenship, 10; *see also mulatto/a; specific African American fictions*

Ai (character from *Of One Blood*), 33–34, 45–46

Alaska, 17

Alegría Peralta (character from "Doña Rita's Rivals"), 107–9, 111–15, 195n43

Alemán, Jesse, 193n8

Alfred Densmore (character from *Cogewea*), 122, 124, 126–27, 134, 139, 141, 145, 147; from Canada, 199n8

Alicia Cherry (character from "The Education of Popo"), 100–106

Alonso, Ana María, 98

Alpers, Svetlana, 163

amalgamation, 15; *see also* miscegenation

Americanization, 153

Ammons, Elizabeth, 35

amnesia, 41

antimiscegenation laws, 16–18, 30–31, 184n49, 184n52

Anzaldúa, Gloria, 99, 118

Aoi Montrose (character from *The Heart of Hyacinth*), 80–81, 86, 88

Ariel (Rodó), 101

Asian Americans, 25, 55–90; Hull-House Labor Museum and, 165–66, 171–72; identity, 68, 69–70; *see also specific Asian American ethnicities*

Asian immigration, 180n15, 181n25

Asiatic Barred Zone, 8, 207n54

assimilation, 2, 7, 16, 129–30, 141; policy, 11; resistance, 132–33

Aubrey Livingston (character from *Of One Blood*), 33, 38–39, 40, 41–42; desire, 187n40; emotions, 49–50

Aubrey Livingston Sr. (Doctor) (character from *Of One Blood*), 33, 34, 37–38

Aunt Hannah (character from *Of One Blood*), 34, 53

Batker, Carol J., 145
Berlant, Lauren, 88, 174
Binet, Alfred, 27–28, 41, 45
Binet, M., 32, 40–41
The Birth of a Nation (Griffith), 14
blood quantum, 119, 128, 130–37,
    201nn44–45, 207n55
Blount (Reverend) (character from *The
    Heart of Hyacinth*), 82, 85
Bourne, Randolph, 7–8
Bow, Leslie, 60, 190n16
Brading, D. A., 96
Breuer, Joseph, 6
Brogan, Kathleen, 35
Brooks, Peter, 63
Brown, Alanna Kathleen, 121, 138, 198n2
Brown, Harry J., 148, 198n4
Brown, William Wells, 29
Brown v. Board of Education of Topeka
    (1954), 180n14
Burke Act (1906), 200n30
Butler, Judith, 18, 184n54

Candace (character from *Of One Blood*), 34,
    44–45, 53–54; substitution of, 186n24
Cannata, Susan M., 123
Carlisle Indian Industrial School, 11, 132,
    208n63; *see also* Pratt, Richard Henry
Carranza, Venustiano, 94
Carrillo, Julián, 192n2
Century Magazine, 23–24, 95, 100, 107, 118
Chance, John K., 97
Charcot, Jean-Martin, 27–28, 45
Charlie Vance (character from *Of One
    Blood*), 33, 34, 51
Cheng, Anne Anlin, 69, 173
Cherokee Nation v. the State of Georgia
    (1831), 201n39
Chesnutt, Charles, 1–2, 29, 179n5, 182n33
Chicanos, 99
Ch'ien, Evelyn, 64
Child, Lydia Maria, 13
Childe, Cromwell, 180n19
Chin, Frank, 60
Chinese Exclusion Act (1882), 8, 11–12,
    180n15, 207n54; extended to Japanese
    laborers, 59
Chinese immigrants, 11, 57, 190n10
Chinn, Sarah E., 153
citizenship, 12, 59, 90; African American
    male, 10; belonging and, 55–56;

Native American, 11, 136, 185n63;
    privatization of, 88
Civil War (1861-1865), 10
Clark, Badger, 121
class *see* cross-class romance
Clifford, James, 165
Cogewea (character from *Cogewea*), 2,
    122–29, 140–42; change of heart,
    199n9; characterization of, 132–33;
    cultural inheritance, 137–38; Jim
    and, 141; marriage and, 199n21;
    relationships, 142–48; Vanishing
    Indian myth and, 200n24
*Cogewea: The Half Blood, A Depiction
    of the Great Montana Cattle Range*
    (Mourning Dove), 2, 3, 24, 119; cultural
    construction of race and, 137–42;
    half-breeds in, 125–30; happy ending,
    123–24; miscegenation and incest in,
    142–48; policy and blood quantum
    and, 130–37; published, 121; *see also
    specific characters*
Cole, Jean Lee, 59, 191n23
Colored American Magazine, 29
consanguineous amalgamation *see* incest
consciousness: double, 44; in *Of One
    Blood*, 35, 43, 45–46, 51, 54; U.S.
    national, 41, 54
Contending Forces (Hopkins), 29
"A Contract" (Watanna), 55–56, 72
Cortés, Hernán, 96
Creelman, James, 193n18
creole identity, 92, 96, 97, 106
cross-class romance, 4, 107–18
cultural adaptation, 145
cultural recognition, 59
cultural relativism, 81

daughter, 152; father-, incest, 23, 68;
    mother-, bonds, 20, 74, 152
Dawes Act (1887), 11, 131, 134, 141
Dawes Rolls, 135–36
Deloria, Philip, 147, 169
democracy model, 7
desire, 19–20, 187n40
Dianthe Lusk (character from *Of One
    Blood*), 32–34, 38, 41, 42, 45, 51; as
    casebook hysteric, 39–40; death,
    187n40; power over, 49–50; substitution
    of, 186n24; trance state, 44
Díaz, Porfirio, 93–94, 96–97, 107, 193n18

displacements, 46–48
Doane, Mary Ann, 45, 186*n*19
domesticity, 172, 206*n*43; idealized, 29
domestic novel, 29, 30–31, 185*nn*61–62
Doña Rita Azpe de Ixtlan (character from "Doña Rita's Rivals"), 107–11, 114, 116–18, 196*n*50; incestuous behavior, 112–13; religious tradition, 196*n*53; representation, 115
"Doña Rita's Rivals" (Mena), 3, 20, 99–100, 106, 107–18; see also *specific characters*
Du Bois, W.E.B., 44, 166, 188*n*46, 205*n*25, 207*n*51

Eaton, Edith, 57, 190*n*13
Eaton, Winnifred, 23, 173; adoption and cultural hybridity and, 79–90; citizenship and, 55–56; half-caste trope used by, 89–90; identity and, 56; incest and, 60–65, 67, 80–81, 90; Japan portrayed by, 55–57, 59; mother and, 74; paternal appetite and object relations and, 65–73; psychoanalysis of fiction of, 67; race rhetoric and, 65; romance of recognition and, 62–65; sibling eroticism and, 73–79; see also Watanna, Onoto
"The Education of Popo" (Mena), 99, 100–106, 117; see also *specific characters*
Ellison, Ralph, 30
endogamy, 13, 16–17, 71, 160; see also incest
Eng, David, 60
enredados, 111–12, 196*n*47
Enríquez, Andrés Molina, 97–98
ethnic, term use, 202*n*2
European immigrants, 7, 11, 25; children and, 153–54; incest and, 159; intermarriage, 206*n*34; racial romance and, 149–52; whiteness, 164–65; see also Hull-House Labor Museum
exogamy, 13, 16–17, 71, 92, 160; see also miscegenation

Fallaw, Ben, 97
family: community model, 127–28, 136–37; cultural, 151–52; half-breed and, 125; half-castes and, 68–69; mixed-race American, 6; models, 6, 153–54, 172; multigenerational model of, 155–56; romance, 18–22, 45, 73; see also kinship; nation-as-family rhetoric
Family of Man theory, 181*n*30

fantasies, 19, 46–48
"A Father" (Watanna), 61, 191*n*25
father-daughter incest, 23, 68
fatherland, 56, 72, 76, 82
Faulkner, William, 5, 30
Felice Adams see Dianthe Lusk
Felman, Shoshana, 51
female: abjection, 38; narrative strategies, 21–22
femininity, or feminization, 56, 88; of Africa, 44–45; Eastern, 57, 59, 60; hysteria and, 40; in *Of One Blood*, 28, 37–39, 40–42, 44–45, 52, 56; Reuel's, 41–42
Ferenczi, Sándor, 28
Ferens, Dominika, 59
Fernando Arriola (character from "The Education of Popo"), 101–2
Fiedler, Leslie, 16, 183*n*45
Fisher, Dexter, 179*n*4, 198*n*1
Flatley, Jonathan, 36, 174
foreignness, 55–56, 60
"Frenchy" LaFleur (character from *Cogewea*), 122, 127, 134, 139, 143–45
Fresonke, Kris, 136–38
Freud, Sigmund, 5–6, 27–28, 37, 45, 179*n*7, 184*n*56; family romance theory, 18–19; fantasies and displacements, 46–48
Fuentes, Carlos, 118
Fusco, Coco, 9, 174
Fuss, Diana, 64

Gamio, Manuel, 97–98
García Canclini, Néstor, 116
gender, 17, 26; half-castes and inequality, 88; oppression, 3; slavery and, 26–47
General Allotment Act of 1887, 11
"Gentlemen's Agreement" (1907), 59, 69, 181*n*26, 207*n*54
ghosts, 48
Gillman, Susan, 31, 46–47
Gilman, Charlotte Perkins, 37
Goldberg, David Theo, 8–9
"The Gold Vanity Set" (Mena), 194*n*22
gothic elements, 35, 187*n*32
Great Migration, 181*n*22
Griffith, D. W., 14

Hagar's Daughter: A Story of Southern Caste Prejudice (Hopkins), 29
half-bloods, 14, 182*n*37

half-breeds, 14, 120, 124, 133, 146–48, 182*n*37, 199*n*7; caught between two worlds, 125–30; immigrants and, 144

"A Half Caste" (Watanna), 20, 56, 61, 62–68, 73, 77; incest in, 71; racial melancholia in, 69–70, 71–72

"The Half Caste" (Watanna), 70, 71

half-castes, 14, 56, 63, 182*n*37, 189*n*3; Easton, W., and, 89–90; family and, 68–69; foreignness and, 60; gender inequality and, 88; identity, 70; psychoanalysis of, 70–71; romance, 71

Halverson, Cathryn, 139, 146 198*n*4

Harkins, Gillian, 16

Harper, Frances E. W., 13, 29

Hawaiian independence movement (1898-1900), 10

healing: acknowledgment of past and, 35–36; psychic and social, 41

Hearn, Lafcadio, 57

The Heart of Hyacinth (Watanna), 56, 59, 61, 73–79, 80–89; *"He knelt in a rapt silence beside her"*, **87**; Hyacinth, **58**; *"Now come, little one: come, give me that welcome home"*, **84**; *see also specific characters*

Hemings, Sally, 6

Herron, Carolivia, 5

hidden self, 40

"The Hidden Self" (James, W.), 41

Homestead Act, 201*n*40

Hopkins, Pauline, 3, 4, 10, 18, 20, 22–23, 27, 172, 185*nn*4–5; address to readers, 52–53; Africa portrayed by, 46; multiculturalism and, 28–29; name use, 188*n*52; occult in works of, 37; psychology and psychoanalysis and, 28, 42–43, 44, 45; "return to Africa" used by, 46–48, 51, 189*n*60; stereotype reversal, 48; U.S. portrayed by, 46; *see also Of One Blood; specific works*

Hrdlička, Aleš, 15, 130, 181*n*23

Huerta, Victoriano, 93–94

Hughes, Henry, 15

Hull-House Labor Museum, 24–25, 149, 173; Addams's death and, 203*nn*4–5; cultural miscegenation of objects, 161–63; endogamy and exogamy, 160; limits of inclusion, 163–72; maintenance, 203*n*8; meaning and relation, 152–57; men absent from, 158–61, 205*n*24;

miscegenation without sex and, 157–61; multiculturalism and, 155, 160, 162–63; parent-child bond and, 153–54; race at, 207*n*51; racial romance and, 156, 170; "Russian Spinning," **158**; services and departments, 150–51; "Spinning with Wool Wheel," **156**; "Weaving an Indian Blanket," **168**; women and, 152–53, 163–64

Hyacinth (character from *The Heart of Hyacinth*), **58**, 80–89

hybridity: adoption and cultural, 79–90; identity and, 82–83, 127, 133; Mexico-U.S. relations and, 106; Mourning Dove and, 128–29, 133; *see also* multiculturalism

hypnosis, 27–28, 38, 41

hysteria, 27–28, 39–40, 41, 185*n*2

I Came a Stranger: The Story of a Hull-House Girl (Polacheck), 157

identification fantasies, 19

identity, 172–73; Anglo-Saxon, 6; Asian Americans, 68, 69–70; blood and, 119, 128–29, 136; collective, 145; creole, 92, 96, 97, 106; cultural, 6; Eaton, W., and, 56; half-castes, 70; hybrid, 82–83, 127, 133; interracial romance and, 61; mestizo/a, 99; Mexican American, 105, 193*n*12; Mexican symbols, 95, 98; Mourning Dove expanding, 120–22; multiracial, 14; Native American, 120, 128, 131–32, 140, 200*n*30; as process, 169; racial, 21; *see also* national identity; nation-as-family rhetoric

immigrants, 6, 144, 202*n*2; first-generation and second-generation women, 25; Native Americans and, 199*n*16; race-based limitation on, 8; *see also* European immigrants; *specific immigrants*

Immigration Act: of 1917, 8, 207*n*54; of 1924, 12

incest, 3, 10, 36, 171, 186*n*11; African American fiction and, 68, 69; in *Cogewea*, 142–48; Doña Rita and, 112–13; Eaton, W., and, 60–65, 67, 80–81, 90; European immigrants and, 159; father-daughter, 23, 68; in "A Half Caste," 71; miscegenation *versus*,

15–18; mother-son, 106; in *Of One Blood*, 34–35; secrecy and, 67–68; under slavery, 13–14; tragic-mulatto/a motif, 30–31; *see also* sibling eroticism
inclusion model, 7
Indian Citizenship Act (1924), 136
The Interpretation of Dreams (Freud), 28
interracialism *see* miscegenation
interracial relationships, 26, 60–61, 130
interracial romance, 1, 3, 19–21, 24, 26, 57, 191*n*18; identity and, 61; Mena and, 103–4; second generation, 59–60
interracial sex, 14, 15, 20, 35, 151, 183*n*41
Irwin, John T., 183*n*45

Jackson, Helen Hunt, 120
Jackson, Shannon, 167
James, Henry, 6, 101
James, William, 6, 28, 41, 45, 188*n*46
Janet, Pierre Marie Félix, 27–28, 41
Japan, 55–57, 59
A Japanese Blossom (Watanna), 59, 190*n*17
Japanese immigrants, 3, 11, 190*n*10; labor, 59
A Japanese Nightingale (Watanna), 61
Jefferson, Thomas, 6
Jen, Gish, 5
Jesús María (character from "Doña Rita's Rivals"), 107, 109–12, 115–18, 196*n*54; representation, 113–14
Jim Crow era, 8, 14, 27, 35, 36
Jim LaGrinder (character from *Cogewea*), 2, 122–23, 125, 129, 138, 141
Jim Titus (character from *Of One Blood*), 33, 34
John Carter (character from *Cogewea*), 122, 127, 134, 138–39, 143, 145
Johnson-Reed Act (1924), 12, 136
Julia (character from *Cogewea*), 122, 134, 138–39, 143
Jung, Carl, 28

Kallen, Horace, 7, 8
Kiku (character from "A Half Caste"), 62–66, 68, 71–72, 77; objectification of, 67
Kiku (character from "Miss Lily and Miss Chrysanthemum"), 74–79
kinship, 124, 128–29, 141, 145; cultural, 152; meaning lost, 13–14; Mourning

Dove, 134–36, 146–48; rules, 16–17; systems, 135
Klein, Melanie, 67
Knowles (character from *The Heart of Hyacinth*), 81
Komazawa "Koma" (character from *The Heart of Hyacinth*), 80–89
Koshy, Susan, 59
Krupat, Arnold, 123, 139

La Malinche, 96
Lape, Noreen Groover, 190*n*17
Lawrence, D. H., 94
Lears, T. J. Jackson, 161
Leonard, Karen, 184*n*52
Lévi-Strauss, Claude, 17
Lincoln, Abraham, 1
Lone Star, 5, 177
Long, John Luther, 23, 57
Longfellow, Henry Wadsworth, 121
The Love of Azalea (Watanna), 59
Loving v. Virginia (1967), 17
Luciano, Dana, 31, 47
Lukens, Margaret, 140

McClintock, Anne, 194*n*21
McDowell, Deborah, 44–45, 47
McWhorter, Lucullus Virgil, 121–22, 123, 148
Madame Butterfly (Long), 23, 57
Madero, Francisco, 93–94
magical realism, 36
marriage, 199*n*21; European immigrants and, 206*n*34; mixed blood, 124; mulatta's, 30; rules, 17
Martín (son of La Malinche and Cortés), 96
Mary (character from *Cogewea*), 122, 124, 134, 143–46; cultural inheritance, 138–39
masculinity, 88; in *Of One Blood*, 28, 37–38, 41–42, 44, 46, 50, 56; Western, 57
Masters (character from "A Contract"), 55–56, 72
Matsukawa, Yuko, 190*n*7
melting pot model, 7
men: African American citizenship, 10; Hull-House Labor Museum and absence of, 158–61, 205*n*24; white privilege, 67–68

Mena, María Cristina, 3, 4, 10, 18, 20, 23–24, 91–92, 172–73, 192n2, 194n22; background, 94–95; colonial and revolutionary romances, 107–18; interracial romance and, 103–4; irony, 195n34; *mestizaje* perspective, 98–100; mestizo in Mexican history and, 95–100; Mexican Revolution romanticized by, 117–18, 197n57; Mexico portrayed by, 91–93; multiculturalism and, 118; neo-imperial romance and, 100–106; *see also* "Doña Rita's Rivals"; "The Education of Popo"; "A Son of the Tropics," 197n57; "The Sorcerer and General Bisco," 197n57; "The Soul of Hilda Brunel," 195n43; *specific works*

mestizaje, 92–93, 193n12, 194n28; Mena's perspective on, 98–100; resistant, 118

mestizo/a, 14, 91, 94–95, 182n37; identity, 99; in Mexican history, 95–100

Mexican Americans, 12, 25, 91; Hull-House Labor Museum and, 165–66, 171–72; identity, 105, 193n12

Mexican-American War (1845-1848), 10, 12, 92

Mexican-"Indian," 97, 114, 128, 130, 194n22

Mexican Revolution (1910-1917), 12, 91, 92, 97; Mena romanticizing, 117–18, 197n57

Mexico: identity symbols, 95, 98; Mena's portrayal of, 91–93; mestizo in history of, 95–100

Mexico-U.S. relations, 91, 92, 94–95, 193n8; cultural influences and, 103–4; hybridity and, 106; popular culture and, 101–2; rejection of colonial and neo-imperial, 105

Michaels, Walter Benn, 16, 136, 180n17, 191n18

Michaelsen, Scott, 174

Mijolla, Alain de, 19

mind-body connection, 28, 38

Mira (character from *Of One Blood*), 33, 34, 37–38, 44–45, 49–51

miscegenation, 3, 36, 171, 183n41, 186n11; in *Cogewea*, 142–48; incest *versus*, 15–18; model of, 25; national identity and, 10; Native Americans and, 130–31; of objects, 161–63; sexless, 157–61; under slavery, 13–14; *see also* antimiscegenation laws; interracial

relationships; interracial romance; interracial sex

"Miss Lily and Miss Chrysanthemum: The Love Story of Two Japanese Girls in Chicago" (Watanna), 61, 73–80

Miss Numè of Japan (Watanna), 190–91nn17–18

mixed blood, 7, 8, 56, 120, 200n32; marriage, 124; one drop rule, 201n41

mixed-race Americans, 21; choice facing, 2; couples, 20; family, 6; psychology, 125; women, 26

"A Modern Lear" (Addams), 204n17

Molly Vance (character from *Of One Blood*), 33

mongrelism *see* miscegenation

Monroe Doctrine (1823), 93; *see also* Roosevelt's Corollary

Moraga, Cherríe, 5

Morrison, Toni, 30

mother: daughter-, bonds, 20, 74, 152; Eaton, W., and representation of, 74; lost, 75; son-, incest, 106

motherland, 56, 61, 72, 74–75, 80, 82, 86

Mourning Dove, 2, 4, 10, 18, 24, 119, 172; autobiography, 198nn1–2; cultural construction of race and, 137–42; family-community model, 127–28, 136–37; half-breed descriptions, 125–30; hybridity and, 128–29, 133; identities expanded by, 120–22; kinship and, 134–36, 146–48; stereotypes and, 128–30; *see also Cogewea*; *specific works*

mulatto/a, 14, 29, 31, 182n37; marriage, 30; paradox of racialization and, 39; *see also* tragic-mulatto/a motif

multiculturalism, 35, 180n12; economic logic of, 180n17; genealogy of, 7–9; Hopkins and, 28–29; Hull-House Labor Museum and, 155, 160, 162–63; institutionalization of, 151; Mena and, 118; Native Americans and, 124, 140, 146; nonsexual model of, 152; origins, 174–75; strong, 9, 175; twenty-first-century, 176–77; *see also* hybridity

multiracial nation model, 5–6

municipal housekeeping, 153, 204n13

Murphy, Gretchen, 93

national identity, 5–6, 7, 27, 59, 61, 129; affect and, 177; hierarchical models

of, 100; miscegenation as precondition of, 10; multiracial, 68; recognition of repressed half of, 39; women and, 60
national psyche, 36–46
nation-as-family rhetoric, 6, 22–23, 25, 54; historicizing, 10–14; *Of One Blood* and, 29–31, 39
Native Americans, 10, 25, 119, 127, 135; boarding schools, 132; citizenship, 11, 136, 185n63; exploited, 126, 147; future, 131; Hull-House Labor Museum and, 165–67, 169–70, 171–72; identity, 120, 128, 131–32, 140, 200n30; immigrants and, 199n16; miscegenation and, 130–31; multiculturalism and, 124, 140, 146; psychology and, 202n57; textiles, 167, 169; *see also* kinship
Native American-U.S. policy, 8, 119, 121–22; *see also* assimilation; blood quantum
Naturalization Law (1790), 165–66
Ned Winterbottom (character from "The Education of Popo"), 103, 105, 195n39
neurasthenia, 186n18
New Era Magazine, 29
Norman Hilton (character from "A Half Caste"), 62–65, 68, 71, 77; abandonment of, 72; language of conquest, 66–67

objectification, 39, 65–67
object relations, 65–73
occult, 37
Office of Indian Affairs, 132, 133–34
Of One Blood (Hopkins), 3, 20, 22–23; consciousness in, 35, 43, 45–46, 51, 54; femininity, or feminization in, 28, 37–39, 40–42, 44–45, 52, 56; geographic shift, 46–48; gothic elements in, 35, 187n32; incest in, 34–35; masculinity in, 28, 37–38, 41–42, 44, 46, 50, 56; national psyche imagined, 36–46; nation-as-family rhetoric and, 29–31, 39; pathology and, 28–29, 31; plot summary, 32–54; racialization in, 39, 44, 45; racial melancholia and, 36, 40, 47; time, narration, and uncanny in, 48–54; tragic-mulatto motif of, 29–31; unconscious and, 35, 37, 38, 40, 41, 43–46, 51–52; U.S. as portrayed in, 27, 46, 54; *see also specific characters*

Okihiro, Gary, 60
O-Kiku-san (character from "A Contract"), 55–56
Omi, Michael, 164–65, 192n35
orientalism, 4, 16, 60, 71, 81, 193n8
Other, 6, 176, 177; within Self, 172–73
Otten, Thomas J., 32, 44
Owens, Louis, 123

Pan-Americanism, 192n4
parent-child bond, 153–54, 155–56, 204–5nn19–20
passive voice, 49–50
paternal appetite, 65–73
pathology, 28–29, 31, 40
Peralta, Ángela, 195n43
Pérez-Torres, Raphael, 118
Perry, Matthew, 56–57
Pershing, John J., 94
Pfister, Joel, 202n57
Piatote, Beth, 122–23
Piedad/La Palma (character from "Doña Rita's Rivals"), 107, 115–18
Plessy v. Ferguson (1896), 8, 27
pluralism *see* multiculturalism
Polacheck, Hilda Satt, 156–57, 164, 167, 170, 205n29
power relations, 35, 36, 53
Pratt, Richard Henry, 11, 132, 201n35; *see also* Carlisle Indian Industrial School
The Principles of Psychology (James, W.), 28
Progressive Era (1890-1914), 152; policy in, 130–37; women, 26
Próspero "Popo" Arriola (character from "The Education of Popo"), 100–106, 195n34
psychoanalysis, 27–28; of Eaton, W., works, 67; of half-castes, 70–71; Hopkins and, 28, 42–43, 44, 45
Psychoanalysis and Black Novels (Tate), 51
psychology, 27–28, 36, 41; Hopkins and, 28, 42–43, 44, 45; mixed-race Americans, 125; Native American, 202n57; race and, 40, 69
The Psychopathology of Everyday Life (Freud), 28
Puccini, Giacomo, 57

Quintasket, Christal *see* Mourning Dove
Quintasket, Christine *see* Mourning Dove

race, 202n1; cultural construction of, 137–42; Eaton, W., and rhetoric of, 65; at Hull-House Labor Museum, 207n51; immigration and, 8; object relations and, 67; psychology and, 40, 69; suicide, 131; *see also* mixed-race Americans
racial dualism, 44
racial formation, 164–65, 192n35
racialization, 39, 44, 45, 69
racialized women, 1; abjection, 67–68; exploitation of, 2–3, 14
racial melancholia, 173; "A Half Caste" and, 69–70, 71–72; *Of One Blood* and, 36, 40, 47
racial romance, 2-26, 147, 171, 172; desexed, 152–53; European immigrants and, 149–52; functions of, 2–3; Hull-House Labor Museum and, 156, 170; power of, 173–74
racism, 8–9, 35, 36, 80–81; gendered, 60
Reconstruction era, 35, 43
Reid-Pharr, Robert, 30
Retamar, Roberto Fernández, 195n37
Reuel Briggs (character from *Of One Blood*), 32–34, 38–39, 46, 48, 53, 187n43, 188n53; feminization, 41–42; melancholia and, 40; powers, 51–52; return to Africa, 46–48, 51, 189n60
Richard Lorrimer (character from *The Heart of Hyacinth*), 83, 85
Riggs, Lynn, 5
Rodó, José Enrique, 101
Rody, Caroline, 74
Rohrbach, Augusta, 42–43
Rohy, Valerie, 44, 187n32
romance, 19, 20, 185n59; colonial and revolutionary, 107–18; cross-class, 4, 107–18; family, 18–22, 45, 73; half-castes, 71; neo-imperial, 100–106; of recognition, 62–65; *see also* interracial romance; racial romance
Roosevelt, Theodore, 7, 8, 13
Roosevelt's Corollary to the Monroe Doctrine (1904), 93
"Russian Spinning," 158
Russo-Japanese War (1904-1905), 57, 59
Rydell, Robert, 181n30
Ryder (Mr.) (character from "Wife of His Youth"), 1–2

Said, Edward, 60, 193n8

Saks, Eva, 183n40
Sano, Kiyokichi: "He knelt in a rapt silence beside her," 87; *Hyacinth*, 58; "Now come, little one: come, give me that welcome home," 84
Saunders (character from *The Heart of Hyacinth*), 82, 83, 85
Sayles, John, 5, 177
Scheidel, Walter, 186n24
Schrager, Cynthia, 38
Sedgwick, Eve, 19–20
seduction, 191n32
sexual hierarchy, 18
Shakespeare, 101–2, 105, 195n35
Shimikawa, Karen, 69
sibling eroticism, 56, 186n24; adoption and, 79–90; Eaton, W., and, 73–79; Mena and, 115-17; Mourning Dove and, 122, 141-43
Silent Bob (character from *Cogewea*), 125, 144–45
Simmen, Edward, 102
Sino-Japanese War (1894-1895), 57, 59, 85
slavery, 27, 35, 36; miscegenation and incest under, 13–14
Smithsonian Institution National Museum of Natural History, 15
Sollors, Werner, 4, 64, 179n5, 200n25
Sommer, Doris, 14, 100
"The Sorcerer and General Bisco" (Mena), 197n57
The Souls of Black Folk (Du Bois), 44
Spanish-American War (1898), 10
Spence, Mark, 136–38
Spencer, Herbert, 1, 181n30
Spillers, Hortense, 13–14, 68
"Spinning with Wool Wheel," 156
Starr, Ellen Gates, 150
Stavans, Ilan, 96
Stemteemä (character from *Cogewea*), 126, 128, 138, 140, 145, 147–48
Stowe, Harriet Beecher, 38–39, 189n67
Studies in Hysteria (Freud), 28
Sui Sin Far *see* Eaton, Edith
Sundquist, Eric, 183n45, 189n60

Taft, William Howard, 12, 13, 181n29
Tate, Claudia, 29, 51, 185n61
Taylor, Diana, 21, 57, 101
Telassar (hidden city from *Of One Blood*), 33–34, 43–44, 46, 188n53

The Tempest (Shakespeare), 101–2, 105, 195*n*35
textiles, 149–51, 154–55, 163, 167, 169
Tolstoy, Leo, 6
Toscani, Oliviero, 175–77, 208*n*6
tragic-mulatto/a motif, 29–31, 182*n*36
transnational cosmopolitanism, 7–8, 91–116, 172, 176, 198
Treatise on Sociology: Theoretical and Practical (Hughes), 15
Treaty of Guadalupe Hidalgo (1848), 12, 93
"True Americanism" (Roosevelt, T.), 7
Turner, Frederick Jackson, 146, 169
Twenty Years at Hull-House (Addams), 154, 157, 159

The Unclassified Residuum (Binet, M.), 32, 40–41
Uncle Tom's Cabin (Stowe), 38–39, 189*n*67
unconscious, 35, 37, 38, 40, 41, 43–46, 51–52
United Colors of Benetton, 9, 152, 175–77, 208*n*5
United States (U.S.), 6, 10; Hopkins's portrayal of, 46; national consciousness, 41, 54; *Of One Blood*'s portrayal of, 27, 54; wealth, 196*n*52; *see also* citizenship; Mexico-U.S. relations; national identity; nation-as-family rhetoric; Native American-U.S. policy
U.S. Training and Industrial School in Carlisle, Pennsylvania *see* Carlisle Indian Industrial School

Vanishing Indian, 120, 121, 123, 129, 131, 138, 142; myth of, 124, 146, 200*n*24
Vasconcelos, José, 97–98
Vidal, Gore, 177
Viehmann, Martha L., 120, 137
Villa, Francisco "Pancho," 94, 97
Vizenor, Gerald, 142, 147
Voice of the Negro, 29

Walker, Alice, 30

Walter Palmer (character from "Miss Lily and Miss Chrysanthemum"), 77–79
Washburn, Marion Foster, 161–62, 163, 164, 206*n*43
Washington, Booker T., 185*n*4
Watanna, Onoto, 4, 10, 18, 20, 53, 172, 190–91*nn*17–18, 191*n*25; biography, 57; pen name, 3, 190*n*7; *see also* Eaton, Winnifred; *specific works*
Waters, Tiffany, 135
"Weaving an Indian Blanket," 168
"Weaving with Navajo Loom," 207*n*59
whiteness, 180*n*13; European immigrants and, 164–65; expansion of category of, 8; privilege and, 38, 67–68
"The Wife of His Youth" (Chesnutt), 1–2, 179*n*5
Wilson, Elizabeth, 159
Wilson, Harriet, 29
Winant, Howard, 164–65, 192*n*35
Winona: A Tale of Negro Life in the South and Southwest (Hopkins), 29
womanhood, 38–39
women: authors, 13, 185*n*61; first-generation and second-generation immigrant, 25; Hull-House Labor Museum and, 152–53, 163–64; mixed-race, 26; national identity and, 60; objectification of, 39, 65–67; Progressive Era, 26; prostitution, 157, 159; silencing of, 52; *see also* female; racialized women
The Wooing of Wystaria (Watanna), 59
World's Columbian Exposition (1893), 45, 74, 181*n*30, 203*n*6, 206*n*42, 208*n*63

The Yellow Wallpaper (Gilman), 37
Yezierska, Anzia, 128
Yoshido Yamashiro (character from *The Heart of Hyacinth*), 83
Yuri (character from "Miss Lily and Miss Chrysanthemum"), 74–79

Zamora, Lois Parkinson, 36
Zapata, Emiliano, 94, 97

About the Author

Jolie A. Sheffer is an assistant professor of English and affiliated faculty in American Culture Studies at Bowling Green State University. She has published essays in *MELUS*, the *Journal of Asian American Studies*, and in *Sport, Rhetoric, Gender, and Globalization: Historical Perspectives and Media Representations*, edited by Linda K. Fuller.

CPSIA information can be obtained at www.ICGtesting.com
Printed in the USA
BVOW010451281112

306638BV00002B/50/P